A Hands-on Guide to Creating a
Successful and Sustainable Business

Greening
Your
Business

About the Author

Dan Sitarz is an attorney, author, lecturer, educator, and business entrepreneur. In 1992, in cooperation with the United Nations Conference on Environment and Development, he wrote and edited the popular abridged version of the central agreement of the Earth Summit: *Agenda 21: The Earth Summit Strategy to Save our Planet*. This book was selected as one of the top 25 Environmental Reference Books by the Sierra Club and one of the top 21 Books for the 21st Century, jointly by the International Center for Environment and Public Policy of the California Institute of Public Affairs, The Commission on Environmental Strategy and Planning of the World Conservation Union (ICUN), and the World Future Society.

In cooperation with the President's Council on Sustainable Development, in 1997, Sitarz wrote and abridged the Council's voluminous reports into a concise book for the general public: *Sustainable America: America's Environment, Economy, and Society in the 21st Century*; (with a foreword by then-Vice President Al Gore). This book was honored as one of the top three environmental books of 1997 by the World Future Society.

Since 1999, he has taught and lectured widely as guest lecturer on sustainability and environmental issues for the Environmental Studies Program and the Environmental Resources and Policy PhD Program at Southern Illinois University in Carbondale, Illinois. He also served as project advisor for the first detailed sustainability assessment of the University in 2000 and was instrumental in the University's signing of the Talloires Declaration on Sustainability in Higher Education. He was one of the initial founders and a director of Southern Sustainability (now the Southern Illinois Center for a Sustainable Future), and he has assisted numerous organizations and businesses seeking to further sustainability goals, including the Land for Learning Institute, the Center for Neo-Tropical Conservation, and many others. He has also advised many entrepreneurs and small business owners on green business and sustainability issues.

Additionally, in the 1980s, Sitarz founded Nova Publishing, which has become one of the premier providers of simplified legal information in America. Its books, software, and legal products are in all major bookstores, Staples, Office Depot, and OfficeMax. Nova also provides content for several major legal service providers on the Internet, notably FindLegalForms.com and LawGuru.com. He has written over 30 business and legal books, all designed to assist entrepreneurs and the general public in navigating the complexities of business and legal issues. His business and legal books have been praised by the *Wall Street Journal*, *Forbes*, CNN, and many others.

A Hands-on Guide to a
Successful and Sustainable Business

Greening
Your
Business

DANIEL SITARZ

EARTHPRESS
RESOURCES FOR A BETTER WORLD

ISBN 13: 978-1-892949-46-2
Book with CD-Rom   price: $29.95

Cataloging-in-Publication Data
     Sitarz, Dan, 1948-
     Greening Your Business: a hands-on guide to creating a successful and sustainable
     business / by Daniel Sitarz -- 1st ed. --Carbondale, Ill.:
     : EarthPress, c2008
     p. ; cm + CD-ROM (4.75")
     Includes bibliographical references and index.
      1. Industrial management--Environmental aspects--United States. 2. Business enterprises--
     Environmental aspects--United States. 3. Sustainable development. 4. Social responsibility of
     business. I. Title.

     HD30.255 .S58 2008
     658.4/08--dc22   0810

1st Edition; 1st Printing / October, 2008

EarthPress Green Business Policies

EarthPress takes seriously the impact of book publishing on the Earth and its resources. EarthPress is committed to protecting the environment and to the responsible use of natural resources. As a book publisher, with paper as a core part of our business, we are very concerned about the future of the world's remaining endangered forests and the environmental impacts of paper production. We are committed to implementing policies that will support the preservation of endangered forests globally and to advancing 'best practices' within the book and paper industries. EarthPress is committed to preserving ancient forests and natural resources. Our company's policy is to print all of our books on recycled paper, with 100% post-consumer waste content, de-inked in a chlorine-free process. In addition, all EarthPress books are printed using soy-based inks. As a result of these environmental policies, EarthPress and its parent company, Nova Publishing, have saved hundreds of thousands of gallons of water, hundreds of thousands of kilowatts of electricity, thousand of pounds of pollution and carbon dioxide, and thousands of trees that would otherwise have been used in the traditional manner of publishing its books.

EarthPress (through its parent company, Nova Publishing Company) is very proud to be one of the first members of the Green Press Initiative, a nonprofit program dedicated to supporting publishers in their efforts to reduce their use of fiber obtained from endangered forests. EarthPress (also through its parent company, Nova Publishing Company) is also proud to be an initial signatory on the Book Industry Treatise on Responsible Paper Use (see: www.greenpressinitiative.org). In addition, EarthPress uses all compact fluorescent lighting; recycles all office paper products, aluminum and plastic beverage containers, and printer cartridges; uses 100% post-consumer fiber, process-chlorine-free, acid-free paper for 95% of in-house paper use; and, when possible, uses electronic equipment that is EPA Energy Star-certified. Nova's freight shipments are coordinated to minimize energy use whenever possible. Finally, all carbon emissions from EarthPress office energy use are offset by the purchase of wind-energy credits that are used to subsidize the building of wind turbines on the Rosebud Sioux Reservation in South Dakota (see www.nativeenergy.com). We strongly encourage other publishers and all partners in publishing supply chains to adopt similar policies.

Dedication

This book is dedicated to my children, Justin and Jessica, and all the other children of the world, in whose hands the future rests. The book also is dedicated to my beautiful and very patient wife and partner, Jan, without whose encouragement, help, support, and true love, this book would not have been possible.

EarthPress
Resources for a Better World
1103 West College St.
Carbondale, IL 62901
Orders: (800) 462-6420 or
Editorial: (618)457-3521
www.earth-press.com

Distributed by:
National Book Network
4501 Forbes Blvd., Suite 200
Lanham, MD 20706
1-800-462-6420

Table of Contents

INTRODUCTION to Greening Your Business 9

Part One: The Basics of Greening Your Business

CHAPTER 1: The Challenge of Sustainable Business 12
  Bad News and Good News 15
CHAPTER 2: Why Green Business? 23
  Cost Savings 24
  Waste Reduction 25
  Employee Motivation 26
  Customer Loyalty 27
  Competitive Advantage 27
  Product and Service Design 29
CHAPTER 3: Green Business Concepts 31
  Pollution Prevention 31
  Cleaner Production 32
  Lean Manufacturing 33
  Eco-Efficiency 33
  Design for the Environment and Green Chemistry 34
  Extended Product Responsibility 35
  The Natural Step 35
  Factor Four 36
  Natural Capitalism 36
  Cradle-to-Cradle Design 37
CHAPTER 4: Green Business Tools 39
  Environmental Management Systems 39
  Eco- or Process-Mapping 41
  Cost Payback and Return on Investment Analysis 43
  Life Cycle Assessment 45
  Environmental Accounting 47
  Environmental Certification and Reporting Programs 48
CHAPTER 5: The Path to Greening Your Business 49
  Read through this Entire Guide 49
  Evaluate Various Green Actions 50
  Conduct a Company-Wide Green Assessment 50
  Develop and Implement Your Green Business Plan 51
  Consult Additional Resources 52

Part Two: Green Business Action Plans

CHAPTER 6: Green Business Energy Use 54

The Price of Carbon 55
Basic Business Energy Efficiency 57
Carbon Footprints and Energy Use Assessment 63
Energy Efficiency and Assessment Resources 65
Renewable Energy Use in Business 69
Carbon Offsets 74
Government Incentives for Energy Efficiency 75
Lighting Energy Efficiency 77
Business Energy Efficiency Plan 83
Energy Use Worksheet 86
Energy Survey Worksheet 87
Business Carbon Footprint Worksheet 88
Energy Use Process Map 89
Energy Efficiency Action Worksheet.. 90
Economic Analysis of Energy Efficiency Measures 95
Energy Efficiency Economic Analysis Worksheet 97

CHAPTER 7: Green Business Water Use 98

Business Water Conservation Resources 99
Business Water Efficiency Plan 100
Water Use Assessment 102
Water Consumption Worksheet 103
Water Survey Worksheet 104
Water Use Process Map 105
Water Conservation Action Worksheet 106
Economic Analysis of Water Use Efficiency Measures 110
Water Conservation Economic Analysis Worksheet 112

CHAPTER 8: Green Business Waste and Recycling 113

Waste Reduction Measurement Tool 117
Business Waste Reduction Plan 118
Waste Assessment 121
Waste Expense Worksheet 123
Waste Survey Worksheet 124
Waste Generation Process Map 125
Waste Reduction Actions 126
Waste and Recycling Action Worksheet 128
Dealing with Recycling 133
Dealing with Hazardous Waste 136
Hazardous Waste Regulations for Large Quantity Generators 143
Typical Hazardous Wastes Generated by Small Businesses 144
Economic Analysis of Waste Reduction Measures 145
Waste Reduction Economic Analysis Worksheet........................148

CHAPTER 9: Green Business Travel and Transportation 149
Business Travel and Transportation Efficiency Plan 151
Business Transportation Carbon Footprint Worksheet 153
Travel and Transportation Action Worksheet 154
Economic Analysis of Travel and Transportation Measures 158
Travel and Transportation Economic Analysis Worksheet 161

CHAPTER 10: Green Business Office Equipment and Computing 162
Office Equipment and Computing Efficiency Plan 165
Equipment and Computer Survey 167
Equipment and Computer Action Worksheet 168

CHAPTER 11: Green Business Supply Chains and Purchasing 173
Life Cycle Assessment Software 176
Green Business Purchasing Plan 179
Supply Chain Process Map 181
Supply Chain Worksheet 182
Supply Chain and Purchasing Action Worksheet 183
Supply Chain and Purchasing Questionnaire 184

CHAPTER 12: Green Business Building Design 186
Green Building Incentive Programs 189
Green Building Rating Programs 190
New Green Building Construction 193
Green Building Remodeling 195
Greening Your Leased Property 196
Green Building Cost Analysis 199
Green Building Plan 200
Green Building Action Worksheet 202
Economic Analysis of Building Upgrades 208
Building Upgrade Economic Analysis 209

CHAPTER 13: Green Product and Service Design 210
The Concepts Behind Green Design.....................................212
The Basic Rules of Green Design 216
The Green Design Process 219
Sustainable Products and the Bottom of the Pyramid 223
Green Product Design Plan 225
Limited Life-Cycle Assessment Worksheet 226
Green Product Design Worksheet 227

CHAPTER 14: Green Business Eco-Labeling and Certification 233
U.S. EPA Energy Star Program 234
Energy Star Product Categories 238
National Environmental Performance Track 239
Green Seal Program 241

Green Seal Environmental Standards 242
Green Seal Green Reports Available 242
Scientific Certification Systems 243
SCS Certifications Available 243
Global Eco-Labeling Network..244
European Union Eco-Labeling Program 245
Forest Stewardship Council 246
Marine Stewardship Council 246
Chlorine-Free Products Association 246
Greener Choices EcoLabels Center 247
EcoLabeling.org 247

CHAPTER 15: Environmental Management Systems................................248
Basic Environmental Management System 250
ISO 14001 Environmental Management Systems 252

CHAPTER 16: Green Business Sustainability Reporting 257
The Global Reporting Initiative and Ceres Principles 259
General Sustainability Report Guidelines 261
Other Sustainability Reporting Standards 262

CHAPTER 17: U.S. Environmental Regulations 263
Major Categories of U.S. Environmental Regulations...........................266
Additional U.S. Environmental Regulations 277
Environmental Regulation Compliance Worksheet 278

CHAPTER 18: Preparing Your Green Business Plan 279
Develop a Green Mission and Policy Statement 279
Determine Each Person's Responsibilities 280
Green Plan Responsibility Worksheet 282
Prepare Your Green Business Plan and Manual....................................284
Green Business Plan cover sheet 285
Basic Contents of Green Business Plan Manual 286
Performance Monitoring Worksheet 287
Implement and Monitor Your Green Business Plan 288
Beyond Greening Your Business 289

Bibliography of Green Business Books and Publications 290

Appendix A: Installation Instructions and Contents of CD 294

Appendix B: Resources for a Greener Business...................................299

Index 313

Introduction to Greening Your Business

This book is based on four simple premises. First, human civilization faces an array of profound environmental problems that have already begun to negatively affect the foundations of life on this planet—with human-induced climate change at the very top of the list. Second, business, in all its forms, is the only force on earth with enough reach, clout, personnel, and assets to confront and correct the most serious environmental problems that face humanity. Third, every single business in the world has both the ability and the opportunity to thrive and prosper by becoming more sustainable in every phase of its operations and, in doing so, become part of the solution to these critical problems. And finally, though creating a "green" and sustainable business can be an immensely complex task, the basic steps to doing so can be made both straightforward and understandable to any business owner.

This final premise is the task of this book: to provide owners of any business—from the tiny one-person proprietorship to the largest of corporations—a clear and comprehensive road map to creating a business that is part of the solution to our shared environmental, social, and economic problems. Part One of this book provides a background on the need for greener business practices and the myriad benefits to greening your own business. An overview of the various theoretical approaches to developing sustainable businesses and a quick look at some green business tools are also presented. The step-by-step method outlined in Part Two of this book provides a blueprint with which business owners may assess their own company's operations and prepare a comprehensive environmental plan for taking their business green. Every element of a business's impact on the environment will be examined—energy and water use, waste generation, transportation, computing and office equipment, supply chains and purchasing, building practices, and product and service design. Most importantly, the real-world steps that will need to be taken are presented in a clear, concise, and straightforward manner.

Definition break: When this book refers to "greening" a business, it is a reference to the continual process of moving towards an elusive goal—a business that produces no waste, is adaptable to innovation, uses the minimum of energy, matter, and the least toxic materials, and uses those materials in such a way that they may be easily reused or disposed of with no harm to the environment—a sustainable business.

Although this book can be used by businesses of any size, it is primarily intended for smaller and medium-sized businesses. Many, but by no means all, large corporations are already confronting many of the issues that are considered in this book. Naturally, large corporations have far more assets and personnel to address these issues and many have already adopted many of the practices and policies that are outlined. Additionally, nearly all of the available books regarding green business practices are geared toward the senior management of very large, even multinational, firms. These materials have fostered a dramatic move among these large corporations toward a more sustainable ecological footprint. In many respects, a few of the world's largest corporations are leading the way toward the greening of business, in particular, Interface Inc., led by its visionary CEO, Ray Anderson.

However, for medium and small businesses—which comprise 90 percent of the businesses in the world and represent more than 60 percent of all global economic activity—there has been little practical guidance available on the basic steps and systematic process involved in greening a business. In the U.S. alone, according to the Bureau of the Census, fully 5.4 million of the 6 million businesses now operating have 20 or fewer employees. In fact, an enormous 60 percent of all of the businesses in America—nearly 3.7 million in all—have fewer than 5 employees. For smaller businesses, both the choice—and the action necessary—to create a successful and sustainable business may be in the hands of a single person. Many small and medium-sized business have already taken great strides toward minimizing their impact on the natural world. Whatever the size of your business and whatever steps you may have already taken, there are many more opportunities awaiting as you begin the journey to a greener and more sustainable business.

To assist you as you begin this journey, many questionnaires, worksheets, and guidelines are provided that are designed to help business owners in the rewarding process of greening their businesses. Many of these aids, as well as other valuable resources, are provided in Appendices A and B and on the CD that accompanies this book. The many ideas, concepts, facts, and statistics noted in this guide can all be found, and further explored, in the publications listed in the bibliography or in the resources noted in Appendix B.

It is the deep desire of those who worked on this project that this guide help to show the way for businesses to save money, save energy, save resources, and maybe—just maybe—save the world.

Part One

The Basics of Greening Your Business

Chapter 1

The Challenge of Sustainable Business

Business drives the global economy like never before. Trillions of dollars flow around the world as businesses, large and small, meet the growing needs of people everywhere. Business, in all its manifestations, has an enormous, almost overwhelming, impact on every facet of life on Earth, and one of its greatest impacts is on the natural world. Global climate change, acid rain, deforestation, overfishing of the oceans, air and water pollution—all of these serious problems are negatively affected by how it is we humans go about our business. And, in turn, the impacts of many of these environmental issues are growing at increasingly exponential rates—from deforestation to overfishing the oceans to fresh water shortages to loss of biodiversity to concentrations of CO_2 in the atmosphere. If we have any hope of solving the profound problems that will confront humanity in the next few decades, our collective solutions will also need to grow at exponential rates. For that to happen, humanity will need to enlist every possible source of assistance. Chief among these is the sector that employs the most people, uses the most technology, has the greatest impact on the natural world, and is at the very heart of many of the environmental troubles we collectively face—the business sector—including heavy and light industry, high and low tech businesses, ancient and cutting-edge businesses, and the enormous businesses of forestry, farming, fishing, and extraction of oil, gas, and minerals. Each and every one of these types of businesses can begin to examine its own powerful impact on our fragile planet and begin to develop new plans, methods, policies, and means to insure that all business—including yours, whatever it may be—is actively engaged in creating a better and, ultimately, sustainable world. Thousands of businesses around the world have already discovered that, instead of aggravating and intensifying the profound problems that humanity faces, business can become an integral part of the solution—and in doing so, become an enormous force for positive change.

Why are you in business? Most people in the business world would answer that question with a reference to the product or service that their business provides—building homes, making pizzas, repairing cars, manufacturing computers, operating a web business, creating . . . well, just about anything. The North American Industrial Classification System lists literally thousands of different businesses that provide a mind-boggling array of goods and services to today's consumer. But if you dig a little deeper into the underlying motivations that drive people in the world of business, a different and more powerful perspective emerges. People are generally "in business" for much more personal and more profound reasons—to make money, of course, but often simply and primarily to provide a better life for their loved ones. They are in business to do the best job that they can do—regardless of what their business may be. They want the efforts they make in their careers to make a difference. They want the work they do to be meaningful. Ultimately, the overwhelming majority of people want simply this—to make the world a better place.

From the street peddler to the CEO, from the storekeeper to the industrialist—these powerful motivations are the true common denominator that unite businesses all across the world. But the daily pressures that face a business person to merely stay in business are enormous and these basic ideals are often lost in the struggle to operate a successful business in today's world of rising energy and health care costs, increasing competition, challenging social problems, and escalating environmental concerns. Around the world, thousands of business owners have found that they can better face the challenges that confront commerce and, simultaneously, begin to make the world a better place by operating their businesses with a new and different ethic—by greening their businesses.

Greening your business is the challenging and highly rewarding task of pursuing the path to sustainability. Over the past few decades, in what writer Paul Hawken, in his book *Blessed Unrest*, describes as "the largest movement in the world," millions of people across the globe, including thousands of businesses, have been pursuing a goal of sustainability. A very elusive concept, *sustainability* has suffered from many attempts at a clear definition. "Meeting the needs of the present generation without compromising the ability of future generations to meet their own needs," the somewhat cumbersome definition from the 1992 Earth Summit and the earlier Bruntland Commission, is one of the most common. But the clearest, most succinct definition that I've seen comes from a presentation at an environmental education conference by folklorist Susan Fowler. Susan accompanies all of her wonderful storytelling with sign language. She was struggling to come up with appropriate signs for "sustainability," and hit upon a simple solution. The sign language description for "extinction" is the two signs of "death" and "forever." In a flash of insight, Susan signed "life" and "forever" as sign language shorthand for sustainability—life forever—the diametrical opposite of extinction. Life forever—the valiant attempt to keep life, in all of its myriad variety, flourishing for as long as humanly possible, and for as close as we can get to forever, is as clear a definition of sustainability as I have seen.

Sustainability is generally accepted as having three critical components: economic, environmental, and societal. The central question that is posed by sustainability is: how to bring a higher quality of life (economic) to the masses of humanity (societal) without destroying the natural foundations upon which life on Earth is built (environmental). This particular question in turn becomes the central goal of the greening of business by adding one crucial word (shown following in italics). How can we *profitably* bring the benefits of a better quality of life to all humanity without destroying the natural world? This single question, perhaps more than any other, may be the most important that humanity has ever grappled with. And it is one that this current generation of humans, for better or worse, has the profound responsibility of answering—for we are today at a climactic point in history when inaction and the continuation of the status quo will surely provide an answer if humanity does not.

Sustainability is often referred to as "sustainable development" to emphasize the crucial component of ensuring that the benefits of modern society accrue also to the developing world. "Sustainable progress" is perhaps a clearer definition of the task. Can we continue to spread the progress that perhaps 20 percent of humanity has enjoyed in the last 50 years—in health care, education, communication, transportation, food, shelter and basic comforts—to the remaining 80 percent of humanity, but do so in ways that, ultimately, do not do irreparable harm to the natural world? As China and India and other developing countries accelerate their efforts to pull their people out of deep poverty, the answer to that question will be answered—for better or worse—in the next few decades.

Imagine for a moment that the world of business is organized to accomplish this task and, in the process, also provide enormous employment opportunities for humanity and make a profit, while simultaneously sustaining, indeed enhancing, the intertwined web of life that we have collectively inherited. Imagine a world where business is actively working to eliminate poverty; reverse environmental degradation; spread the benefits of health care to everyone; and provide educational opportunities worldwide. In fact, each and every individual component of this seemingly overwhelming undertaking is already a reality today somewhere in the world. There are businesses that are able to provide goods and services without adding pollutants to the atmosphere; businesses whose purpose is to clean or even create fresh water; businesses that have created products that mimic natural products by using nature's instruction manual and modeling their product design on animal or plant life; businesses that are thriving by supplying goods and services in a safe and clean manner; and thousands of businesses around the world that are designing the technology and products that can harness the renewable sources of energy that surround us. The greatest challenge of the twenty-first century is to make certain that this future unfolds for the entire world. It is the challenge of sustainability. It is the challenge of the greening of business.

This book is about possibilities and opportunities—the endless possibilities and enormous opportunities that can come from answering this challenge by taking your business on the road to sustainability. The greening of your business can be a quest, an adventure even, as you work to build a leaner, stronger, and healthier business. As science has been telling us about human health in recent years, in order to become healthier we need to cut out the fat, become more active, and lower our bodies' intake of harmful chemicals and additives. To create a sustainable business is to follow that same general plan: cut the inputs of energy and raw materials to an absolute minimum, make the business more resilient to change and risk, and eliminate toxic materials wherever possible. The results, as with a successful human fitness plan, can be stunning. Reductions of energy use can be well upwards of 70 percent; materials use can likewise often be reduced by half, or even more. Waste can, in some cases, be virtually eliminated or, better yet, sold for a profit or converted into additional useful products. Hazardous chemical use can be dramatically reduced or eliminated. And best of all, by creating a company that is healthier, a company that is poised for the future, a company that is lean and strong, you will almost inevitably generate greater profits, while eliminating many risks.

Like a highly trained athlete who is deeply in tune with her body, you will also begin to understand your business as never before. You'll understand intimately where all of your material inputs come from, where every kilowatt of your company's energy is used, how your supply and distribution chain operates, the exact make-up of each of your products, the intimate details of the services you provide, and precisely what materials comprise your waste stream. At each step of your journey towards sustainability, you will find ways to do things better, more efficiently, more effectively, safer, and with dramatically less waste and energy. You will be joining thousands of other businesses and millions of people around the world in the quest to align business with the real needs of humanity.

Bad News and Good News

With the greening of business however, as with many jokes, and most issues in the modern world, there is good news and bad news. Since it is always nice to end up on a positive note, we'll start with the bad news:

Every environmental problem that we face today as a society has its root cause in a conscious business decision.

Let's repeat and emphasize that:

Every environmental problem that we face today as a society has its root cause in a conscious business decision.

Skeptical? Stop for a moment and consider the major ecological problems we collectively face—the long and sometimes overwhelming list of environmental problems that stand directly in the path of our imagined future:

- Global warming and fossil fuel use
- Water pollution and lack of fresh water
- Air pollution and acid rain
- Biodiversity and habitat loss
- Overfishing and ocean pollution
- Topsoil loss and overuse of crop chemicals
- Depletion of natural resources and deforestation
- Toxic chemicals and hazardous waste, and, finally,
- Abject human poverty

If you look at the core causes and not just the symptoms of this wide range of problems, you find that a business decision falls at the heart of every one of these problems. Start with the greatest challenge that humanity faces: climate change. Nearly everyone now accepts the 2007 consensus opinion from the fourth and latest United Nations Intergovernmental Panel on Climate Change (IPCC) that, based on a review of over twenty-nine thousand observational data studies of the Earth's climate, **"Warming of the climate system is unequivocal, as is now evident from observations of increases in global average air and ocean temperatures, widespread melting of snow and ice, and rising global average sea level."** And the consensus scientific opinion of the IPCC is that 90 percent of that warming is caused by human activities.

The changes to the climate that are now taking hold around the world—melting Arctic and Antarctic ice, melting glaciers, increasingly violent storms, more droughts and floods, shifting growing seasons, spreading desertification, increasing stresses on habitat, dying coral reefs, the spread of tropical diseases, rising sea and land temperatures—are all a direct result of the introduction of increasing amounts of greenhouse gases into the earth's atmosphere. These increasing gases are, themselves, a result of an enormous range of human activities that are fostered, indeed, made possible by business.

Fine, but aren't we talking about all human activities, basically the sum total of all of our own individual actions, not just business actions? Modern life quite simply requires each of us to engage in activities that are, to some extent, harmful to the environment. To solve these problems, each of us needs to change our ways individually, right?

This position has been one of the central and traditional responses to all of our shared environmental problems: that we each need to work harder to make certain that our own personal actions have less impact on the earth and to take more individual responsibility for our actions. We each need to achieve a higher level of consciousness about the consequences of our own personal activities in order to solve all of the critical environmental problems.

While this is certainly true as far as it goes, it does not reach the heart of the problem: there is a conscious business decision at the very core of every environmental problem we face. We may seek and achieve a more spiritual path in our relationship with creation and then individually strive to live with a smaller environmental footprint, but if modern industrial society does not provide the tools necessary for all of us to do that, en masse, then our valiant individual efforts can be quickly overshadowed by our neighbor's purchase of a new Hummer 2 or China's current construction of a new coal-fired power plant every few days. This does not, in any way, diminish the enormous value of individual efforts. We need far more environmental enlightenment; we need far more people living simply; we need far more environmental education. We need all these things and much more. But the central issue, the issue that most often gets overlooked and, in fact, ignored is that we need much, much better business decision making to truly confront and solve the enormous range and complexity of environmental problems that we face. Until the enormous impact of business on our planet becomes truly green and fully sustainable for the long term, all other attempts to solve our common environmental problems will, quite simply, fail.

But, wait a minute, doesn't government have a major responsibility in this process?

While this also is true, much of the legislation regarding environmental problems has been increasingly shaped, in large part, by the influence of business on the political process. Government action in attempting to raise the mileage standards on autos and light trucks in the United States is a good example. Despite the overwhelming public consensus and the clear need to do so in order to combat the release of CO_2 into the atmosphere, conscious business decisions have led to sustained efforts to prevent the passage of legislation that would effectively begin to confront this critical, and increasingly imminent, problem. Even the recent, and long overdue, passage in the U.S. of mandated increases in fleet mileage standards was delayed and ultimately diluted by intense lobbying pressure from the auto industry. The decisions by business leaders to fund lobbying efforts to challenge legislative efforts on the grounds of the economic pain it would cause (raising mileage standards might cost us up to $200 per vehicle!) or the technological difficulty of meeting such standards (sure, we can make a Prius efficient, but, of course, we make SUVs, too) are just that: business decisions. And those business decisions are not only the root of the problem, they are also often the main roadblocks to effective solutions—even governmental-based solutions.

Of course, effective governmental policies can greatly accelerate the move to a sustainable society. Regulations and laws can work to prevent business from using the environment as its "free" waste dump—a business practice that economists like to obscure by referring to it as a "negative externality." Governments can provide powerful incentives to push business in a particular direction: tax breaks, direct payments, research funding, and subsidies of all kinds. Government can also help provide the public (and business) with the information that it will need to effectively confront the problems that society faces. In fact, throughout this book, we will look at many, many sources of very valuable government information and assistance that can be used effectively in all stages of greening your business. Unfortunately, however, compared with the speed at which business can bring solutions to bear on a particular problem if it is a perceived obstacle, governmental action is often grindingly slow. And time is a luxury that, unfortunately, is no longer on our side in the race to halt environmental degradation and climate change.

Returning to our list of problems, the use of fossil fuels in modern society continues, in part, because of a long line of business decisions to prevent the development of effective alternatives from being widely available to the public. Seemingly mundane efforts by business to retain subsidies and tax breaks for the oil, gas, and coal industries—an amount totaling in the tens of billions of dollars—have the effect of making the introduction of reliable alternatives all the more difficult, and have effectively stalled the rapid deployment of solar, wind, and other renewable energy technologies around the world, but particularly in America.

Comparable business decisions by other outmoded businesses seeking to retain their dominant positions and wring the last dollar out of old, outmoded, and dirty factories, processes, and machinery have ominously delayed the introduction of dramatically cleaner and, most importantly, currently available technologies. Despite the easy availability and enormous long-term cost and energy-use advantages of fluorescent lighting, Mr. Edison's incandescent light bulbs are still being produced by the millions—many of them on very, very old machinery. Most of the electricity being sold in the greatest industrial country the world has ever known is still being produced by boiling water with burning coal fires—some of it supplied by power plants constructed before World War One, and paid off long, long ago. Despite the wide availability of far better and more energy-efficient technology, the vast majority of vehicles being produced around the world in the twenty-first century are powered by a technology developed in the 1800s. Around the world, short-sighted business decisions, geared to increase next quarter's profits and supported by seemingly sound economic arguments, are preventing a tidal wave of new, better, and dramatically cleaner human technologies from replacing the technologies of the status quo.

Additionally, nearly continual business efforts to roll back the requirements of the U.S. Clean Water Act in America threaten to undo decades of progress in cleaning waterways, lakes, and wetlands. Business and agri-business decisions that fail to make the efficient use of fresh water a priority greatly exacerbate the growing problems surrounding fresh water. Business decisions to block efforts to expand the protections of the U.S. Clean Air Act have the effect of preventing further progress in reducing air pollution and acid rain. Rapid and increasing development of raw land threatens habitat in every state and nation and leads to often overwhelming pressure on entire species to survive. Business decisions to increase the takes from industrial fishing fleets lead directly to the decimation and collapse of fisheries worldwide. Business decisions to use our waterways and oceans as dumps leads to the enormous worldwide pollution of the oceans that is only now beginning to be quantified. Agricultural business decisions over spans of decades have led to massive soil loss, ocean dead zones from overfertilization, and to pesticide and herbicide residues entering the human food chain on a massive scale. Every one of our extractive industries—those of mining, forestry, fishing, and oil and gas extraction—are harvesting nonrenewable and renewable resources at increasingly nonsustainable rates. Business decisions keep extremely hazardous chemicals in our society even in the face of acceptable nontoxic alternatives. Most of these detrimental business decisions were, and are, based on simple and seemingly sound economics. In the recent past, it was just simply easier to ignore the environmental problems that such decisions fostered. This litany of problems caused by shortsighted business decisions, unfortunately, goes on and on and on. There are hundreds, if not thousands, of excellent books that expand upon each of these important issues.

But enough of the bad news. This book is about the good news.

Interestingly, the good news is surprisingly familiar:

Greening Your Business

Every environmental problem that we face today as a society has its root cause in a conscious business decision.

Yes, the good news is the same as the bad news. But by looking at that statement from a new and entirely different perspective, this news becomes fiercely optimistic good news. Because if the base causes of our environmental predicament are ultimately the direct result of shortsighted, uninformed business decisions, then the solutions to those very same problems *must* be possible with better, more informed business decisions. Business—the full spectrum of global commerce—is where the solutions to our global environmental problems lie. What needs to change then, is the fundamental way that basic business decisions are being made. To accomplish this, a new perspective needs to be injected directly into the heart of the business decision-making process—a green perspective.

Smarter and more principled business decisions can immediately confront and begin to correct the entrenched and very complex problems that we collectively face. Business can lead the way in eliminating any additional emissions of greenhouse gases into our atmosphere. Business need not wait for governmental regulation to begin to lead the way in halting air pollution and acid rain. Business can begin—today—to stop habitat loss and increase the biodiversity on this planet. Sound business decisions can stop ocean pollution and prevent overfishing; stop top soil loss and the overuse of crop chemicals; reverse deforestation and dramatically slow the depletion of our shared natural resources. Moral and thoughtful business decisions can eliminate toxic chemicals and hazardous waste from ever even entering the world. And finally, business can step up and lead the way in alleviating the abject human poverty that threatens to overwhelm vast portions of humanity. There can be no greater business purpose than to commit to providing solutions to these deep and challenging problems.

Business drives the global economy in ways that were solely the realm of governments in the very recent past. As recently as 1970, 70 percent of the money flowing into the developing world came from government and only 30 percent came from business and the private sector. Today, that situation is more than reversed—80 percent of the money flowing to the developing world is from business and the governmental input has fallen to just 20 percent. The economic, social and environmental impact of business on both the developed and the developing world is enormous and growing every day. Paul Hawken, author of *The Ecology of Commerce* and co-author of *Natural Capitalism*, perhaps said it best: "Business is the only mechanism on the planet today powerful enough to produce the changes necessary to reverse global environmental and social degradation." Business has a once-in-a-lifetime opportunity to lead humanity into a sustainable future. Of all the tasks we have assigned to business, this one is the greatest, the most profound.

The task of setting the world on a sustainable course is enormous, but it is also an opportunity of unmatched scale. It is difficult to conceive of the magnitude of the opportunities that are presented by restructuring the global economy to become sustainable, but a few visionaries have tried. Lester Brown, director of the Earth Policy Institute, states, "Restructuring the global economy so that economic progress can be sustained represents the greatest investment opportunity in history." Stuart Hart, professor of management in sustainable enterprise at Cornell University, writing in the *Harvard Business Review*, echoes those sentiments: "Sustainable development will constitute one of the biggest opportunities in the history of commerce." And finally, getting to the heart of the issue, Fisk Johnson, CEO of S. C. Johnson & Sons, Inc., says: "There is no inherent conflict between making the world a better place and economic prosperity for all."

Business, in all its myriad forms—from the smallest mom and pop enterprise to the largest multinational corporation—is where the ultimate solutions to these deep societal problems must lie. However, as Albert Einstein cautioned, "We can't solve problems by using the same kind of thinking we used when we created them." Rather, business will need to begin to use a better, more informed kind of thinking to solve the problems that we all, collectively, face—a better and more informed kind of business thinking—green business thinking.

That, fundamentally, is the focus of this book: to provide a straightforward, pro-active, and hands-on method for making better and more informed business decisions and to add a crucial, and often missing, environmental viewpoint to that decision-making process. By adding such an environmental perspective, business leaders of every stripe can begin to bring business decision making more in line with the concept of sustainability, and, by doing so, move human society progressively closer to the best possible future that we can imagine.

Greening your business will provide a multiplier effect to your efforts to reach that brighter future. Your work to create a more sustainable business will have a powerful ripple effect—flowing out in all directions from your enterprise—positively impacting its employees, its community, its investors, its competitors, its suppliers up the supply chain and customers down the supply chain. These effects will, in turn, influence all of those players to themselves take more positive steps toward achieving a sustainable future.

The process of greening your business is a major undertaking. It will constitute a new direction for your business and for you personally. The steps taken will take time, money, and a commitment to operating your business in a new and different manner. At the core of this process will be a reimagining of what your business really is and what, ultimately, it should be. Again, from Paul Hawken, writing in *The*

Greening Your Business

Ecology of Commerce: "To create an enduring society, we will need a system of commerce and production where each and every act is inherently sustainable . . . We must design a system . . . where the natural, everyday acts of work and life accumulate into a better world as a matter of course, not a matter of conscious altruism." But for now, at least, it will still take a conscious decision to take the first step—and the next—toward that sustainable system of commerce. Taking the action necessary to begin greening your business involves steps that anyone—in any business—can take today to make a difference in the quest for a better future.

All of us in the world of business need to understand the importance of taking these steps toward sustainability and, also, the critical urgency in taking them now. As we rapidly approach the peak of human population, the peak of oil production, and the tipping point of catastrophic climate change, the next few decades will very likely determine the future trajectory of humanity. That direction will be decided, in large part, by the combined decisions made by all of those involved in the business of the world. Each of us, as members of the world's business community, will have few opportunities in our lifetimes to make a decision as profound, far-reaching, and fundamentally important as the one we make in deciding to take our business down the path to sustainability.

Chapter 2

Why Green Business?

Creating a sustainable and greener business can have a dramatic and profound positive impact on our shared environment, but most business owners must also look at the pragmatic details of greening a business. How will it affect my business? Does it make economic sense to "green" my business? Is it a good business decision to begin to work towards creating a sustainable business? You run a business and you run it to make a profit. As much as you might support environmental issues and sustainability, first and foremost, your business needs to be successful. Can it be both green and successful?

The general public perception is that making our life-styles and our businesses more environmentally sensitive will, almost by definition, be more expensive than the status quo of business as usual. It is commonly assumed that there will be an "environmental premium" assessed for doing the right thing. Hybrid cars must cost more; organic produce must be more expensive; products that are nontoxic must be higher priced than their hazardous equivalents. All of us have a variation of this perception ingrained into our thinking, including our thinking about how we should run our business.

Unfortunately, for the most part, it simply isn't true. Common sense should tell us (if we listen) that food produced with fewer chemical pesticides and herbicides and with more efficient use of water should actually be cheaper; cars that are lighter and more energy-efficient should probably be less expensive, rather than more; products with fewer toxins and less hazardous waste should actually cost less to produce. The misperception that green = expensive itself has been fueled by many status-quo business interests in an effort to convince the public, government regulators (and, perhaps, themselves) that it would be much too expensive for them to _____ (you fill in the blank):

Upgrade the fuel economy of the cars they produce
Make products without the toxic chemicals they use
Treat the waste water leaving their factory
Mine minerals without damaging the environment
Grow crops without chemical pesticides/herbicides
Build homes without using hazardous non-renewable materials
Produce milk without bovine growth hormones and antibiotics
Produce enough energy without using coal, oil, or natural gas
Et cetera, et cetera, ad infinitum

But, as more businesses every day are realizing, the real world impact of greening a business is actually far different and almost universally positive. There are manifold powerful benefits to making your business more sustainable and greener.

Cost Savings

The cost savings associated with running a cleaner, more efficient business are the first and most obvious benefit to greening your business. Real money can be saved (and applied directly to your bottom line) when you take the steps necessary to look at your energy, water, and material inputs and trim them in every way possible. The task of looking at these inputs in detail can nearly always highlight dramatic savings that might otherwise be overlooked. The same careful examination of business transportation can almost always clearly illuminate striking savings possibilities in fuel usage. The complete analysis of how your business uses energy, water, and other inputs and a comprehensive exploration of how to reduce each and every one of these inputs is a critical component of greening your business. Such a careful look at your entire business operation can also provide a clear basis for better and more accurate costing and pricing of the products and services that your company provides. By looking at your business operations in a new green way, direct and measurable cost savings are not only possible, but highly probable.

Related to reducing your businesses inputs is operating your business in a leaner, more efficient manner. Lean manufacturing or production is a business concept that has been implemented in nearly all large corporations over the past few decades. Operating in a leaner mode by introducing "just-in-time" inventory methods (where new orders are fulfilled with inputs that have just been received by your company) can have many clear benefits. Lean, just in time operation reduces the cash that you will have invested in inventory. It also generally shortens the time between buying your material inputs and payment for your ultimate output of products. It can lower equipment needs by streamlining your production processes, and in turn, make it easier to increase or decrease your production runs. Lean production can also often reduce the size of facility needed. Tighter inventory controls can improve audit performance, reduce inputs, and make it easier to recycle any waste.

Implementing a lean and green system also can foster an overall culture of waste elimination among employees and management. Such attention to your supply chain can alert you in advance to any likely problems or upcoming price increases or shortages in the materials that your business may use. Finally, green operations tend to lend themselves to continual improvement in the entire production or manufacturing process. Green operation can also be applied to service businesses by, again, examining the entire process that your business uses and carefully looking for every possible place to reduce inefficiency and waste.

The real and often immediate cost savings associated with running a more energy-, materials-, and waste-efficient business are one of the prime reasons for greening your business. By operating a more efficient business, it will be nearly inevitable that you will be more successful and profitable in clear and quantifiable ways.

Waste Reduction

A detailed look at the waste stream of any business will show the owners the true cost of the waste they produce and make plainly evident the maxim that "waste is money." Looking at waste from a new, sustainable perspective can often show how waste, rather than being an expense item, can instead become an income item— that what may have been your company's waste in the past can be an important input for another company's industrial process—that, in fact, it isn't really waste unless and until you actually waste it.

By looking at your company's waste stream in detail, you will begin to understand the true cost of waste: that every single thing that your company disposes of— every single thing that leaves your business not as a saleable product, from used packaging, to trimmings, to waste oil, to smoke stack emissions, to plant effluents— was initially purchased. When purchased materials become waste, you are quite literally throwing away money. Waste not only doesn't make environmental sense, it just doesn't make business sense either. How to reduce, sell, or eliminate waste in your business is a major component to greening your business.

Employee Motivation

Introducing a green business culture to your enterprise can also have a dramatic effect on your employees' motivation and morale. It is far more rewarding personally to work for a company that is making every effort to operate in a clean, honest, and progressive manner than to work for a company that is polluting its environs, ignoring regulations, and wasting material and energy. Improving your employees' (and your own) pride in their work and in their company can build a highly motivated work force that is more loyal, has less turnover, and is much more involved in the process of innovation. This employee motivation and involvement can drive additional cost savings as you move your company toward a greener and leaner future.

You will also begin to attract the best and the brightest employees—those who share your values and commitment to actively creating a better world. As the best employees are drawn to your company, you'll also notice that they will tend to stay longer—thus reducing your costs of retraining new employees. You will have far less turnover as your employees find much greater satisfaction working for a company that mirrors their own personal values. People want to make a positive difference with their lives and their work. They want their lives to be meaningful. If they are able to find this in their work, this satisfaction will translate into increased productivity as they apply their efforts to helping the company become ever more environmentally and socially responsible.

Increased employee commitment to a greener company mission will also provide you with an excellent early warning system regarding potential problems, as your fundamental shift in focus to greener operations will foster a closer appraisal of all aspects of your company by its employees. You and your employees will be more likely to notice aspects of your business that can be improved once the mission of the company is directed toward a continual improvement of the environmental impact of the business.

A cleaner, more efficient business, one that has reduced its waste stream and its use of toxic substances, will also offer its employees a much healthier and safer workplace atmosphere that will in turn inspire greater employee confidence in and loyalty to your company. A healthier and safer business will also be a workplace that is far less prone to accidents, spills, or other emergencies. You will find that the benefits that accrue to your business from the process of striving for sustainability will begin to show up in ways that you never anticipated. And those benefits will continue to grow as your outlook on your business changes to a more hands-on approach to finding and exploiting every possible measure to green your business.

Customer Loyalty

Much as your shift to a greener business can motivate your employees, doing so will generally also foster a sense of loyalty in your customer base. People simply like to do business with companies that care about the impact of their products and their operations on their communities, their regions, and the wider world. By understanding your business at a deeper level, you will also begin to better appreciate your customers' needs and can help them understand the goals that your new green business direction is striving to fulfill. As a conscientious business, your products or services will have greater appeal to a public that is itself struggling to live in a more sustainable manner. Without resorting to "greenwashing" your efforts, you can begin to position your business as a leader in its field or community and increase its market position in relation to other less motivated business competitors.

By holding true to your new mission of creating a sustainable business, you will develop a customer trust in your business that is, in many ways, priceless. By being honest with your customers and the public about the new direction of your company and the actual steps that you are taking, you will likely avoid any sustained attacks on your company or your company's image regarding current social and environmental issues or problems related to the type or makeup of the products that you sell. The community or communities that you work in will also likely respond in positive ways to your new and smarter way of doing business. By working steadily to provide a better quality of life through your business, you will find that your reputation in your industry, your community, and with your customers will be pleasantly enhanced.

Competitive Advantage

By adopting a cleaner, greener, and leaner business model, you will begin to appreciate what green businesses worldwide have already noticed: green business has a distinct competitive advantage over most of its traditional "brown" competitors. By reducing or eliminating the environmental compliance costs of a business, green business owners are finding that they are more flexible in how they can operate. Because their businesses are operated in a more efficient and streamlined manner, their overall costs are often much less than their dirtier competitors. This efficiency in operations can have benefits beyond the bottom line. More efficient and cleaner operations will most likely find their insurance premiums falling rather than rising as the health and safety benefits of the new operations methods begin to take effect.

Greening Your Business

If raising outside capital is important to your business, the cleaner and greener a business is, the better the access to capital will become. Banks and investors find clean, green, and well-run companies much more appealing than companies that are continually struggling to comply with government regulations, dealing with rising energy, water, and materials costs, and shouldering the high costs and dangers of handling and disposing of hazardous substances. Because you will be ahead of the curve in insuring that your operations are run in a clean and safe manner and that your products are safe and nontoxic, you will be well-poised to avoid any surprises as new environmental, health, and safety regulations are enacted. Likewise, a cleaner, greener business is less likely to be confronted by legal surprises, such as lawsuits stemming from product toxicity, violations of state or federal regulations, and other expensive legal difficulties. As an environmentally sensitive business, you will be able to differentiate yourself—in vibrant and cutting-edge fashion—from any of your stodgy status-quo competitors.

The greening of your business can also provide a competitive advantage as you may seek to expand your business. Increasingly, large corporations are examining their entire supply chains to insure that all of their suppliers are certified as environmentally sound businesses. We'll examine certification programs in Chapter 4 and again in Chapter 14. There is also a growing tendency for financial analysts to upgrade the investment quality of a firm based on its perceived environmental performance and sustainability. Increasingly stringent environmental regulations are also taking hold in some regions—from tougher air quality regulations in California to comprehensive take-back packaging rules across Europe—and, as a green business, you will be poised to enter these markets more quickly and with less retooling than other businesses with less advanced leadership.

Finally, climate change is poised to dramatically affect all businesses across the world—creating, at once, the largest change in business and the largest new market (for carbon) in a century. Governments around the world are gearing up for major initiatives to confront climate change. Europe already has a market in place for trading carbon emissions, and the Chicago-based Climate Exchange is set to trade greenhouse gas emissions on a large scale with a commodities-like market exchange, with hundreds of companies already registered to trade. Sooner rather than later, carbon emissions emanating from business will begin to be inventoried and then regulated as a pollutant. A recent U.S. Supreme Court case confirmed that the U.S. EPA has such regulatory authority. Carbon taxes are another distinct possibility as the world struggles to find ways to wean itself from fossil fuels. Whether via carbon trading or taxes, a market price for carbon will be created that will have major effects all across the business world. Large corporations are already taking steps to adjust to this eventuality. By beginning the process of examining your carbon emissions and seeking ways to lessen them now, you will be years ahead of competitors that ignore this reality. All of these advantages to greening your business will provide your new lean and clean business with distinct competitive advantages over competitors.

Product and Service Design

As you examine your business from the ground up with an eye toward building a greener, more sustainable operation, you will enter into the process of carefully analyzing each of the products or services that your company provides. As you look at each product or service through the lens of sustainability, you will begin to seek better and more sustainable product or service design—design that has the least impact on our fragile planet. This will move you into the exciting world of *design for the environment, cradle-to-cradle design,* and *biomimicry*—three relatively new ways to look at human products and services in a manner that seeks to bring the delivery of products and services more closely in line with the rules of the natural world, rather than the rules that govern the economic realm. This area is actually the heart and soul of creating a sustainable business—the fundamental examination of what your business really is and how best to operate that business. Reimagining your business can be the most exciting part of the process. We'll examine these and other green business concepts in the next chapter and again in Chapter 13.

Moving your business in a greener direction is a process, a continual process that has as its central goal the profitable and productive delivery of goods and services in a manner that has the least possible harmful impacts on the world around us. As you begin this process with your own business, you will begin to reap all of the additional benefits that a greener business can provide—dramatic cost savings from reduced energy, water, and material inputs; striking reductions in waste and, perhaps, new income streams from the recycling of any remaining waste; greater employee pride, motivation, health and safety; more customer loyalty stemming from your new commitment to operating your business in a less harmful manner; greater competitive advantage in the marketplace over other less environmentally sensitive companies; and exciting new possibilities for improved product and service design.

Naturally, the costs to implement all of the various green business practices are not free. Oftentimes the initial costs may, in fact, be rather steep. Part of operating a greener business, however, is beginning to take a longer view of your business—a view that stretches farther into the future than you may be used to looking. By taking a longer view of your business and by examining the full cost of operating your business in an inefficient and less-than-green manner, you will begin to adopt a new business point of view that looks at the longer-term costs and benefits of each of your activities. Yes, it may be expensive up front to change all of your company's lighting to all compact fluorescent lighting (or, better yet, all LED lighting), but when you look at the long-term savings—in terms of actual costs of energy use, the resulting reductions in emissions, and other very real benefits— the up-front expenses begin, in many cases, to look like real bargains. There will, of course, be many balancing acts you will have to perform. You can't implement all of the innovative green techniques, policies, and operations at once. You will, of necessity, have to develop a long-range plan to achieve all of the various ideas that you will find in this guidebook.

The fundamental benefits of green business are really very simple to understand. Jeffrey Hollender, CEO of Seventh Generation, the fastest growing brand of environmentally friendly cleaning and personal care products in the U.S., with sales over $100 million annually, explains: "You generally make more money when you do the right thing. When you do the wrong thing, people sue you, governments fine you, sales plunge, disgusted employees sabotage you, community groups start picketing you, reporters show up . . . . And, ultimately . . . pollution is waste; waste represents inefficiency; and inefficiency is simply not profitable. It's that simple."

Business owners are often lulled into a feeling that the current status quo is a permanent condition—that what has been true in the past will be true in the future. History, of course, teaches us just the opposite. Change is the only real certainty. In the modern world, where technology is changing daily and other very powerful forces—from population, to health care issues, to religion, to peak oil, to climate change—are putting increasing pressure on society, those businesses that are able to act on change, in fact, thrive on change, will be the ones that will prosper. Greening your business is ultimately about changing your business—about making your business better. Greening your business is a long-term commitment to enter into the process of continually moving your business in a new and sustainable direction. It is a direction that you will find is highly rewarding, both for your business and, ultimately, for yourself personally.

Chapter 3

Green Business Concepts

In the realm of green business, a host of brilliant thinkers have devised various frameworks to explore how we can successfully create a business atmosphere that fosters progress towards sustainability. In the 1970s, the concept of pollution prevention took hold in environmental regulation reform. In the 1980s, Swedish doctor Karl-Henrik Robèrt outlined a fundamental approach to these issues that he titled The Natural Step. In the 1990s, the Factor Four concept was introduced by Ernst Von Weizsacker and Amory and L. Hunter Lovins. In 1993, Paul Hawken developed a similar powerful approach to business in his book, *The Ecology of Commerce*. In 1999, Paul Hawken, Amory Lovins, and L. Hunter Lovins joined forces to expand upon these concepts in their book, *Natural Capitalism*. Exciting new concepts like biomimicry and cradle-to-cradle design have also emerged. Many other frameworks and approaches have been created and discussed, often using a similar set of parameters by which to examine business practices. The approach in this book to greening your business is a hands-on amalgam of many of these theoretical concepts. Let's take a look at these various concepts and their interrelationships.

Pollution Prevention

One of the earliest manifestations of greening a business was the concept of *pollution prevention*. This simple idea was that it is cheaper and easier to prevent pollution in the first place than to treat it, dispose of it, or handle it later, whether at the smoke stack, the landfill, or the end of the pipeline. Reducing pollution at its source was the key to this concept. Strategies for examining industrial processes were developed to attempt to eliminate pollution or waste at each step. Adopting pollution prevention has direct, immediate and measurable benefits for any business. It will often dramatically reduce a company's operational cost by reducing or eliminating waste storage or disposal costs. Employee health and safety costs are also lowered if there is less exposure to toxic materials. Prevention of pollution also reduces a business's environmental compliance costs. Complying with environmental regulations regarding pollution is expensive. Preventing pollution in the first place turns out to be extremely cost effective. Long-term liabilities and cleanup costs are also reduced if less pollution is produced in the first place. The first step on the road to a sustainable business is to prevent pollution.

Cleaner Production

This focus on pollution prevention led businesses to examine *cleaner production* methods. Introduced in 1989 by the United Nations, "cleaner production" is the U.N. term for reducing the environmental impacts from processes, products, and services by using better management strategies, methods, and tools. Cleaner production includes activities such as pollution prevention, waste minimization, phase-out of toxic materials, and eco-efficiency (which we'll examine later in this chapter). Four elements have been identified that define cleaner production:

The Precautionary Principle
This concept provides that a business must itself first prove that a substance or activity will cause no harm before introducing it into the marketplace. This approach is particularly important if a product or activity has the potential to cause severe or irreversible harm. In legal terms, this places the burden of proof on the business that wishes to introduce any potentially harmful products to the market. A corollary is that a lack of scientific certainty about the potential harm is not an excuse to do nothing about it.

The Preventive Approach
This is an adoption of the earlier concept of pollution prevention and reducing pollution at its source—source reduction.

Democratic Oversight
The principle highlights that business should reflect a concern for its workers, its customers, and the community at large. This concern should be manifested in more transparency (a favorite U.N. term) that allows all parties more information about the waste and products that the business produces. With more information, these stakeholders (another beloved U.N. term) will have a better ability to become involved in the decision-making process.

Life-cycle Approach

Cleaner production techniques require a holistic approach that looks at all phases of production throughout the life of the product, from the manner in which its raw materials are obtained, to its actual production processes, and on through its distribution, sale, and eventual disposal.

These four elements introduced to the world of business a new way of thinking about industrial processes. It was an attempt to look for ways that products could be made with less damage to humans and the environment.

Lean Manufacturing

A related concept, *lean manufacturing*, was initially developed by Toyota to minimize waste in its production facilities. Toyota identified seven separate sources of waste: defective products, overproduction of products, unnecessary transportation, delays in production or time spend waiting, inventory waste, unnecessary motion in the production process, and overprocessing of materials. By addressing each of these waste issues, a company's operations can become leaner and far less wasteful in its use of energy, water, and raw materials.

These first attempts to address waste, pollution, and environmental issues in the business world did not look deeply into the issue of sustainability. These early efforts were designed to eliminate the low-hanging fruit of waste and pollution and were laudable goals as far as they went. Valuable techniques and practices from each of these concepts are integrated into the methods outlined in this book to green your business. But to have a truly green business is to look deeper into what a business produces or provides and attempt to align the product or service itself more closely with environmental principles. The next concepts were developed in an attempt to do just that.

Eco-Efficiency

Introduced in 1992 in the book *Changing Course: A Global Business Perspective on Development and the Environment*, by industrialist Stephan Schmidheiny and the World Business Council for Sustainable Development, *eco-efficiency* was a natural extension of the concepts of cleaner and leaner production. It incorporated all of the pollution and waste prevention notions of these earlier ideas and then went beyond them to begin to look more closely at how products are actually produced and the processes involved in their manufacture. To be eco-efficient is to produce products that are more durable, more repairable, and more able to be efficiently recycled than previous products. This concept addressed a major issue with modern consumer society: the throwaway aspect of much of the goods that are produced.

Eco-efficient manufacturing also introduced the concept of closed-loop systems. Borrowing from our understanding of natural systems—in which waste from one process becomes fodder for the next process—eco-efficient manufacturing provides that the waste from one process can become the raw materials for the next production activity. Ideally, an eco-efficient product, once used, can be disassembled or reassembled to become another useful product. Eco-efficiency began to more fully introduce a life-cycle perspective into the manufacturing processes of modern society—an attempt to look at the entire life of a product— from raw materials to eventual disposal or, preferably, reuse of the product itself or its materials.

This concept was a neat fit with the mantra of reduce, recycle, and reuse. Eco-efficiency, in its best form, should provide for a reduction in the material and energy intensity of goods or services. It should also provide for a reduction in the use of toxic materials, improved recyclability of products, maximum use of renewable resources, and greater durability (and thus longer life) of the products produced. The concepts of eco-efficiency are integrated into the various guidelines that are presented in this book. Other newer concepts have continued to expand upon these core principles.

Design for the Environment and Green Chemistry

The U.S. Environmental Protection Agency has adopted an advanced version of eco-efficiency that they term *Design for the Environment* (or DfE). This program stresses redesign of manufacturing processes to eliminate waste, lessen toxicity, and provide for improved recyclability and reuse. The Office of Pollution Prevention and Toxics at the U.S. EPA uses life-cycle assessments and various chemical assessment tools and expertise to examine possible substitutes to hazardous materials. This program has examined the use of detergents, lead solder, flame retardants, paints, and many other products. The growing field of chemical sustainability and *green chemistry* is the focus of this particular version of eco-efficiency. Green chemistry is an effort to use chemistry to design products that are nontoxic and have no hazardous by-products or waste. A component of this program is the right to display the DfE logo on recognized products that have been designed to ensure that their ingredients and finished products are on the green end of the health and environmental spectrum. We'll look at green chemistry concepts in more detail later in this book when we look at product design and related issues in Chapter 13.

Extended Product Responsibility

This concept, also known as *extended producer responsibility* refers to the idea that those entities that produce a product should be responsible for that product throughout the entire life of the product. This places the obligation for eventual disposal of a product on the producer. The first legislative effort using this concept was initiated in Germany in the 1990s and required producers to either reuse their packaging or pay for the recycling of it. German manufacturers were required to take back their packaging from the ultimate consumer and very quickly developed better, more efficient, and more recyclable packaging, often-times entirely eliminating unnecessary and redundant packaging. Following the success of the German laws, the European Union soon followed suit. This concept is primarily used as a regulatory tool to encourage (or force) businesses to behave responsibly, but it can be used successfully as an overall design concept as well.

The Natural Step

In the 1980s, Swedish physician Karl Henrik Robèrt and a group of Swedish scientists developed a new and more scientific and systematic approach to looking at business sustainability issues. In a concept that he termed *The Natural Step*, Dr. Robèrt looked to the underlying theories of thermodynamics and outlined four requirements for a sustainable society (which he termed "system conditions"):

- The natural world should not be subjected to increased concentrations of substances extracted from the earth's crust (i.e., minerals, oil, gas, etc.).

- The natural world should not be subjected to increased concentrations of substances produced by society (such as PCBs, insecticides, nuclear waste, and other chemicals or compounds not found in nature).

- The natural world should not be subjected to degradation of its capacity for renewal (such as by overfishing the oceans, destroying topsoil, deforestation, mountain top–removal mining and other similar activities).

- Humanity should not be subjected to conditions that systematically undermine their capacity to meet their needs (most particularly abject poverty).

These system conditions are intended not as a prescription that must be rigidly followed, but rather as a compass that can lead business owners to examine their companies in a new light and then determine for themselves how to align their businesses with these basic concepts. Part of the Natural Step process is envisioning the environmental ideal of a product or service, one that meets all the Natural Step conditions, and then "backcasting" or working backwards to try to take the necessary steps to achieve such an ideal. The Natural Step has been adopted as a guide by many businesses worldwide to help them fundamentally rethink how their businesses operate. It provides a sound scientific basis for the greening of any business.

Factor Four

In the 1990s, an additional concept, *Factor Four*, was developed by Ernst Von Weizsacker of the Wuppertal Institute for Climate, Environment, and Energy and by L. Hunter and Amory Lovins of the Rocky Mountain Institute. Factor Four is actually a fairly simple concept to grasp: if you double the life of a product by making it more durable, you decrease by half the amount of materials used to provide that product over its productive life. If you additionally decrease by half the amount of materials that are required to produce this more durable product in the first place, you again decrease the materials used by 50 percent. This more efficient use of resources can, if implemented widely, radically reduce material use by 75 percent. The Factor Ten concept is an extension of this that would provide a 90 percent reduction in material usage. Hundreds of examples are provided in this ground-breaking book to show the effectiveness of this bold, innovative concept.

Natural Capitalism

In 1999, a variation of this concept was introduced to the U.S. by Amory Lovins, L. Hunter Lovins, and Paul Hawken in their best-selling book, *Natural Capitalism: Creating the Next Industrial Revolution*. This book refined the concept of Factor Four and introduced new strategies of its own, some of which had been proposed by Paul Hawken in his earlier 1993 book *The Ecology of Commerce: A Declaration of Sustainability*. The four main points of Natural Capitalism, a set of principles for a sustainable economic system, are:

Radical Resource Productivity
This strategy involves deliberately making our resource use far more efficient by effectively getting the same amount of use or value from a product or process while using far less energy or materials. It is an extension of the Factor Four concept.

Biomimicry
This strategy envisions the actual redesign of products or processes on more biologically based designs, thus enabling closed-loop systems of production and the elimination of toxic and hazardous substances—production that mimics the

biology and design of nature. This concept was popularized in 1997 by author Janine Benyus in her book: *Biomimicry: Innovation Inspired by Nature*. It envisions a thorough study of nature in an effort to emulate or take creative inspiration from the elegant processes of nature and apply them to human industry.

Service and Flow Economy

This natural capitalism strategy calls for a dramatic shift from selling goods for customers to use to simply providing those same customers with the services that those goods actually provide. This concept is also referred to by the lengthy term of "dematerialization," emphasizing the attempt to dramatically lessen the use of materials by continually taking them back from the consumer and remanufacturing them in some manner. Interface Inc., the largest manufacturer of carpet in the world, led by its innovative and visionary CEO, Ray Anderson, has aggressively and very successfully adopted this strategy for leasing and taking back its carpet products rather than simply selling them to customers.

Investing in Natural Capital

This strategy calls for increasing our investments in preserving, restoring and actually expanding the natural capital of our planet. This embraces the further concept of eco-system services: the idea that the natural systems of our planet —the water cycle, the carbon cycle, the oceans, the forests, the plains, the mountains, etc.—provide humanity with an enormous array of services that we take for granted because we don't have to pay for them. Such eco-system services include providing our oxygen, sequestering our carbon, cleaning our fresh water, decomposing our waste, regulating the climate, pollinating our crops, and many more services that we underappreciate because they are assigned no value in our current economic system.

Cradle-to-Cradle Design

The Natural Step, Factor Four, Natural Capitalism and Biomimicry together introduced several new concepts into the business sustainability debate, chief among them the concept of redesign. To achieve sustainability, the human production of goods requires a reexamination from the ground up (in fact, from below the ground in the case of oil, gas, and mineral production) in a concerted effort to dramatically reduce the environmental impact of all products' material use. Architect William McDonough and scientist Michael Braungart expanded on this principle by introducing the *cradle-to-cradle* concept, explained in their 2002 book *Cradle to Cradle: Remaking the Way We Make Things*. This idea is meant to replace the current cradle-to-grave analysis of product life that looks at a product from genesis (cradle) to disposal (grave) and attempts to lessen the environmental impact along this linear lifespan. The cradle-to-cradle concept develops a life-cycle view of products in which a product is designed to emulate the cyclical nature of biological processes. What we perceive of as waste, in the natural world nearly always represents food for other organisms. This process of designing products to be cyclical over their life-cycles was termed *eco-effectiveness* in opposition to the earlier, more linear concept of eco-efficiency. Eco-efficiency was seen as striving to be less bad, while eco-effectiveness is seen as striving to be more good, as in healthy and sustainable. While some of the differences in approach stem from semantics, cradle-to-cradle thinking incorporates an innovative strategy that encourages a fundamental redesign of much of our industrial production so that the materials used may become either "biological nutrients" that may later be returned to the ecosystem with no harm, or "technical nutrients" that may be used continuously in closed-loop systems of production.

Each of these theoretical approaches to greening a business has effective elements that can help a business progress along the road to sustainability. The process of greening a business is a long-term process and a particular business may start at any point along the continuum in this process. Your business may have already taken steps to lessen energy use or revamp its operations to become more transportation-efficient. You may have already begun to address water use, recycling, and even redesign. But no business can yet claim to be entirely sustainable; no business can yet claim not to violate any of the four system conditions delineated by The Natural Step; and no business can yet consider itself entirely deep green. All business owners can learn more about how their own business operations impact our shared environment and how they can strive to lessen that impact in ways that are both attainable and profitable.

Part Two of this guide will provide a wide range of tools and techniques to assist in that process. Those tools and techniques have been adopted from a fusion of all of the various theories that have been developed to help businesses achieve sustainability. Some of them are simple and easily adopted, and others are much more advanced and require rethinking your business at a far deeper level. Chapters 12 and 13 on green building and green product design, in particular, will look at the latest concepts and practices to help you radically rethink your business, including a closer look at the Natural Step, Natural Capitalism, Biomimicry, and Cradle-to-Cradle Design. Regardless of whether your business has already taken some steps toward sustainability or whether you are only now considering such a move, once you commence the process of greening your business, you'll begin to understand that it is not a destination, but rather a journey—a journey that you will be taking with millions of others who are working to create a sustainable future.

Chapter 4

Green Business Tools

Across the globe, each year more and more business owners are beginning to understand the enormous immediate and future competitive advantages that accrue to businesses that become more environmentally conscious. These business leaders understand that the advantages stem not from the simple expediency of greenwashing their businesses in the public's eye, but rather from the pragmatic and fundamental overhaul of their entire business operations and their alignment with the core concepts of green business practices.

A short aside: No modern businesses have actually achieved full sustainability in their entire operations. Full sustainability would be an enterprise that is fully powered by renewable energy from product input to distribution; and whose product or service is created in such a way as to enhance, rather than detract from, the natural world, and then be reused in its entirety in the way that nature reuses material. Many businesses, however, have achieved remarkable success from their green efforts.

Environmental Management Systems

One of the initial efforts to provide a comprehensive framework for businesses to use to implement environmental practices into their operations was the development of environmental management systems. The development of environmental management systems in the later years of the twentieth century was spurred by an attempt to quantify improvements (or regressions) in the environmental performance of companies. Initially, the focus of environmental management systems was primarily on compliance with environmental regulations. As such, although it introduced some environmental consciousness into business decision making, it was somewhat limited in its impact. The development of global standards in environmental management did boost the recognition of the need for greater efforts on the part of business in the sustainability arena. The most widespread environmental management system is that used by the International Organization for Standardization: ISO 14001. This system was developed as an environmental adjunct to the successful ISO 9000 Quality Management Program that provides tools and certification for businesses that are in compliance with the various business and industrial quality standards.

The benefits of establishing an environmental management system for your business are many. Such a program puts environmental issues directly on the table and increases awareness of them at every level of a company. By quantifying environmental issues, it becomes much easier to see the cost and other benefits that can stem from taking a more pro-active approach. Naturally, this will lead to cost savings as environmental issues are identified and handled in a more systematic way, reducing toxics, materials, and energy and water use, lowering compliance costs, and reducing health and safety threats.

Environmental management systems generally consist of the following steps:

- Develop a company-wide environmental policy
- Communicate environmental requirements to everyone in the company
- Establish clear and measurable targets and goals
- Set up a clear structure for responsibility to meet those goals
- Provide training and awareness for everyone in the company
- Document your efforts carefully
- Develop an emergency response plan
- Monitor and measure your results
- Correct any deficiencies and prevent any noncompliance

In recent years, the focus of environmental management systems has broadened to encompass a wider range of issues than mere regulatory compliance. We will look into environmental management systems in more depth later in this book in Chapter 15 and provide the basics for developing your own strategy.

Beyond mere compliance with environmental regulations, businesses began to seek a proactive method for approaching sustainability issues. To this end, a series of tools was developed to help businesses analyze their operations. Among these, eco-mapping or process-mapping, cost payback analysis, life-cycle assessment, and environmental accounting are, perhaps, the most useful.

Eco- or Process-Mapping

The purpose of *eco-mapping* is to provide small companies and organizations with a visual, simple and practical tool to analyze and manage their environmental behavior. It involves making a map of a company's premises—for example, a shop floor, a workshop, or an office—to create an understanding of how materials, energy or water are used in the current environmental situation. Eco-mapping was developed in Europe by Heinz-Werner Engel as part of an International Network for Environmental Management initiative. *Process-mapping* is a similar visual representation of the entire process involved in creating a particular product. Both of these similar concepts provide a framework through which to define, highlight, and prioritize environmental issues. The visualizations can then serve as a guide for taking action to lessen the overall environmental impact of the premises or processes.

The development of detailed environmental management systems can seem unnecessary and daunting to small companies. Despite their value, such systems tend to be somewhat bureaucratic in nature. In contrast, process-mapping is a relatively simple and immediately available tool that can provide a clear picture of the environmental flows of energy and materials in your company. It also enables you to quickly involve your employees and other management directly in the process of thinking about the environmental impacts of the business. Process-mapping provides a systematic way for you to conduct an on-site review of your business with an eye to improving its environmental performance. Process-mapping is effective for examining your company's energy use, water use, waste flows, and material supply chains.

Each of the chapters in this book relating to those four topics provides information that will help you develop a process map for energy, water, waste, and materials for your own company. You can also use them to identify accident areas and environmental risks, or to plan for building upgrades. You will probably want to return to your process maps at least annually and draw new ones to visualize your progress in addressing the issues that your process map has illuminated.

The concept is simple: draw a simple visual map of a particular aspect of your business with a view to illustrating the flow of energy, materials, or waste through your company. The technique is also simple: Grab a sheet of paper and a pencil and start drawing. A clear process map of any phase of your business shouldn't take more than an hour of you and your employees' time. Here are a few basic pointers for preparing your process maps:

- Like most maps, make your process map as it is seen from above.

- Try to draw the area involved (the shop floor, the office, the entire site) to scale as much as possible without getting too obsessive about it. It should simply provide a view that is clearly recognizable and in rough proportion.

- If your process map gets too complicated, it will be difficult to follow. You may need to break it down into two or several maps of different areas of your business. Keep it simple and clear.

- Develop some type of symbols to identify problems. These should be simple—like a big circle around something or exclamation points!!!

Here is a simple process map of the waste collection in a pizza parlor and some possible waste reduction suggestions:

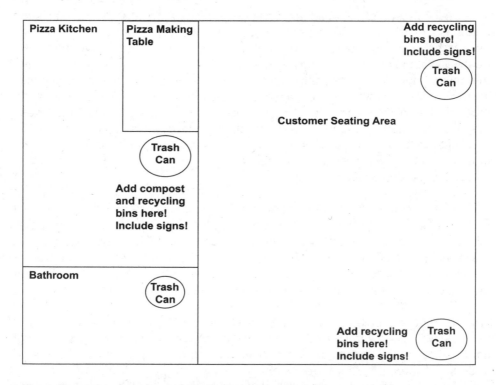

Add compost bin and signs in kitchen to collect food scraps.
Add recycling bins and signs in seating area to collect recyclable items.
Add recycling bins and signs in kitchen to collect recyclables.

Cost Payback and Return on Investment Analysis

For business owners to make rational business decisions about which green business actions are the most cost-effective to implement, cost/benefit analysis provides a useful set of tools. There are various levels of this type of analysis, from very simple to extremely complex. A highly simplified form of cost/benefit analysis is called *simple cost payback analysis*. In this method, the total first cost of the improvement is divided by the first-year cost savings (in energy or water use, etc.) produced by the improvement. This method yields the number of years required for the improvement to pay for itself. This type of analysis is somewhat similar to life-cycle costing—a process that attempts to take the longevity of a purchase or investment into account during the purchasing decision-making process.

While many green business investments appear to be more expensive than less environmentally sound choices, a careful long-term analysis of them most often reveals that the greenest upgrades or investments are often the most cost-effective over the long term. A study by Lawrence Berkeley Laboratory examined the additional costs required to upgrade new building construction to be more green and comply with the latest green architectural and building standards. This study determined that although the green upgrades did indeed add about 10 percent to the cost of building, they also added over 10 times the cost of the upgrades to the value of the building. In other words, although the initial outlay to build green might be $10,000, the added overall financial value to the building was often $100,000 or more.

The Federal Energy Management Program of the U.S. Department of Energy has made available a wide array of very useful web-based and/or downloadable cost calculators that can be used to assess the potential cost benefits for a variety of energy and other environmental investments. Their BUILDING LIFE-CYCLE COSTS software program analyzes capital investments in buildings based on annual energy cost savings. Typically, this software is used to evaluate alternative designs that have higher initial costs but lower operating-related costs over the project life than the lowest-initial-cost design. It is especially useful for evaluating the costs and benefits of energy and water conservation and renewable energy projects. The life-cycle costs of two or more alternative designs are computed and compared to determine which has the lowest total life-cycle cost and is therefore more economical in the long run.

ENERGYPLUS software is another building energy simulation program (available from the U.S. EPA) that is designed for modeling buildings with associated heating, cooling, lighting, ventilating, and other energy flows.

Greening Your Business

WATERGY is a spreadsheet program that uses water/energy relationship assumptions to analyze the potential of water savings and associated energy savings. The spreadsheet allows input of utility data (energy and water cost and consumption data for the most recent twelve months) and facility data (number and kind of water consuming/moving devices and their water consumption and/or flow rates). It then estimates direct water, direct energy, and indirect energy annual savings, as well as total cost and payback times for a number of conservation methods.

These and other software programs are provided free from the U.S. Department of Energy. The website for these calculators is found at: **www1.eere.energy.gov/ femp/information/access_tools.html.**

Short of using these sophisticated software analysis programs, a simple cost payback analysis divides the capital cost of a particular action (such as the installation of water-saving toilets or solar panels) by the net annual savings produced by the action. The capital costs would include the cost of the equipment or material itself, the cost of any necessary prep work to install the equipment, and the actual cost of the installation of the equipment. The net annual savings would include any avoided costs (such as less water use or less energy consumption or, possibly, lower disposal costs) and any annual additional revenue (such as any net-metered energy sold back to a utility). The formula provides a payback period in years. A very simple example is the purchase of a low-flow faucet. Its capital cost is $100 and the net annual savings is $20 in lower water and sewer bills. Its payback would be 100 divided by 20 or 5 years, assuming no increase in rates (a somewhat doubtful assumption).

This type of analysis can also include calculations to discount dollar amounts over time and other more sophisticated approaches, but the basic idea is to provide a tool to evaluate investments on an equal footing. In the recent past, businesses insisted on a payback from energy or waste-reduction investments of less than two years. This unreasonably fast payback requirement naturally put such green investments at a distinct disadvantage compared with other business investments. Payback periods are now viewed from a longer-term perspective and paybacks up to 10 years or longer may now be accepted as reasonable for environmental investments, if other factors are also considered, such as avoidance of carbon regulation, retention of the best employees, or rapidly escalating, but unpredictable, energy costs.

Related to cost payback analysis is *return on investment analysis*. While cost payback allows a business owner to determine how long a particular investment will take to be paid back from the revenue gains or expense reductions of the investment, return on investment provides the business with a percentage return calculation that can be measured against other potential investments. In the area of green business, this allows a business to accurately assess the real bottom line impact of a decision to pursue environmentally sound upgrades to the business's operations. This calculation takes the net annual savings of an action and multiplies that amount by the life of the equipment, less the capital costs of the equipment. This first step provides a figure for the net actual return. This figure is then divided by the capital costs. This calculation provides the return on the investment over the life of the equipment. This can then be divided by the life of the investment in years to provide an annual return on investment rate.

Let's take another, closer look at our faucet upgrade. The net annual savings was $20. If the life of the faucet is 15 years, this yields a $300 lifetime savings from lowered water and sewer expenditures. Less the initial cost of the faucet itself $100 (the capital cost) leaves a net monetary return of $200. Dividing this by the initial cost of $100 provides a total lifetime percentage return on investment of 200 percent, which is then divided by the life of the equipment in years (15) to provide an annual return on investment rate of 13.33 percent—a very reasonable rate of return in today's world. This very basic example shows how you can quickly evaluate investments in green business upgrades and equipment against other business investments. Simple worksheets with programmed formulas that allow you to input your own figures for both cost payback and return on investment analysis and have the calculations completed for you are provided on the CD that accompanies this book.

The simple economic analysis worksheets that are provided for some green business situations in this book are just that—simple. They are not intended to provide a sophisticated economic analysis of your green investments. Cost payback and return on investment analyses can get extremely complicated in many situations. The simple worksheets in this book, for example, do not attempt to bring the time value of money into the calculations at all. There are numerous cost payback and return on investment calculators and software on the Internet that can allow you to make much more sophisticated analyses of your potential green business investments. Please see the list of resources in the Appendix and investigate these sources if you wish to make more detailed examinations of your green business investments.

Life-Cycle Assessment

Life-cycle assessment is another useful tool in greening your business. It is a comprehensive analysis of the environmental impact of a product or service throughout its entire existence. In most cases, this is a cradle-to-grave analysis. By looking at impacts throughout a product's entire life cycle, life-cycle assessment provides a comprehensive view of the environmental aspects of the product and a more accurate picture of the true environmental trade-offs in product and process selection and design. The ISO 14001 environmental standards use life-cycle assessments to determine the overall impact of a business on the environment. Green Seal certification also uses this method of analysis in determining the environmental impact of a given product or service. Any business, however, can use this analytic tool to determine the base environmental impact of its products or operations and then work to eliminate the environmental problems that such an assessment highlights. We'll look further at life-cycle assessments in Chapters 11 and 13 and at Green Seal and other certification programs later in Chapter 14.

A life-cycle analysis of a product would include a look at where the raw materials come from, the impacts of manufacturing the product, how the product is actually distributed and used, and the ultimate disposal or reuse of the product. A classic example, at the consumer level, is the analysis of what type of bag to use for your groceries—the paper or plastic conundrum. By looking at the entire life-span of a particular product, businesses can get a better picture of the overall impact of their operations on the environment.

The complete analysis of a product's life can be amazingly complex. Computer software has been developed to make this task much easier. GaBi software, developed by PE International, is the world leader in such tools and has a wide range of life-cycle assessment tools available, from very user-friendly versions that do not require any in-depth understanding of the assessment modeling process to very complex and detailed software that provides an analysis of all of the following areas of concern:

- Greenhouse Gas Accounting
- Life-cycle Assessment
- Life-cycle Engineering
- Design for Environment
- Energy Efficiency Studies
- Substance Flow Analysis
- Company Ecobalances
- Environmental Reporting
- Sustainability Reporting
- Strategic Risk Management
- Total Cost Accounting

There are many other programs available that address life-cycle assessment and a wide array of resources regarding them is provided in Appendix B of this book. We'll also touch on this concept again in Chapter 11 when we look at the latest internet-based life-cycle assessment software available. A very basic limited life-cycle assessment worksheet is also provided in Chapter 13 on green design.

Environmental Accounting

Environmental accounting is a tool that helps businesses understand the overall impact of environmental issues on their bottom line. Our concern here is with company-level environmental accounting. Environmental accounting can also be addressed at both the global and national levels in an attempt to integrate the costs and benefits of various natural resources, eco-system services, and energy sources into national and international systems of accounts. At the company level, environmental accounting provides a method to quantify the costs and benefits of the environmental impact of a product, service, or process. Environmental costs are typically not well represented with customary accounting practices. Although they directly impact a company's bottom line, they were not traditionally considered as a separate item to be tracked. Environmental costs were often obscured in overhead accounts or were otherwise overlooked. For example, under traditional accounting systems, the environmental regulatory compliance costs or the costs of waste disposal are not typically allocated to the overall cost of the production of a particular product. Such costs are more often simply recorded as general overhead expenses of the business. These very real costs are, however, directly related to how a product or service is produced and should be taken into account when assessing the bottom line for that product or service. By illuminating and allocating these and other environmental costs, company-level environmental accounting attempts to make these costs more visible to decision makers, thus enabling them to take action to lessen their impact on the environment and the company's bottom line.

A related accounting tool is referred to as *triple bottom line*—looking at all the impacts of a company's product or service on people and the planet as well as the basic economic impact of business decision making. This approach allows businesses to begin to focus on their impact in these often overlooked areas of business. The triple bottom line concept mirrors the three prongs of sustainability— environmental, economic, and societal impacts.

Typically, the environmental costs (such as waste disposal or energy inefficiency) that a business incurs provide no added value to either the products or services that a business provides. By separating these costs out in internal accounting practices, you can begin to clearly see ways to eliminate them.

The EPA Guide *Introduction to Environmental Accounting as a Business Management Tool* is included as a PDF file on the accompanying CD. Additional resources regarding the use of environmental accounting are also provided in Appendix B of this book.

Environmental Certification and Reporting Programs

Finally, in recent years, a wide range of *environmental certification* and *reporting programs* have also been developed to begin to measure and evaluate how and if businesses are effectively addressing sustainability and environmental concerns. These environmental reporting and certification schemes were developed to help standardize the analysis of business environmental performance. Among the most prominent are the following:

• The Global Reporting Initiative developed by CERES in cooperation with the United Nations

• ISO 14001 Standard for Environmental Management by the International Organization for Standardization

• SA 8000 Social Accountability Standard by Social Accountability International

• LEED standards for Leadership in Energy and Environmental Design by the U.S. Green Building Council

• Energy Star and National Environmental Performance Track programs from the U.S. Environmental Protection Agency

• United Nations Global Compact on corporate responsibility

• Green Seal and many other nonprofit environmental certification programs

Green building certification under LEED and the other standards will be outlined in Chapter 12. We'll look at environmental certification and its related concept of eco-labeling in Chapter 14. ISO environmental management systems will be covered in Chapter 15, and we'll examine sustainability reporting in Chapter 16.

These and other business tools are constantly being developed and refined in an ongoing effort to bring the environmental and social impacts of business into parity with the formerly exclusive focus of the business world on the economic role of commerce and industry.

Each of these various green business tools will be discussed and, in many cases, integrated into the processes outlined in Part Two of this book for creating a successful and sustainable business.

Chapter 5

The Path to Greening Your Business

The process outlined in this book for taking your business on the road to a green and sustainable future will allow you to analyze every aspect of your business. The list of business operations that can be optimized by greening your business is detailed and complex. This chapter will provide a basic outline of the various steps that are provided for greening your business. This book is intended to be a hands-on guide to the entire process of greening your business. At each stage in the process, you will be given questionnaires, worksheets, and other tools to help you in developing an overall plan that you can actually implement for your own business. These aids are all provided on the accompanying CD as both fillable PDF forms and text forms to make the process as streamlined as possible. Ready? Follow these steps on the path to greening your business:

Read through this Entire Guide

Before you can effectively begin the process of greening your business, you will need a thorough understanding of what that will actually entail. You should read through this entire manual, even if you skim through it the first time. This will give you an overview of the steps and the details that you will be addressing in your development of a company green plan. It will be much easier to develop your company's approach to greening once you know the scope and range of the possible items that you may want to address in your green business plan. A quick look at the contents of the Appendices and the CD will also help you to see the very wide range of tools, assistance, organizations, websites, and other resources that are available.

Evaluate Various Green Actions

The heart of your green business efforts is detailed in the second part of this book. Each separate chapter in Part Two: *Green Action Plans* will help you investigate and determine how to prepare a plan of action for every phase of your company's operations. In these chapters, you are provided with various worksheets, assessments, and plans that you can use to decide how aggressively you want to dive into the process of greening your business. All of the following chapters also provide tools to use to assess the economic impact that your proposed actions will have on your firm. Here are the main areas for which an action plan can be developed and implemented:

- Energy Use
- Water Use
- Waste and Recycling, including Hazardous Materials
- Travel and Transportation
- Office Equipment and Computing
- Supply Chain and Purchasing
- Building Design
- Product and Service Design

This list of actions starts and ends with the most far-reaching and complex actions that your business may decide to undertake. How your business uses energy and how your products, services, and buildings are designed are at the heart of greening your business. In Chapter 13, you will be asked to evaluate, from a green perspective, every product that you now produce or use, and every product that you intend to introduce in the future. This challenging task will help you highlight the fundamental nature of actually operating your business in a green manner.

In addition to developing action plans for all of your core business elements, four additional chapters provide information relevant to the green management of your business and its interactions with the wider community:

- Eco-Labeling and Certification
- Environmental Management Systems
- Sustainability Reporting
- Environmental Regulations

Conduct a Company-Wide Green Assessment

For each phase of your company's operations, an important part of your action plans will be to take a careful look at your current business practices. In order to understand the present state of your company's environmental performance, you will need to undertake a deep and comprehensive assessment of all aspects of your business's operations. Energy use, water use, waste stream content, supply chain details, durability and recyclability of products, and other aspects of your company will need to be carefully assessed and documented in order to set a baseline of environmental performance from which you will be able to measure improvement. Each chapter in Part Two of this book provides worksheets and surveys to assist you in this audit process. All of the worksheets and other forms are provided on the accompanying CD in both fillable PDF format and text format.

Develop and Implement Your Green Business Plan

The preparation of a company green business plan that specifies the environmental policy, goals, action plans, and responsibilities will help guide your company in the direction of greater sustainability. This plan can contain information regarding your company's waste management, energy management, and water management plans, as well as details regarding your company's material inputs and outputs, supply chain elements, travel and transportation activities, product design plans, and potential building plans. Details regarding how to prepare your plan are outlined in Chapter 18.

Develop a Company Environmental Policy Statement

The first part of this process is to develop a company environmental policy. This part of the process will show your employees, customers, investors, and supply chain that managing environmental issues is a high priority in your company, and will outline your commitment to placing sustainability issues at the heart of your business. This declaration of your intentions needn't be long or wordy. In fact, it should be straightforward and to the point. It should include a consideration of what you are trying to accomplish and a brief outline of how you intend to accomplish your goals. This is not meant to be a statement of your complete plan for greening your business, but rather more of a mission statement of your commitment to operating your business in a more thoughtful and farsighted manner.

Determine Each Person's Responsibilities

The next step is to outline in some detail who in your business will have the particular roles and responsibilities necessary to effectively attain your company's environmental goals. A clear definition of who is responsible for what part of the company's plan will afford accountability and motivate you and your employees to take personal responsibility for environmental performance. Every business is unique and must work out these roles and duties in a way that best fits into its particular organization and culture. If your business is managed and operated by you alone, you already know who has the responsibility for its greening, but if you have any employees at all, you will need to delineate each person's responsibilities.

Prepare the Green Plan

This step in your progress is fairly straightforward and can essentially consist of compiling the work that you have already completed as you have assessed your current operations and developed your plans for action. A little work may be necessary to put all of your individual assessments and action plans into a final format. The final plan that you put together will be the blueprint (greenprint?) that you will follow as you green your business.

Implement Your Green Business Plan

Finally, you'll need to begin work on the actual steps necessary to fully implement your company's plan. Using the details of the actions that you have decided to include in your plan, you will set goals to achieve and targets to reach in your efforts to maximize your greening efforts. And then you will put the entire plan in motion. This step will be both the most difficult and most fulfilling of the process as you'll begin to reap the myriad benefits associated with greening your business.

Consult Additional Resources

A detailed bibliography is provided, listing all of the green business books that were consulted in preparing this book. Many websites are mentioned throughout this book relating to various green business topics and tools. You need not retype these various web addresses into your web browser software to access these sites. The CD that accompanies this book has a PDF document titled: BOOK WEB ADDRESSES that provides an interactive list of all the web addresses that are cited in this book. Appendix B of this book additionally provides a number of additional resources to assist you in your efforts to green your business. Organizations, websites, governmental assistance, and other useful sources are provided. As you progress along the road to sustainability you may want to look at a particular area or concept in more depth. These additional resources should point you in the right direction. In addition to the various worksheets, charts, Excel spreadsheets, and questionnaires that are contained on the CD that accompanies this book, numerous useful publications are also included (in PDF format) to provide further information on particular topics. You may view on your computer or print them out if necessary (using double-sided printing on 100% recycled paper, of course).

Part Two

Green Business
Action Plans

Chapter 6

Green Business Energy Use

The greatest challenge and the source of some of the greatest opportunities in greening your business will come in the area of business energy use. Energy, at least for the present, is inextricably linked to carbon emissions that are fueling the dramatic changes to the world's climate that we are already beginning to experience. According to the Energy Information Administration of the U.S. Department of Energy, in 2006, America's consumption of energy contributed 5.8+ billion tons of carbon dioxide to the earth's atmosphere. By comparison, non-energy sources contributed less than 110 *million* tons of CO_2. Human energy use is, by far, the main culprit behind climate change—literally the fossil-fuel-belching smoking gun, pointed directly at the earth's climate. As such, reining in energy use and changing basic energy sources—from old fossil-fuel-based to new renewable—are at the very heart of any efforts to effectively green the business world.

The growing consensus among both the scientific and business communities is that humanity must, at a *minimum*, reduce its greenhouse gas emissions by around 80 percent in the next few decades in order to begin to stabilize the global atmosphere's carbon dioxide content and, hopefully, avoid the worst manifestations of climate change. To reach this astonishing reduction will require an almost unimaginable transformation of the world's energy infrastructure. Whether you agree with this assessment or not is completely irrelevant to its coming impact on your business. The immense changes that will be required to meet this goal will devastate some businesses and provide enormous opportunities for others. Like any sweeping change, those businesses that begin now to prepare for this transformation will be on the winning side. Those that ignore this inevitable future will falter and eventually fail. The best time for your business to begin its transition to a ruthlessly energy-efficient future was, well . . . 1978. The second best time is today.

The Price of Carbon

Most economists believe that the only way to achieve this magnitude of change in the global use of fossil fuels is for a monetary price for carbon to take hold in the marketplace. The carbon emissions of fossil fuel use already have a genuine cost—they are altering the earth's climate in potentially catastrophic ways. This is a real cost, one which all of humanity will eventually pay. The problem is, however, that this is not, as yet, a monetary cost. The actions that put the carbon in our atmosphere have no negative impact on those businesses that are doing so. There is no actual monetary price to pay—other than the proverbial piper—for damaging the earth's climate.

How to put a price on carbon is at the center of intense debate around the world—a debate that is at the heart of sustainability. A carbon price can be adopted in two basic ways, both initially instituted by government action. First, government can impose a *carbon tax* of some type. This idea was proposed by President Clinton in 1993 as a Btu-based tax and met with immediate, strenuous, and vocal opposition; it was subsequently swept off the legislative table for nearly a generation. Although there are already some types of carbon taxes already in place (gasoline taxes are an obvious example), most observers feel that the public, so far at least in America, would not support a government-imposed tax on carbon. This may or may not be true, but what is undoubtedly true is that politicians tend to believe that new large tax programs are the third rail of governance—touch them and you're pretty much dead. If potential carbon tax revenues were earmarked for a clear environmental use—say subsidizing wind power—public acceptance might increase appreciably. Another method to gain public acceptance of a carbon tax is the concept of tax-shifting—basically replacing a current tax (like the income tax, for example) with the new tax (the carbon tax). The rationale for this is that an income tax acts to curtail work by taxing the proceeds of that work. Do we really want to discourage work? That doesn't really make economic sense in the long term. Better that we tax something we don't want—like, say, carbon in our air. Even the most desperate and extreme climate change deniers don't advocate adding more carbon dioxide to the atmosphere. A carbon tax would provide a marketplace price for carbon since any reduction in carbon emissions by a carbon taxpayer would reduce the tax by a certain dollar amount, which then becomes the market value of carbon.

The other, and at present more likely, method to achieve a market price for carbon is by adopting some type of mechanism that would allow the marketplace to provide a value for carbon. This second method, preferred by most businesses as more workable and more desirable than a carbon tax, would most likely come in the form of a *cap-and-trade* system. This type of trading scheme has been used successfully (mostly) for controlling sulfur dioxide emissions from coal-fired power plants in the U.S. The basic idea is for government to set a cap on the total amount of emissions allowed. Then the government provides (or preferably sells) emitters credit allowances that allow them to emit a certain amount of the total. Then you simply let the marketplace take over by setting up a system to trade the credits—and voilà!—we have cap and trade. Those companies that can reduce their emissions in a cost-effective manner can sell their allowances to those companies that can not. In so trading the allowances, the marketplace will, as marketplaces do, arrive at a presumably fair price for the credits. The final, and crucial, piece of the system is that every year, the allowed emissions level is reduced, which should, at least in theory, increase the value of the remaining credits and spur further efforts to reduce emissions. In 2005, the European Union introduced a somewhat flawed carbon cap-and-trade system. It is still a work in progress. The Chicago Climate Exchange has set up a voluntary commodities-type exchange in anticipation of a future government-imposed carbon trading system in the U.S.

For business purposes, however, it really doesn't matter at all how governments around the world decide to develop a price for carbon. The important matter is that they will—and sooner rather than later—most likely in the next few years. How your business anticipates this development and makes plans to confront this coming inevitability will, in all likelihood, determine whether your business will still be around to celebrate New Year's 2020.

Energy use is a huge part of most businesses' expenses, and carbon emissions are tied directly to that expense. According to the U. S. Department of Energy, energy use represents 30 percent of commercial building operating costs, and energy use by commercial buildings contributes 15 percent of U. S. greenhouse gas emissions or about 1 billion tons of CO_2. Transportation contributes another 1.8 billion tons; industry in general about 1.6 billion; and electric generation a whopping 2.3 billion tons. If carbon quickly achieves a market value of $40 a ton (not an unlikely prospect), do a little math, and suddenly, to paraphrase the late U.S. Senator Everett Dirksen, we're talking about real money—potentially a quarter of a trillion dollars annually in the U.S. alone. In 2004, General Electric committed itself to reducing its carbon footprint by just 1 percent by the year 2012. By 2008, the company had already achieved a 9 percent reduction and, in the process, saved over $100 million in energy costs, money that literally would have gone up in smoke had the company's management not made the decision to act.

With energy prices and concerns about global warming on the rise, more public attention is being focused on how companies are controlling their energy consumption. At present, few companies report on their energy use and energy management strategies in their annual reports, securities filings, or on their corporate websites. Recently, however, shareholder proponents like the Sierra

Club Mutual Funds and New England Friends Funds (Quakers) began filing shareholder resolutions with major big businesses, asking them to assess the "rising regulatory, competitive, and public pressure to increase energy efficiency" and to report on their progress in addressing energy efficiency measures in their businesses. These energy-efficiency shareholder advocates got a boost in October 2005, when Wal-Mart announced that it would invest $500 million a year in technologies to reduce its stores' greenhouse gas emissions by 20 percent within 7 years, and double the fuel efficiency of its vast fleet of trucks. Wal-Mart is the world largest retailer, with 3,800 stores in the United States and 6,000 worldwide.

As Wal-Mart CEO Lee Scott explained at the time, "If you had told me 12 or 18 months ago that we would be doing a focus on the environment, I would have told you that would be a good public relations campaign, nothing more. But the truth is, the more we learned, the more opportunity we saw for Wal-Mart." Wal-Mart is not alone. The Home Depot and Lowe's arrived at the same conclusion four months later. Having received energy efficiency shareholder proposals for their 2006 annual meetings, they agreed to issue detailed reports on their energy management programs in exchange for having the resolutions withdrawn. These efforts have been followed by many other large corporations joining the ranks of businesses finally taking action to reduce their carbon footprints. Across the board, big business is beginning to understand that energy efficiency is the future and that if they fail to initiate energy efficiency measures, they will suffer both in the marketplace and in their relationships with customers and shareholders. This pressure will ripple down the supply chains of all big corporations and begin to have serious repercussions on those businesses that have not begun to take serious steps to deal with energy efficiency.

Basic Business Energy Efficiency

Without question, energy use is the most important area to be dealt with in greening your business. Maximizing the efficiency of energy use is the key to operating your business in the most cost-effective and environmentally sound manner possible. It is also the area where the greatest cost savings can be found. The Electric Power Research Institute estimates that an aggressive drive to reduce energy costs can reduce electricity use by 25 to 45 percent. In the words of Andreas Schlaepfer, of the reinsurance giant, Swiss Re: "If you've never focused on energy efficiency before, achieving a 30 percent reduction is simple." Amory Lovins, coauthor of *Natural Capitalism*, Director of the Rocky Mountain Institute, and longtime champion of energy efficiency, goes even further and believes that potential cost-effective electricity savings of 75 percent are not only possible, but probable.

Greening Your Business

How to identify areas in your business where such dramatic efficiencies are possible and how to actually adopt policies and plans that take advantage of these enormous energy efficiency opportunities are key components of greening your business. Energy use is an integral part of every aspect of any business's operation, often imbedded in ways that are difficult to detect.

The quest for energy efficiency in any business entails a careful look at two main areas. First, you need to examine how exactly your business uses energy and investigate every possible way to reduce or eliminate that use of purchased energy. Second, you will also need to look closely at any possible ways to replace that purchased energy (generally, fossil fuel–derived) with renewable energy sources, either those that your business may be able to install onsite or those that may be purchased from other producers. This two fold process is, necessarily, different for every individual business, but nearly all businesses share certain elements of energy consumption that can be examined for improving energy efficiency.

Lighting is a critical component of every small business and can be a source of immediate energy savings. Many retailers and offices spend half of their electric bills on lighting, so it makes sense to address lighting first to reduce your energy costs. Efficient lighting pays for itself quickly. Due to continually improving equipment, lighting usually provides the highest return on investment of major upgrades. Lighting upgrades such as installation of compact fluorescent lamps and light-emitting diode (LED) exit signs are relatively simple to implement and can reliably deliver dramatic cost savings. You should always upgrade your lighting before making any changes to your heating or cooling systems because increasing your lighting efficiency lowers your air conditioning requirements. Employees must be able to see to perform their jobs, and objects and spaces must be aesthetically pleasing to encourage sales, but businesses often overlight some areas and underlight others and generally use older, outdated and inefficient lighting. Besides saving money from lower electric bills, lighting upgrades will improve lighting quality, which can boost worker productivity and enhance the appearance of your merchandise (if you're a retailer). We'll look at lighting energy efficiency in greater detail later in this chapter.

Proper heating, ventilating, and air conditioning are another key element to maintaining a comfortable, healthy, and productive work environment. Collectively, these systems account for approximately 40 percent of the electricity used in commercial buildings and are the source of many opportunities for energy efficiency upgrades. You can start by bringing your building back to its original design performance with simple steps, such as cleaning your equipment and replacing any filters. Reducing the amount of heated or cooled air that escapes from your building through cracks in windows or ducts will reduce your heating and cooling costs. Window films, shades, and awnings will reduce heat gain in the summer. You can take advantage of landscaping measures, such as adding trees and vines to block direct sunlight. You can take simple steps to ensure that lights and office equipment are not left on by accident. Once you reduce the overall heating and cooling requirements in your business, you might then look at upgrading to smaller and more efficient heating and cooling units. Later in this chapter, you'll find tools to assess your current energy consumption and evaluate the specific systems that your business operates that drive that usage.

Business travel and transportation consume huge amounts of energy and are areas where immediate savings can usually be found. How your business can be more energy efficient in all areas of transportation needs is addressed in Chapter 9.

When business owners think of energy consumption, they naturally focus on building operations (such as lighting and air conditioning) and building components themselves, but not necessarily on their energy-consuming office equipment and appliances. We'll look separately at the wide array of opportunities for energy efficiency in office equipment and computers in Chapter 10.

If you plan on upgrading your existing facility, energy-efficiency improvements are one of the first places you should focus. Upgrading your building, by installing improved insulation, roofing, doors, and windows, can have a dramatic impact on your energy bills. Many of these upgrades for energy efficiency are a major investment that should be evaluated on a cost payback or return-on-investment basis, rather than merely on the lowest initial cost. Over the life of the building, the operating savings in energy alone will far outweigh the initial cost of most building efficiency improvements. In the case of new construction for your business, it will always be less costly to do it right the first time than to make even more costly upgrades later. We'll look more at green building design in Chapter 12.

Retail Businesses

Retail companies spend nearly $20 billion on energy each year. A 10 percent reduction in energy costs for the average retailer can boost net profit margins by nearly 2 percent and sales per square foot by $25. Retail buildings are everywhere, outnumbering office buildings two to one. They range from small shops in strip malls to large department stores, and occupy more total space than any other segment of the commercial market. If you operate a retail business, you may use vast amounts of energy to create inviting spaces for your customers. Eye-catching signage and merchandise displays, plus heating and cooling needs, all contribute to high energy costs in retail buildings. Lighting is the biggest energy expense for retailers—37 percent of total energy use. In a highly competitive business, you may feel that you are hard pressed to lower your operating costs without affecting customer service and satisfaction, but you can often can reap big savings by starting small. For instance, more than 90 percent of retail buildings use standard fluorescent bulbs, which consume more energy than compact fluorescent lamps and require more frequent replacement. Standard fluorescent lights also throw off more heat, which adds to cooling needs. Using compact fluorescent to light retail spaces can provide fast returns on the initial investment. Another simple way to lower lighting costs is through the use of solid-state LED technology for exit signs. LEDs consume very little energy and last up to 10 years or more, saving both energy and maintenance costs.

Retail buildings can reduce energy costs even further by looking at how the windows, doors, roofing, heating and cooling, and other building systems work together for the most efficient energy use. New high-performance retail buildings can consume up to 50 percent less energy than comparable buildings, with designs that integrate energy-efficient lighting fixtures with daylighting systems to substantially reduce electric lighting and cooling loads. Additional energy-smart choices about the building site, envelope, and mechanical systems are factored into the design and contribute to the savings. The best news is that the same energy improvements that lower utility bills also foster a more comfortable retail space, with better lighting, temperature control, and indoor air quality. That means employee morale and retention improve, and customers are more likely to return often. We'll look more at green building design in Chapter 12.

Office-Based Businesses

Office buildings consume operating budgets as voraciously as they consume energy. Office building energy bills are the highest of any commercial building type. While heating, ventilation, air conditioning, and lighting are still the big power consumers, office equipment now accounts for almost 16 percent of an office building's energy use. We'll look specifically at ways to reduce energy use in office equipment and computer use in Chapter 10.

Reducing energy use and costs in an office can be challenging, particularly since workers and tenants are often unaware of overall building expenses. Using energy-efficient design and technologies can cut energy costs by as much as 50 percent. By incorporating efficient lighting and daylighting systems, as well as advanced windows, roofing, insulation, and mechanical and ventilation systems, you can cut your building operating costs and enhance the comfort and performance of your employees and boost productivity. Many of the same measures that improve a building's energy performance also make it a more comfortable place to work. Employees benefit from the use of daylighting and nontoxic chemicals, with better temperature control, ventilation, and indoor air quality. With the high cost of labor, payback on energy features is shortened even further when savings from reduced absenteeism are combined with energy cost savings. Energy-efficient building features also help building owners attract and retain tenants.

In existing buildings, renovations that replace older systems with more efficient technology can yield savings of up to 30 percent, with the same positive impact on building comfort. A quick way to realize savings of 10 percent or more—at little or no cost—is to effectively operate and maintain existing systems. Simple behavioral changes, such as turning off lights when leaving a room, help reduce energy use. Automated controls like occupancy sensors and programmable thermostats ensure reduced energy use in unoccupied offices or infrequently used areas like conference rooms.

Lodging Businesses

Reducing operating costs can be particularly challenging in the lodgings industry, where the bottom line is directly tied to guest service and satisfaction. From large convention hotels, to local motels, to tiny bed and breakfast inns, owners and operators are challenged to lower energy costs without lowering the quality of their service. In the face of rising energy costs, you must continue to meet your guests' expectations for comfort and energy-intensive amenities like air conditioning or heated pools. The largest chunk of a lodging's energy use—42 percent—is for heating water. Guest showers, pools, hot tubs, and especially laundry operations account for almost half of a hotel's energy bill. Many smaller lodgings are finding that energy-efficient technologies and processes offer bottom-line savings without any adverse impact on guests. In fact, many are finding that their energy-saving, environmentally friendly choices actually appeal to their guests and that their energy consciousness is further rewarded with repeat reservations.

Many hotels have successfully implemented water and energy-saving programs like offering guests the option of reusing towels and linens throughout their stay. Other options for saving water and energy include energy-efficient laundry equipment, low-flow showerheads, and solar water-heating systems. For guest rooms, you can preset temperature ranges, lower or raise the temperature during the day (depending on the season), and use control devices that automatically adjust room temperature and lighting when guests are present.

Renovations to existing lodging businesses—replacement of inefficient boilers, lighting, and other systems—can save up to 30 percent on annual energy costs. Even bed and breakfasts in historic buildings are finding ways to reap bottom-line savings from energy improvements without marring the charm or historic features of the building. Implementing no-cost and low-cost solutions can yield savings of up to 10 percent or more. Controlling the temperature and lighting in unoccupied guestrooms—manually or with controls—delivers small savings that make a difference when multiplied over many rooms and many days. You can also implement energy awareness programs to educate cleaning and maintenance staff about energy-saving measures.

Food Service Businesses

If you operate a facility that serves food, perhaps a restaurant, grocery store, or convenience store, there may be opportunities for saving energy and money from more modern, energy-efficient commercial food service equipment. For food service businesses, refrigeration equipment alone can typically account for 25 to 60 percent of electricity consumption. A 10 percent reduction in energy costs for the average limited-service restaurant can boost net profit margins by as much as 4 percent and sales per square foot by $17. The same 10 percent reduction in energy costs for the average supermarket can boost net profit margins by even more—as much as 16 percent and sales per square foot by $44. There is dramatically more energy-efficient equipment on the market today. Simply replacing old electric deep fryers, hot food holding cabinets, gas and electric steam cookers, and refrigerators and freezers can often pay for itself in energy savings alone.

All Businesses

Regardless of what type of business that you operate, you will find that there are enormous potential savings from aggressively looking for and implementing energy efficiency measures. For all businesses, the process then is, first, to investigate any and all uses of energy in your business and look for ways to lower or eliminate the actual energy use; and, second, to look for methods that can be efficiently used to lower or eliminate your need for purchased fossil fuel energy by using your own possible renewable energy sources, like wind, sunshine, or geothermal energy.

To break the energy issue down into workable components, this chapter first addresses the assessment of your current energy use and the calculation of your energy carbon footprint. Tools that you can use to determine your energy carbon footprint are also explained and provided to help you fully understand your carbon exposure (your business's exposure to the coming increases in the cost of carbon emissions). The greater your carbon footprint, the greater vulnerability your business has to price increases, regulations, and other changes that will accompany a market price for carbon. The availability and range of various energy efficiency assessment software tools will be examined. Then we'll examine some particular energy issues, including renewable energy and green power. We'll look more closely at one energy use area that affects all businesses—lighting—and investigate ways to lessen your lighting energy needs. (Note: business travel and transportation issues are discussed separately in Chapter 9, and energy-reduction issues that are a component of building and product design are discussed further in Chapters 12 and 13.)

Carbon Footprints and Energy Use Assessment

In the last few years, the concept of carbon footprints has gained mainstream acceptance as a method to calculate the carbon emissions of any given operation or activity. The concept of an ecological "footprint" was first developed in 1996 by Mathis Wackernagel and William Rees at the University of British Columbia. The purpose of the footprint tool was to provide a simple yet comprehensive way to account for the flows of energy and materials to and from any given activity. As first used, this tool was based on the idea that, for each item of material or energy consumption, a certain amount of land was required to provide both the resources necessary and the waste disposal required. This provided an easily-understood view of the impact of economic activities on the earth. This tool was later adapted and refined to be used as a method to analyze the carbon emission impact of economic activities and determine the overall carbon footprint of these activities.

Carbon footprinting is now being implemented around the world and is generally recognized as a standard by which to measure the total carbon emissions of an activity, product, or service over its entire lifetime. The measurement generally takes into account emissions from three sources: *direct emissions* (those actually emitted onsite); *indirect emissions* from any purchased energy (such as electricity or heat); and *other indirect emissions* attributable to a business's activity, product, or service (all of those offsite, such as emissions from the mining of the raw materials and from the distribution, use, and disposal of a product). For example, the carbon footprint for this book would include the emissions attributable to the production of the paper and ink, the transportation of the paper and ink to the printing plant, the indirect emissions from the energy used at the printing plant to produce this book, the indirect emissions from the transportation of the book to any central warehouse and on to the online or actual bookstore, and finally, the emissions attributable to the final disposal of the book.

When illuminated by a tool such as a carbon footprint, the huge amount of imbedded energy use necessary to produce most products becomes glaringly evident. Carbon footprinting shows how deep and intrenched the reliance on cheap energy has become in our society and how very difficult it will be to cure our collective addiction to fossil fuels. Carbon footprints also provide a relatively standardized method to compare very different business operations and products. A complete carbon footprint requires a life-cycle assessment of the operation or product and can be a very complex matter. In the above example regarding the carbon footprint of this book, the assessment could go much deeper and involve the emissions attributable to the construction of the paper and printing plants, the manufacture of the plant's equipment and the trucks necessary for the transportation, the actual manufacture of the ink and any chemicals used in the paper production, and on and on. The simple personal carbon footprint calculators found on the Internet (including the very basic ones provided later in this chapter and later in Chapter 9) generally limit the calculations to standard measures attributable only to the fossil fuel use of the activity itself, for example, the emissions from the gas required to drive a car a certain number of miles.

In coming years, as carbon emissions become regulated and achieve a market price, the determination of a business's carbon footprint will take on much more importance. How a carbon tax is applied and how a carbon emission credit allowance is calculated will rely, in large part, on the same type of calculations that determine a business's carbon footprint. For the present, examining your company's carbon footprint allows you to clearly see your direct impact on the environment and begin to visualize ways to lessen that impact. Carbon footprints can often surprise business owners by illuminating carbon emissions that may have been overlooked. The boot manufacturer, Timberland, expecting that its main carbon emissions came from transportation, was startled by the revelation that the manufacture of the raw materials used for its products was the main source. The real value of a carbon footprint analysis is to point to areas where energy use can be reduced and money can be saved for a business, while simultaneously reducing the company's environmental impact.

Determining the carbon footprint of your own business can also be a very complex and time-consuming process. Many new consulting businesses have evolved in the last few years to provide such assessments to businesses around the globe. Due to its complexity, full life-cycle assessments have been beyond the resources of most small and medium-sized companies. However, the World Resources Institute and the World Business Council for Sustainable Development have joined forces in the Greenhouse Gas Protocol Initiative, which provides the best and most widely accepted information available on the measurement of carbon and other greenhouse gas emissions. They have developed an excellent set of user-friendly Excel spreadsheets that can be used to determine carbon emissions for a variety of standard business operations, such as:

- CO_2 emissions from business travel and transportation
- CO_2 emissions from fuel use in facilities
- Emissions from employee commuting
- Greenhouse gas emissions from stationary combustion
- Indirect CO_2 emissions from purchased electricity, heat, or steam

These spreadsheets are available on the CD that accompanies this book (Check the following website to be certain that you have the latest versions: **www.ghgprotocol.org/calculation-tools**.) Additionally, the Greenhouse Gas

Protocol Initiative website provides numerous industry-specific calculation tools, for industries such as pulp and paper, refrigeration and air conditioning equipment, semiconductors, and wood products to name a few.

Later in this chapter, you will be provided with a very simplified carbon footprint calculator for your direct emissions related to the actual energy that your business consumes based on its utility bills (but that does not take into account the multitude of indirect emissions that may also apply to your business operations). Additionally, in Chapter 9, on business travel and transportation, you are provided with a simple transportation carbon footprint worksheet to evaluate the carbon emissions stemming from business travel and transportation.

Appendix B also provides information on some of the available services for obtaining a complete carbon footprint analysis of your business. In Chapter 11, regarding green supply chains and purchasing, we will take a look at some new life-cycle assessment tools (from Earthster.org and the OpenLCA project) that provide low-cost and easy-to use online life-cycle assessments for a wide variety of products. Chapter 12 on green building notes a free life-cycle assessment tool for green construction, and Chapter 13 provides a basic worksheet to prepare a limited life-cycle assessment. The next section on resources also provides information on various available resources for energy efficiency assessments (though not specifically for carbon footprint analyses).

Energy Efficiency and Assessment Resources

There are hundreds of products available to help you assess, track, and implement energy efficiency in your business. The management of energy efficiency efforts is itself becoming big business. The Building Technologies Program of the U.S. Department of Energy's, Energy Efficiency and Renewable Energy Program has developed an online tool that provides a concise evaluation of a wide array of these tools—The Building Energy Software Tools Directory. This directory provides information on more than 300 building software tools for evaluating energy efficiency, renewable energy, and sustainability in buildings. The energy tools listed in this directory include databases, spreadsheets, component and systems analyses, and whole-building energy performance simulation programs. A short description is provided for each tool. You can access this directory at: **www.eere.energy.gov/buildings/tools_directory**.

Department of Energy Best Practices Software
There is also an enormous array of free software available from the U.S. Department of Energy for developing a comprehensive energy efficiency program for your

business. Although much of the software is designed for larger industrial businesses, you should check the Department of Energy Best Practices website for the latest software tools at: **www1.eere.energy.gov/industry/bestpractices/software.html**. Information about particular programs is also provided in Appendix B.

Energy Plus Software

One of the premier energy efficiency software programs provided free by the Department of Energy is EnergyPlus. This is a building energy simulation program for modeling a building's heating, cooling, lighting, ventilating, and other energy flows. It includes many innovative simulation capabilities, such as time steps of less than an hour, modular systems, and plant integration with heat balance-based zone simulation, multizone air flow, thermal comfort, and photovoltaic systems. A fairly high level of computer skill is required, as EnergyPlus software is a stand-alone simulation program without a user-friendly graphical interface. EnergyPlus reads input and writes output as text files. You can download this program at: **www.eere.energy.gov/buildings/energyplus**.

Quick Plant Energy Profiler Online Tool

If you operate an industrial plant or factory of any size, there is an extremely useful online tool provided free by the Energy Efficiency and Renewable Energy Program of the U.S. Department of Energy to help industrial plant managers in the United States identify how energy is being purchased and consumed at their plant and also identify potential energy and cost savings. The Quick Plant Energy Profiler, or Quick PEP, is an online software tool designed so that the user can complete a plant profile in about an hour. After entering the information, the software tailors a customized, printable report that shows the details of energy purchases at your plant, how energy is consumed at your plant, potential cost and energy savings at your plant, and a list of next steps that you can follow to get you started saving energy. This tool is located at: **www1.eere.energy.gov/industry/quickpep**.

The Save Energy Now Initiative

The U.S. Department of Energy, through its Industrial Technologies Program, is also spearheading a broad initiative to achieve a 25 percent reduction in industrial energy intensity over the next 10 years. Available to any industrial facility regardless of size, this program is engaging other federal agencies, leading corporations, states, utilities, universities, and other organizations to accelerate industry adoption of the technologies and practices that will enable increased production with reduced energy requirements. This program provides a wide array of resources to identify and implement the most cost-effective options for energy savings, including a pledge program, plant assessments, standards development, tools and training, and recognition programs.

As a key element of the Save Energy Now initiative, the Department of Energy conducts plant energy assessments to help manufacturing facilities across the nation identify immediate opportunities to save energy and money, primarily by focusing on energy-intensive systems, including process heating, steam, pumps, fans, and compressed air. To date, more than 16,000 manufacturing plants have used these resources to reduce the energy intensity of their operations. As an all-inclusive initiative, Save Energy Now hopes to help all 200,000 U.S. industrial facilities, wherever they currently stand along the energy efficiency continuum, to reduce their energy intensity and carbon footprint to the greatest extent practical. A Save Energy Now CD is available with more than 10 free software tools, and many publications all in one package. Guidance on energy management, including assessment opportunities and corporate energy management, is also provided, with additional information on accessing qualified specialists and industrial assessment centers. Information about this initiative and ordering information for this CD is available at: **www1.eere.energy.gov/industry/saveenergynow**.

Energy Cost Calculators

The Federal Energy Management Program also provides an array of energy cost calculators that allow users to enter their own input values (utility rates, hours of use, etc.) to estimate the energy cost savings from buying more efficient products. Some are Web-based tools; others are Excel spreadsheets provided for download (as indicated.) Access to these tools is at: **www1.eere.energy.gov/femp/procurement/ eep_eccalculators.html**. The tools include online calculators for the following:

* Compact Fluorescent Lamps
* Commercial Unitary Air Conditioners
* Air-Cooled Chillers
* Water-Cooled Chillers
* Commercial Heat Pumps
* Boilers

Downloadable Excel spreadsheets are available for the following products:
* Exit Signs
* Refrigerators and Freezers
* Gas Fryers and Pressureless Steamers
* Hot Food Holding Cabinets
* Beverage Vending Machines and Ice Machines

Building Life-Cycle Cost Software

The Building Life-Cycle Cost Program was developed by the National Institute of Standards and Technology to provide an analysis of capital investments in buildings. The software can be used to conduct economic analyses by evaluating the relative cost effectiveness of alternative designs. Typically, it is used to evaluate alternative designs that have higher initial costs but lower operating costs over the project life when compared to the lowest-initial-cost design. It is especially useful for evaluating the costs and benefits of energy and water conservation and renewable energy projects. The life-cycle costs of two or more alternative designs are computed and compared to determine which has the lowest life-cycle cost and is therefore more economical in the long run. The software also calculates comparative economic measures for alternative designs, including Net Savings, Savings-to-Investment Ratio, Adjusted Internal Rate of Return, and Years to Payback. Although the software is oriented toward building-related decisions, it can be used to evaluate alternative designs for almost any project type in which higher capital investment costs result in lower future operating-related costs. A handbook for this complex program, the Life-Cycle Costing Manual, explains in detail the principles of life-cycle cost analysis and how to use the program. This software and the manual is available at: **www1.eere.energy.gov/femp/information/download_blcc.html**. A number of additional software programs for energy efficiency and life-cycle analysis are available and are outlined in Appendix B.

Utility Company Energy Efficiency Programs

Nearly all utility companies in the U.S. provide support and resources for businesses that want to become more energy efficient. These programs often provide free energy use audits to business customers and specific recommendations for energy efficiency upgrades. The Environmental Technologies Division of the Lawrence Berkeley Laboratory provides access to these programs with a state-by-state listing, which is found at: **http://eetd.lbl.gov/EnergyCrossroads/2ueeprogram.html**.

Online Business Energy Analysis

An excellent online tool for business energy efficiency analysis is provided by Nexus Energy Software, an affiliate of the U.S. EPA's Energy Star program. This tool is a sophisticated software program that uses your answers to an online survey of your business; local climate conditions based on your zip code; and an advanced energy efficiency model, developed from the U.S. Department of Energy, to provide personalized and specific recommendations for improved energy management based upon industry best practices. This free tool is available at: **www.energyguide.com**.

Additional Energy Efficiency Resources

Information regarding many additional energy efficiency resources is found in Appendix B. Three useful energy efficiency guides are also included on the CD that accompanies this book: the U.S. EPA's *Putting Energy Into Profits: Energy Star Small Business Guide* and their *Lean and Energy Toolkit*; and the U.S. Department of Energy's *Hands-on-Solutions to Improve Profits and Productivity: Energy Saving Tips for Small Businesses.*

Renewable Energy Use in Business

One of the system conditions for sustainability, as outlined by the Natural Step Program, is the use of renewable, rather than nonrenewable resources. The use of renewable energy is at the heart of the transition to a sustainable global society. Again, business can lead the way in this effort by becoming first adopters of renewable energy technologies and purchasers of renewable energy from current green power providers.

The two main renewable energy technologies that are immediately available for use by any business are solar and wind. Solar, for business applications, is primarily *solar photovoltaic* panels that produce electricity and *solar thermal* that can be used for heat and heating water. Few power-generation technologies have as little impact on the environment as photovoltaics. As it quietly generates electricity from light, it produces no air pollution or hazardous waste. It doesn't require liquid or gaseous fuels to be transported or combusted. It's highly reliable and needs little maintenance. It costs very little to operate. It's modular and thus flexible in terms of size and applications. And because its energy source—sunlight—is free and abundant, photovoltaic systems can guarantee access to electric power. As the cost to both produce and install solar panels continues to drop, it is becoming more affordable and available. Recent developments in flexible and thin-film solar will dramatically lower the price of solar photovoltaics in the next few years. Nanosolar, a solar film company, is on track to make solar electricity cost-competitive with traditional nonrenewable energy sources. Nanosolar has developed an innovative technology that makes it possible to produce 100 times thinner solar cells at rates 100 times faster than existing technology, thus allowing its low-cost highly competitive solar products to be mass-produced on a global scale. This and many other dramatic innovations are pushing solar to the forefront of energy planning.

Solar thermal technology harnesses the power of the sun to provide solar thermal energy for solar hot water and solar space heating. Solar water heating is achieved, generally, by rooftop solar collectors. Any business that uses heated water can benefit from a solar thermal water heating system. A solar space heating system can also save energy, reduce utility costs, and produce clean energy in the form of heat. A solar space heating system can consist of a passive system, an active system, or a combination of both. Passive systems are typically less costly and less complex than active systems. Passive solar space heating takes advantage of warmth from the sun through design features, such as large south-facing windows, and materials in the floors or walls that absorb warmth during the day and release that warmth at night when it is needed most. Active solar space heating systems consist of collectors that collect and absorb solar radiation combined with electric fans or pumps to transfer and distribute that solar heat. Active systems also generally have an energy storage system to provide heat when the sun is not shining. These two basic types of active solar space heating systems use either liquid or air as the heat-transfer medium in their solar energy collectors. Amazingly, cooling and refrigeration can also now be accomplished with modern thermally activated cooling systems driven by solar energy. These systems can provide for the year-round utilization of collected solar heat, thereby significantly increasing the cost effectiveness and energy contribution of solar installations. The efficiency and reliability of solar thermal systems of all types—water heating, space heating, and cooling—have increased dramatically in recent years, making them very attractive options for any business.

The city of Chicago is leading the way in developing solar electric generating power for business and government buildings. If cold, northern Chicago can successfully deploy solar technologies, solar photovoltaics can be part of any business energy package. Cities across the country are also taking action to make solar energy a more viable option for their communities. As part of a new Solar America Cities program, many municipalities are using innovative approaches to remove market barriers to solar and to encourage the adoption of solar energy technologies at the local level. The U.S. Department of Energy selected 13 cities in June 2007 and an additional 12 cities in March 2008 to help lay the foundation for a solar energy market that can serve as a model for cities around the nation. The cities involved have committed to developing a sustainable solar infrastructure that removes barriers to solar installations and encourages the adoption of solar energy by their residents and businesses. The idea is to dramatically increase the number of solar installations within U.S. municipalities. These cities are taking a comprehensive, citywide approach that lays the foundation for a viable solar market and provides a model for other cities to follow. To see if your city is involved with this program and to see what benefits this program can provide for your business efforts to go solar, please see: **www1.eere.energy.gov/solar/solar_america**.

Wind power also provides a way out of the carbon emissions trap of fossil fuel energy use. Modern wind technologies have been deployed so successfully in Europe that 20 percent of Danish electric power is currently being supplied by wind. Fully one-third of Europe's new electric generating capacity in the next two decades will be supplied by wind power. Spain, Germany, and Denmark lead the world in wind energy production. The U.S., unfortunately, is far behind Europe in harnessing wind power, but that leaves enormous opportunities and potential on the table for those companies willing to lead. Utility-scale wind energy is already cost-equivalent with traditional carbon-emitting energy sources in most areas of the U.S., and, as carbon costs accelerate, wind will become more cost effective than any other power source in the near term. At smaller scales, wind energy has not been as affordable. However, in 2007, the Distributed Wind Energy Technology Program of the Energy Efficiency and Renewable Energy division of the U.S. Department of Energy was able to work with wind technology companies to develop commercial products that reduced the cost of electricity produced by residential-sized turbines to 9.9 cents per kWh. The program also reduced the cost of electricity for business/industrial-sized wind turbines (11 kW to 100 kW) to 10.7 cents per kWh. Take a look at your company's utility bill and see how this compares with your current business energy costs. As fossil fuel energy becomes more expensive, the costs of wind energy are decreasing rapidly. With the latest technology, businesses large and small can quickly and effectively deploy wind technology to begin to harvest their own energy. Check some of the resources at the Wind and Hydropower Technologies website of the U.S. Department of Energy at: **www1.eere.energy.gov/windandhydro**.

Another form of renewable energy is geothermal. In certain areas of the United States, this type of energy is extremely cost-effective and has almost no environmental drawbacks. Large scale geothermal energy production is in place in several areas around the world, such as the Geysers area of California. Such facilities inject water deep into the ground and use the resulting steam to power traditional electricity-generating turbines. The geothermal heat pump, also known as the *ground source* heat pump, is a highly efficient smaller-scale renewable energy technology that is gaining wide acceptance for both residential and commercial buildings. These differ from the more widely used *air source* heat pumps in use in many residential locations. Geothermal heat pumps are used for space heating and cooling, as well as water heating. Geothermal's great advantage is that it works by concentrating naturally existing heat, rather than by producing heat through combustion of fossil fuels. These systems use the constant temperature of the underground earth to cool hot air in summer or heat colder air in the winter. Due to environmental advantages and low initial and operating costs, business use of geothermal energy has skyrocketed in recent years.

At least 300,000 geothermal heat pumps are in operation, mostly in the western states of California, Oregon, and Idaho, with lesser use in Arizona, Colorado, Nevada, and New Mexico. Geothermal energy is also very cost efficient and environmentally sound for such business applications as greenhouses, aquaculture, and agricultural drying. If your business is located in the western U.S., you should investigate the use of geothermal heat pumps further. A good place to start your research is the Geothermal Technologies Program of the Department of Energy at: **www1.eere.energy.gov/geothermal**.

Using your own source of constantly renewable energy can be an enlightening experience. Your business will be that much freer of the restraints that high energy costs entail. A significant advantage of solar water heating, passive solar design, photovoltaic, wind, and geothermal is that they can be installed right where the energy will be consumed. Wind and geothermal systems are commonly installed in specific areas that have the best resources. But solar technologies—which include passive solar designs, solar water heating, ventilation air preheating, and photovoltaics—are applicable almost everywhere, and nearly every business can benefit from them. Note that state and local governments and utilities often provide rebates or incentives that help to make these projects more affordable. Various government incentive programs for both energy efficiency and renewable energy will be discussed on the following pages.

Green Power for Business

The term *green power* generally refers to electricity supplied in whole or in part from renewable energy sources, such as wind and solar power, geothermal, hydropower, and various forms of biomass. Increasingly, electricity customers are being given electricity supply options, either when retail power markets open to competition or when their regulated utilities develop green pricing programs. More than 50 percent of retail customers in the United States, including businesses, now have an option of purchasing a green power product directly from their electricity supplier. In addition, businesses can support renewable energy development through the purchase of green energy certificates. By choosing to purchase a green power product, your business can directly support the increased development of renewable energy sources, which can reduce the burning of fossil fuels, such as coal, oil, and natural gas.

If retail electricity competition is allowed in your state, you may be able to purchase a green power product from an alternative electricity supplier. About a dozen states have implemented electricity competition that allows you to purchase power from competing suppliers. Even if your state is not implementing electricity market competition, you may still be able to purchase green power through your regulated utility. More than 600 regulated utilities spanning nearly 40 states offer green pricing programs. The term *green pricing* refers to an optional utility service that allows customers to support a greater level of utility investment in renewable energy by paying a premium on their electric bill to cover any above-market costs of acquiring renewable energy resources. Finally, whether or not you have access to green power through your utility or a competitive electricity marketer, you can purchase *renewable energy certificates*. Renewable energy certificates (also known as green tags, green energy certificates, or tradable renewable certificates) represent the environmental attributes of power generated from renewable electric plants. A variety of organizations offer renewable energy certificates separate from electricity service. Thus, you need not switch from your current electricity supplier in order to purchase these certificates. See below regarding the Green-e renewable energy certificate certification program.

To determine what green power options are available in your state or locale, you can check the interactive map available on line at: **www.eere.energy.gov/ greenpower/buying/buying_power.shtml**. This resource will show you which organizations offer green power in your state, if there are any utility green pricing programs available, any retail green power products offered, and if any renewable energy certificate products that are sold separate from electricity are available.

Green-e Renewable Energy Certification

The Green-e renewable energy certification program was established in 1997 in order to provide clear guidelines and standards in the emerging voluntary renewable energy market. Currently, the non-profit Green-e Energy program is the most rigorous and respected consumer protection program for renewable energy certificates in the country, serving both individuals and businesses by applying a set of clear standards to the renewable marketplace.

The renewable energy that Green-e certifies goes through a thorough verification process to ensure that it is generated from new projects. This requirement is vital so that renewable energy certificates support new projects that are being built and not being used simply to satisfy an existing state or federal requirement. Certified renewable energy certificates sold to a consumer cannot also be counted toward a state's renewable energy goal. (Note: many states have set *renewable portfolio standards* that provide that a percentage of the state's overall energy use will be supplied by renewable sources within a certain time period.) Individuals and businesses generally want their investments in renewable energy to come from new facilities that are built with their investments.

Any green energy programs that are certified by Green-e are audited twice a year to ensure that they live up to their advertising claims—that their customers are getting what they paid for. Certified energy is accounted for and tracked through the Green-e verification process to ensure that it has not been double-counted. To obtain certification through the Green-e program, the renewable energy produced must come from wind, solar, geothermal, biomass, or low-impact hydropower sources built since 1997. To locate the certified sources of renewable energy credits available for businesses in your state, please see: **www.green-e.org/ about.shtml**.

Carbon Offsets

A carbon offset is a relatively new concept—the purchase of some type of product that will balance, in some manner, the carbon being produced by the purchaser of the offset. Basically, you pay someone else to reduce emissions of carbon dioxide on your behalf. Offsets are being used by individuals, companies, and organizations to mitigate (or offset) their own greenhouse gas emissions from transportation, electricity use, and other sources. Although such offsets are also part of the Kyoto Protocol on Climate Change and function as part of the larger international carbon trading concept, here we are talking about the voluntary purchase of carbon offsets as part of an individual or business effort to become "carbon neutral." By purchasing something that will remove carbon from the atmosphere or provide energy in a noncarbon–producing manner, purchasers of carbon offsets are attempting to alleviate the environmental impact of their own carbon producing ways. The purchase of carbon offsets for renewable energy production are very similar in many ways to the purchase of renewable energy credits.

The most common types of carbon offsets are purchases to support renewable energy projects, such as windfarms, biomass energy, or other renewables. Although offsets may be cheaper or more convenient than reducing one's own fossil-fuel consumption, they are really not a substitute for simply reducing your business's own carbon footprint. In the short-term, however, they may be a way for your business to support viable renewable energy projects and, in a general sense at least, become carbon neutral.

Currently, one of the best offset programs is operated by Native Energy, which uses the money raised from the purchase of carbon offsets to develop a wide array of real-world renewable energy projects, such as wind turbines on Native American lands and family farms, methane plants on family farms, solar arrays, and small scale hydropower. Native Energy offers a wide variety of offset, emissions reduction, and renewable energy credit programs. Their CoolWatts program, for example, offsets 10,000 kWh of fossil fuel energy use for the cost of about $100 annually. Please see their website at: **www.NativeEnergy.com**.

The Green-e program also operates Green-e Climate, a certification program for the sale of carbon offsets (which they term *greenhouse gas emission reduction products*) sold in the voluntary market. The have currently certified three programs worldwide that meet their rigorous standards: 3Degrees Emission Reduction Program operating in China, Brazil, and India; Bonneville Environmental Foundation's GreenTag Program; and the Community Energy Wind Energy Program. For more information, please see: **www.green-e.org/getcert_ghg_ intro.shtml**.

Government Incentives for Energy Efficiency

There are many valuable incentives provided by federal and state programs to encourage energy efficiency. Reimbursements, tax deductions, tax credits, loans, and even direct grants are available for many business energy expenses. Businesses are eligible for tax credits for buying hybrid vehicles, for building energy-efficient buildings, and for improving the energy efficiency of commercial buildings. There are also various credits for producing biodiesel and ethanol, for installing alternative fuel refueling pumps, and for energy-efficient home building. A tax credit directly reduces the amount of income tax you have to pay; a tax deduction reduces the amount of income that is subject to income tax.

For information on various state and federal tax and other energy efficiency incentives, please see the Database for State Incentives for Renewables and Efficiency at **www.dsireusa.org**. Every state has provided some type of incentives. Some of these tax credits are due to expire at the end of 2008, but may be renewed and possibly expanded. Check the IRS website at **www.irs.gov** for additional information. Here is an overview of some of the current federal programs:

Biodiesel/Alternative Fuels
Small producer biodiesel and ethanol credit. This credit will benefit small agri-biodiesel producers by giving them a 10 cent per gallon tax credit for up to 15 million gallons of agri-biodiesel produced. In addition, the limit on production capacity for small ethanol producers increased from 30 million to 60 million gallons. This is effective until December 31, 2008. After that date, check **www.irs.gov** to see if it has been renewed.

Credit For Installing Alternative Fuel Refueling Property
Fueling stations are eligible to claim a 30 percent credit for the cost of installing clean-fuel vehicle refueling equipment (such as E85 ethanol pumping stations). Under the provision, a clean fuel is any fuel that consists of at least 85 percent ethanol, natural gas, compressed natural gas, liquefied natural gas, liquefied petroleum gas, or hydrogen and any mixture of diesel fuel and biodiesel containing at least 20 percent biodiesel. This is effective through December 31, 2010.

Renewable Energy Production Tax Credit
Businesses that produce energy from landfill gas, wind, biomass, hydroelectric, geothermal electric, municipal solid waste, refined coal, or small hydroelectric are eligible for a tax credit of 2.0¢/kWh for wind, geothermal, closed-loop biomass; 1.0¢/kWh for other eligible technologies. The credit applies to the first 10 years of energy production. This credit is scheduled to expire at the end of 2008.

Energy-Efficient Commercial Building Deduction

This federal income tax deduction provision allows a tax deduction for energy-efficient commercial buildings that reduce annual energy and power consumption by 50 percent compared with the American Society of Heating, Refrigerating, and Air Conditioning Engineers (ASHRAE) 2001 standard. The deduction would equal the cost of energy-efficient equipment installed during construction, with a maximum deduction of $1.80 per square foot of the building. Additionally, a partial deduction of 60 cents per square foot would be provided for building subsystems.

Tax Credits for Home Builders

There are additional tax credits for home builders who are constructing energy-efficient new homes. Home builders are eligible for a $2,000 tax credit for a new energy-efficient home that achieves 50 percent energy savings for heating and cooling over the 2004 International Energy Conservation Code and supplements. At least one fifth of the energy savings must come from building shell improvements. This credit also applies to contractors of manufactured homes conforming to Federal Manufactured Home Construction and Safety Standards.

There is also a $1,000 tax credit to the producer of a new manufactured home achieving 30 percent energy savings for heating and cooling over the 2004 Code (at least one third of the savings must come from building shell improvements), or a manufactured home meeting the requirements established by U.S. EPA under the Energy Star program. These tax credits apply to new homes located in the United States whose construction is substantially completed after August 8, 2005 and that are acquired from the eligible contractor for use as a residence from January 1, 2006 through December 31, 2008. Check **www.irs.gov** for renewal information.

Bonus Depreciation

The federal Economic Stimulus Act of 2008, enacted in February 2008, included a 50 percent bonus depreciation provision for eligible renewable-energy systems acquired and placed in service in 2008 (or, in certain limited cases, in 2009). Again, check **www.irs.gov** for more details.

Energy Conservation Subsidy Exclusion

According to Section 136 of the IRS Code, energy conservation subsidies provided by public utilities, either directly or indirectly, are nontaxable: "Gross income shall not include the value of any subsidy provided (directly or indirectly) by a public utility to a customer for the purchase or installation of any energy conservation measure."

Business Energy Tax Credit

For equipment placed in service from January 1, 2006 until December 31, 2008, the credit is 30 percent for solar, solar hybrid lighting, and fuel cells, and 10 percent for microturbines. The geothermal credit is currently 10 percent.

USDA Renewable Energy and Efficiency Improvements Program

The U.S. Department of Agriculture has created a program to offer direct loans, loan guarantees, and grants to agricultural producers and rural small businesses to purchase renewable-energy systems and make energy-efficiency improvements, such as solar water heat, solar space heat, photovoltaics, wind, biomass, geothermal, hydrogen, anaerobic digestion, renewable fuels, fuel cells using renewable fuels. The grants are for 25 percent of eligible project costs and guaranteed loans are for 50 percent of eligible project costs. Grants and loans for 2008 will amount to over $220 million.

Lighting Energy Efficiency

Lighting consumes a tremendous amount of energy and financial resources and accounts for approximately 17 percent of all electricity sold in the United States. Lighting alone amounts to 30 percent of energy use in the typical office and can approach 50 percent in some businesses. Old incandescent lighting consumes more than 75 percent more energy than compact fluorescent lighting. Newer LED lighting consumes dramatically less energy than even compact fluorescent lights, with efficiencies of over 90 percent over incandescent bulbs. The U.S. EPA estimates that if efficient lighting were used in all locations where it has been shown to be profitable throughout the country, the nation's overall demand for electricity would be cut by more than 10 percent. This could save nearly $17 billion in ratepayer bills and result in the following annual pollution reductions:

- 202 million metric tons of carbon dioxide, the primary cause of global climate change. This would be the equivalent of taking 15 million cars off the road.

- More than 1.3 million metric tons of sulfur dioxide, which contributes to acid rain.

- 600,000 metric tons of nitrogen oxides, which contribute to smog.

Lighting is also a primary source of waste heat, which places additional requirements on any building's cooling systems. Excess heat and energy use can often be dramatically reduced by implementing an energy-efficient lighting system. Lighting upgrades are a very low-risk investment with an immediate reduction in energy costs. Upgraded lighting systems can also improve lighting quality to increase occupant comfort and productivity.

In addition to visible light, all lighting systems produce heat. Lighting is typically the largest source of waste heat, often called "heat gain," inside commercial buildings. Improving lighting efficiency reduces this heat gain, which also reduces your building's cooling requirements. Consequently, your existing cooling system may be able to serve future added loads. Lighting also affects the power quality of your building's electrical distribution system. Poor power quality is a concern because it wastes energy, reduces electrical capacity, and can harm equipment and the electrical distribution system itself. Upgrading to lighting equipment with clean power quality (high power factor and low harmonic distortion) can improve the power quality in your building's electrical system. Upgrading with higher efficiency and higher power factor lighting equipment can also free up valuable electrical capacity. This benefit alone may justify the cost of a lighting upgrade.

A lighting upgrade is an investment not only in reducing electricity consumption but also in improving the performance of the building in supporting its occupants. A building's lighting directly affects the comfort, mood, and productivity of its occupants. Improved lighting enhances visual comfort, reduces eye fatigue, and improves performance on visual tasks. Well-designed lighting is likely to improve performance, increase productivity, and reduce absenteeism. As the most visible building system, it also directly affects the aesthetics and image of the building and your business.

Whatever your current lighting, if it was installed over 10 years ago, the chances are very high that you can save considerable energy and money by upgrading to a modern more efficient lighting system. Obviously, all incandescent lighting should be replaced with compact fluorescent bulbs. If you are using T-8 or T-12 lighting, investigate upgrading to more efficient T-5 lighting. You may save energy by upgrading older fluorescent lighting systems to newer, more efficient *high-intensity discharge* (HID) systems, such as sodium or metal halide lighting if your situation warrants. You will need to work with a local lighting contractor to investigate all of the available upgrades to your lighting system.

The fastest and most cost-effective ways to save energy with lighting are:

• Design your lighting quantity and quality for specific tasks and needs

• Convert lighting to compact fluorescent or T-5 fluorescent, if feasible

• Convert fluorescent ballasts to electronic, rather than magnetic

- Maximize your total lighting system efficiency, not just the individual components

- Use automatic controls to turn lights off or dim lights in daylit areas

- Use LED exit signs

Fluorescent and HID Lighting

While a wide range of light sources are available, the predominant types used in commercial and industrial spaces are fluorescent and HID lighting. Historically, fluorescent lighting has been used for high-quality, general-purpose indoor diffuse lighting. Typically, HID lighting has been used for industrial and outside lighting and is generally very energy efficient in lighting large areas. Recently, technical advances and a flood of new products have increased the use of HID in interiors. Although fluorescent sources are still limited by their inability to function in very hot or cold environments or as spotlights, some recent advances in physical size, thermal performance, and light quality are allowing wider application in industrial, manufacturing, and residential environments. For example, linear T-5 lamps, which are relatively new, are becoming popular. T-5 lights are 5/8 inch in diameter, as opposed to T-8 which are 1 inch and T-12 which are 1 1/2 inch. They afford a dramatic reduction in energy use over T-8 or T-12 lights but are difficult to use in retrofit applications because the lamp holder design is different from that of T-8 and T-12 holders.

Fluorescent Ballasts

Ballast selection is also integral to lighting performance. All fluorescent and HID lamps require a ballast to provide the necessary starting voltage and regulate lamp current and power quality. Ballasts determine the lamp's light output, life, and control capabilities. Similar to advances in lamp technology, electronics advances have greatly expanded ballast capabilities and selection. The three types of fluorescent ballasts are magnetic, electronic, and hybrid ballasts. Magnetic ballasts, also known as electromagnetic ballasts, have improved from the standard-efficiency, core-coil ballasts last made in 1989 to higher-efficiency models.

Electronic ballasts have been developed for almost all fluorescent lighting applications to replace their conventional magnetic counterparts directly. Electronic ballasts operate fluorescent lamps at a higher frequency, which improves system efficiency by about 30 percent when used in conjunction with T-8 lamps to replace T-12 lamps and standard magnetic ballasts. Electronic ballasts provide less audible noise and virtually no lamp flicker, while adding dimming capability (with specific ballast models). Electronic ballasts also offer the ability to power up to four lamps, increasing energy efficiency by an additional 8 percent, while reducing the initial cost and maintenance costs.

Hybrid ballasts, which combine features of magnetic and electronic ballasts, are also available. Although these ballasts offer the same efficiency benefits as electronic ballasts, they cannot power more than three lamps. Instant-start circuitry offers an additional 5 percent efficiency compared with rapid-start electronic. Programmed-start ballasts offer increased lamp life compared with instant or rapid-start ballasts. Programmed-start ballasts are designed to soft-start the lamp, which decreases lamp damage.

Reflectors and Diffusers

Another low-cost upgrade is the use of reflector inserts designed to reduce the internal light loss in fixtures by using highly reflective surfaces to redirect light out of the fixture. They can be used in new fixtures or installed in existing fixtures as part of an energy savings retrofit strategy.

Most indoor commercial fixtures use some type of diffuser, a lens or louver over the face of the fixture to block a direct view of the lamp or to diffuse or redirect light. In general, diffusers are simply semitranslucent plastic sheets that hide lamp images and diffuse light evenly across the face of the fixture. Because they spread light in all directions and absorb a large amount of light, diffusers are not only inefficient but also ineffective at controlling glare. By using clear plastic lenses with small prismatic surface patterns instead of diffusers, you can improve both the efficiency and the distribution of light. Louvers are an even better upgrade. New parabolic louver shield designs can provide high efficiency (up to 90 percent) with high visual comfort ratings.

Lighting Controls, Sensors, and Dimmers

Reducing the wattage of the lighting system by using compact fluorescent, T-5, or LED lights represents only half of the potential for maximizing energy savings. The other half is minimizing the use of lighting through automatic controls. Automatic controls are used to switch or dim lighting based on time, occupancy, lighting-level strategies, or a combination of all three. In situations where lighting may be on longer than needed, left on in unoccupied areas, or used when sufficient daylight exists, you should consider installing automatic controls as a supplement or replacement for manual controls.

The most basic controlling strategies involve time-based controls, which are best suited for spaces where lighting needs are predictable and predetermined. Time-based controls can be used in both indoor and outdoor situations. Common outdoor applications include automatically switching parking lot or security lighting based on the sunset and sunrise times. Typical indoor situations include switching lighting in production, manufacturing, and retail facilities that operate on fixed, predefined operating schedules. Time-based control systems for indoor lighting typically include a manual override option for situations when lighting is needed beyond the scheduled period. Simple equipment, such as mechanical and electronic time clocks and photocells, can be independent or part of a larger centralized energy-management system.

Motion sensors are used to detect occupant motion, lighting a space only when it is occupied. Sensors should first be selected based on the range of body motion expected to occur throughout the entire lighted space. Controls for hallways, for example, need only be sensitive to a person walking down a narrow area, while sensors for offices need to detect smaller upper body motion, such as typing or reaching for a telephone. Once sensitivity and coverage area is established, sensors are available in two predominant technology types. Passive infrared sensors detect the motion of heat between vertical and horizontal detection zones. This technology requires a direct line of sight and is more sensitive to lateral motion, but it requires larger motion as the distance from the sensor increases. The coverage pattern and field of view can also be precisely controlled. Passive infrared typically finds its best application in smaller spaces with a direct line of sight, such as in warehouses and buildings with aisles.

Ultrasonic sensors detect movement by sensing disturbances in high-frequency ultrasonic patterns. Because this technology emits ultrasonic waves that are reflected around the room surfaces, it does not require a direct line of sight and is more sensitive to motion toward and away from the sensor. In addition, its sensitivity decreases relative to its distance from the sensor. These characteristics make it suitable for use in larger, enclosed areas that may have cabinets, shelving, partitions, or other obstructions. If necessary, these technologies can also be combined into one product to improve detection and reduce the likelihood of false on-off triggering. All sensors have an adjustable time delay to prevent the lights from switching off when the space is occupied, but there is little activity. Some infrared and all ultrasonic sensors also have an adjustable sensitivity setting.

Daylight dimming is another energy-saving strategy and involves continuously varying the electric lighting level to maintain a constant target level of illumination. Dimming systems save energy by dimming fluorescent lights down to as low as 10 to 20 percent of full output, with the added benefit of maintaining consistent lighting levels. You'll need modern electronic ballasts for your compact fluorescent lights if you will be installing a dimming system. Check with a lighting contractor for additional information on installing these systems.

Greening Your Business

You can use the simple economic analysis tools that are provided at the end of this chapter to check the payback periods and return on investment amounts for your lighting efficiency upgrades. The U.S. Department of Energy's Federal Energy Management Program also provides a detailed online Energy Cost Calculator for Compact Fluorescent Lamps that allows you to determine the payback periods for retrofits of current incandescent lighting with compact fluorescent lighting. This tool is found at: **www1.eere.energy.gov/femp/procurement/eep_fluorescent_ lamps_calc.html.**

Lighting is just one component of any company's energy usage. Let's now take a look at how to assess your business's current energy consumption in all areas and how to develop an overall plan to reduce your energy use and costs. Next, you will find various worksheets to help you assess your current energy use and help you look at numerous ideas and actions that your business can adopt to increase its energy efficiency. Finally, methods to analyze your potential energy efficiency measures on a sound economic basis will be outlined, including cost payback and return-on-investment analyses. You'll use your assessments, action plans, and analyses to develop your eventual Green Business Plan, which will help you in the final phase of actually implementing your new green energy policies and practices into your business operations. This general approach of Assess, Plan, Analyze, and Implement, introduced in this chapter, will be followed in the following chapters on water, waste, transportation, office equipment, purchasing, and design.

Business Energy Efficiency Plan

① You'll need to conduct a comprehensive energy use assessment of your current business operations. There are several worksheets in this chapter that use both a standard data-collection inventory and a process-mapping approach.

An Energy Use Worksheet is provided to allow you to easily collect your past energy use data—generally from your past electric or gas utility billings—and begin to analyze it. Utility bills often include the following data:

- Consumption Charges: Electricity is charged based, in part, on the amount of electricity used (in kilowatt-hours or kWh) in a billing period. The per kilowatt-hour rate for electricity may vary based on the time of year (winter or summer season) and/or the time of day (peak or off-peak hours).

- Demand and Transportation Charges: For many electricity customers (all but small accounts), there will be a demand charge (per kilowatt) in the bill that is based on the peak electricity use each month averaged over a short time period (such as 15 minutes). Your business may pay more for demand costs than consumption costs, although the two costs may be a single line item in your utility bill. There may also be an electricity transportation charge as a line item on your bill.

- Fuel Costs: For natural gas and other fuels, you may be charged for the amount of fuel you receive (for natural gas this is usually based on a per therm price) and a separate delivery charge for the transportation and delivery of the fuel. Fuel charges may vary seasonally and are based on the amount consumed.

Using the energy consumption data that you have collected for your Energy Use Worksheet, you can now complete your Business Carbon Footprint Worksheet. This simple carbon footprint worksheet is only a simple and basic tool that will begin to allow you to understand how your business energy use is directly related to the carbon emissions that are fueling worldwide climate change. Additionally, there is a travel and transportation carbon footprint worksheet provided in Chapter 9 to measure your company's emissions in those areas. Remember that there are numerous additional resources for carbon footprint analysis noted in this chapter, in Appendix B of this book, and on the CD that accompanies this book.

The next part of your business energy assessment is to complete your Energy Use Survey, on which you will list all of the major energy-consuming equipment that your business has in operation. For a small business, this may seem to be a simple task. It may appear that you only have a few pieces of office equipment and some heating and air conditioning to consider. Part of your assessment, however, is to begin to understand the pervasiveness of energy use in business and your business in particular. For larger companies, your energy use audit process will become increasingly complex. You will need to identify the equipment that uses the most energy in your business. In many businesses, a few pieces of the equipment account for the majority of energy consumption. Things to look for include large pieces of equipment and also equipment that runs most of the time or that has periodic, but substantial, start-up energy requirements (such as a bank of electric motors). A typical equipment list at a larger business facility might include machinery in the following categories:

- Natural gas heating/cooling/ventilating equipment (such as heaters, hot water heaters, or boilers) or production equipment

- Electric air compressors, heating/cooling/ventilating equipment (such as rooftop heat pumps and air conditioners), or production equipment (like motor-driven equipment, pumps, fans)

- Fuel oil heating/cooling/ventilating equipment (for example, boilers)

- Office and business-specific equipment (such as computers, printers, refrigeration, or other specialized equipment)

Your energy use assessment and your carbon footprint analysis will provide you with measurable data that can be checked periodically to determine the effectiveness of your eventual energy efficiency measures.

Finally, instructions for an Energy Use Process Map are provided. Use your own graph or other paper to develop your own energy use map. Process-mapping will show you, in graphic fashion, how energy flows through your particular business. This map of how your business uses energy will provide the basis for a careful examination of which energy efficiency methods will be most useful in your particular business. Refer back to the discussion of process mapping in Chapter 4 if necessary.

② Based on the information that you collected in your assessment, you should then formulate an aggressive energy efficiency plan. An Energy Efficiency Action worksheet listing some basic efficiency methods is provided. More detailed energy efficiency actions for specific business operations are provided in other chapters—travel and transportation in Chapter 9, office equipment and computing in Chapter 10, and building and product design in Chapters 12 and 13, respectively. Naturally, all of the energy efficiency ideas are not applicable to all businesses. Choose those actions that are most suited to your particular business. This worksheet is available on the enclosed CD as both a PDF form that may be printed out for your use and a text form. Later, in Chapter 18, the text version of this worksheet will be used to cut and paste the action steps that you choose into your overall comprehensive Green Business Plan. Your plan should be revisited and, if necessary, revised on at least an annual basis. The plan should include a clear method for monitoring and collecting your energy use data. The plan should establish and promote targets for energy efficiency throughout your business. (Remember that you don't need to retype any web address: all of the website addresses noted in this book are found, in interactive format, on the BOOK WEB ADDRESSES document that is on the CD that accompanies this book.)

③ The next element in this process is to evaluate your possible energy efficiency actions on a sound economic basis over a long term, not simply by considering the initial cost of investment. Most energy efficiency measures have a relatively short payback period and provide good returns on your investment. As energy prices continue to escalate, the affordability of efficiency becomes much clearer. To analyze the economic impacts of your energy efficiency measures, you can use the Energy Efficiency Economic Analysis Worksheet that is provided at the end of this chapter.

④ The last step in your energy efficiency plan is to actually implement it. Many energy efficiency methods can generally be implemented fairly quickly. Some will take longer and cost more. Someone in your company should be given the responsibility to implement and oversee the company energy action plan as part of your overall green business plan.

Energy Use Worksheet
(Prepare for past 2 years)

Use the following to complete the Energy Use Worksheet: your business's energy bills for the last two years, including electricity, natural gas, and fuel oil, if applicable. For larger and multi-metered businesses, it may be easier to set up a simple spreadsheet to record this data. Natural gas is usually measured in *therms* which is equivalent to about 29 kWh (killowatts/hour) or 100,000 Btus (British thermal units). Electricity is measured in kWh units, and fuel oil is measured in gallons.

Year:_____	Natural Gas (therms)		Electricity (kWh)		Fuel Oil (gallons)	
	Cost	Amount	Cost	Amount	Cost	Amount
January						
February						
March						
April						
May						
June						
July						
August						
September						
October						
November						
December						
Total						
Average (Total divided by 12)						

Prepare an Energy Use Worksheet for the past two years and then prepare one for every year (or quarter) in the future in order to track the effectiveness of your energy efficiency measures. If your facility or business is large enough, you may wish to break this information down for each electric meter or gas gauge in use at your business. If your business is power-intensive and if you have installed additional submeters, you may be able to monitor power usage much more carefully and evaluate the effectiveness of each efficiency measure separately. The installation of smaller energy monitoring devices in areas of high electricity use is a very cost-effective way to monitor and reduce energy use.

Energy Survey Worksheet

Completed by:	Date:	Business:
Address:	Phone:	Business Sq. Footage:

Energy is:	Energy products used:	Main Energy Use
❑ Generated on-site ❑ Supplied by utility ❑ Other supplier	❑ Electricity ❑ Liquid petroleum ❑ Natural gas ❑ Renewable	❑ Office use ❑ Industrial processes ❑ Commercial/retail ❑ Transportation
Number of employees _____	Number of visitors/ customers: _____	Total average occupancy _____
Occupancy Schedule:	Weekdays: _____am to _____pm	Weekends: _____am to _____pm

Existing Major Energy-Consuming Equipment or Fixtures

Location	Equipment	Type	# Units	Make/ Model	Energy use/kWh	Use/week in hours	Comments

Areas of High Energy Use	Location	Usages

You should prepare this Energy Survey Worksheet initially and then annually if your business is subject to change or expansion. By using the usage information compiled with this worksheet, you will be better able to develop a plan which minimizes energy use for each item of energy-consuming equipment or fixture.

Business Carbon Footprint Worksheet

Note: This very simplified basic carbon footprint analysis only measures the footprint of your directly purchased energy consumption. Its purpose is to start you on the road to thinking about your energy use in terms of the carbon dioxide emissions that are a direct result of your energy consumption. It does not take into account any direct emissions from your business operations, any indirect emissions that are not a result of purchased energy, nor any carbon emissions from your business travel and transportation. A separate Business Travel and Transportation Carbon Footprint Worksheet is provided in Chapter 9. Note also that this worksheet is provided on the accompanying CD in a PDF format that is fillable and will complete your calculations for you. Many more complex carbon footprint calculators are noted in this chapter and in Appendix B.

Type of Usage	Usage Amount	Multiplier	Carbon Footprint in CO_2 Equivalent Pounds of Emissions
Annual Natural Gas Use (in therms)		40	
Annual Electric Use (in kWh)		1.5	
Annual Fuel Oil Use (in gallons)		22	
Total Business Carbon Footprint from purchased energy			

The multipliers for this worksheet are derived from carbon conversion factors provided by the Voluntary Reporting of Greenhouse Gases Program, Fuel and Energy Source Codes and Emission Coefficients, from the Energy Information Administration, U.S. Department of Energy.

Energy Use Process Map
of Energy Inputs and Usage

Refer to Chapter 4 regarding process mapping and then draw your own simple diagram to help you better understand where your business's energy is used and how to locate the best areas for efficiency efforts. Your Energy Use Process Map should include the following details:

• All areas where energy of any type is used in your business

• Electric and/or natural gas distribution systems

• Building heating and air conditioning systems

• Estimate of the type of energy use per area (natural gas, electric, liquid fuel, steam)

• Estimates of percentage of each type of energy used per area

• Areas where immediate cost savings might be found (such as areas where lighting is unnecessary, areas of heat loss, areas that are unnecessarily heated or cooled, etc.)

• Areas where longer-term cost savings might occur (such as areas where oversized machinery could be replaced, areas where older, less efficient equipment could be replaced, areas with machinery in which motors, compressors, or pumps could be replaced, etc.)

Energy Efficiency Action Worksheet

	Already Doing	Should Do	Doesn't Apply
Prepare an Energy Use Worksheet to track business energy use. Update this information on a regular basis to monitor results of energy conservation actions.			
Prepare an Energy Survey Worksheet and Energy-Use Process Map to outline the main energy uses in the business and help identify the best areas for efficiency efforts.			
Prepare your Business Carbon Footprint Worksheet and consider the public reporting of your greenhouse gas emissions. See Chapter 16 on reporting.			
Consider joining the U.S. EPA's Climate Leaders program to work on voluntarily reducing your company's greenhouse gas emissions. For more information, see: **www.epa.gov/stateply**.			
Consider the purchase of carbon offsets or renewable energy credits for your company.			
Develop a company-wide energy efficiency policy and communicate that policy to all management and employees.			
Set a company policy to shut off all lights, machinery, or equipment when not in use, particularly on nights and weekends. Much equipment is idle for up to 90 percent of its life.			
Install energy monitors (as sub-meters) that can provide an accurate display of the cost and energy usage of individual equipment. See, for example, **www.powermeterstore.com**.			
Consider using energy-efficient surge protectors or power strips. The Belkin Conserve Surge Protector works with a remote control. See **www.belkin.com**. The Smart Strip Power Strip automatically cuts power to other equipment when the main switched equipment is shut down. See: **www.bltsltd.net/consumerproducts/**. The Isole Plug Load controller combines a surge protector with a motion detector shut-off. See: **www.wattstopper.com**.			

Consider using simple timer devices to shut off equipment at night and on weekends. These can easily be set to shut off your power strips, and thus shut off multiple pieces of equipment.			
Install motion sensor and/or automatic dimming switches for all lighting.			
To dim fluorescent lighting, you will need to retrofit any older fixtures with newer electronic ballasts.			
Use task lighting to light only areas that are in use, rather than an entire room.			
Install reflectors to increase the effectiveness of any lighting fixtures. This simple retrofit can reduce lighting needs by up to 50 percent.			
Replace incandescent light bulbs with compact fluorescent lamps, wherever appropriate.			
Upgrade to T-8 (1 inch diameter) fluorescent lamp tubes with solid-state electronic ballasts that are more efficient than older T-12 (1.5 inch diameter) tubes with magnetic ballasts.			
Use T-5 fluorescent lighting if you are considering a complete retrofit of lighting.			
Always buy Energy Star qualified products for your business. The Energy Star label indicates the most efficient computers, printers, copiers, refrigerators, televisions, windows, thermostats, ceiling fans, and other appliances and equipment.			
If you need to purchase new equipment, buy equipment that is durable and can be easily upgraded. Consider also whether the product has online manuals that reduce the need for printed manuals, if the equipment is recyclable, and whether the manufacturer has a take-back policy.			
Even better, investigate the leasing of any business equipment that you may need.			
Clean refrigerator and cooling coils and condensers twice a year. Replace door gaskets if a dollar bill easily slips out when closed between the door's seals.			

Install an insulation blanket on water heaters 7 years of age or older, and insulate the first 3 feet of the heated water "out" pipe on both old and new units.			
Set water temperature only as hot as needed (110-120 degrees).			
Insulate hot and cold water lines in any areas they pass through that are not heated or cooled.			
If buying a new water heater, always buy the most efficient model possible. In areas of infrequent use, consider tankless water heaters to reduce "standby" storage costs and waste.			
Even better, install a solar thermal water heating system for your business.			
Make sure your heating, ventilating, and air conditioning (HVAC) systems are operating at peak efficiency. Consider using an annual maintenance contract.			
Regularly change (or clean if reusable) HVAC filters every month during peak cooling or heating season.			
Install a programmable thermostat to automate your HVAC system and set it to significantly scale back heating and cooling when the business is not in operation. These units generally offer a 50 percent rate of return on the cost of the original investment.			
Control direct sun through windows depending on the season and local climate. During cooling season, block direct heat gain from the sun shining through glass on the east and especially west sides of your business.			
Depending on your facility, options such as solar screens, solar films, awnings, and trees can help prevent summer heat gain.			
During heating season, with the sun low in the south, unobstructed southern windows can contribute solar heat gain during the day.			
Plug all leaks in your building's outer shell with weather stripping and caulking. Use expandable foam to fill any gaps.			

Use fans. Comfort is a function of temperature, humidity, and air movement. Moving air can make a somewhat higher temperature and/or humidity feel comfortable. Fans can help delay or reduce the need for air conditioning, and a temperature setting of 3 to 5 degrees higher can feel as comfortable with fans. Each degree of higher temperature can save about 3 percent on cooling costs.			
Use reversible fans that pull hot air up in summer and push hot air down in winter.			
Use natural ventilation whenever possible to lighten the load on your HVAC system—open the windows!			
Consider installing double-paned windows. These generally can reduce heating and cooling costs by over 30 percent.			
Seal and repair all leaks in your building's HVAC duct works. Insulate any duct work that passes through unheated or uncooled spaces.			
Isolate any unused space in your business building and close the heating and cooling vents to those areas.			
Completely seal and insulate any unused exterior windows that are not used or are not necessary for good lighting.			
Install automatic door closers to close and seal doors.			
Use exterior insulating covers in the winter months for any air conditioners.			
Upgrade the energy efficiency of your older equipment. Modern equipment is much more energy efficient, often with less than half of the energy use of older equipment. Efficiency upgrades for motors and drives for equipment, air compressors, lighting, and other energy-consuming equipment often have rapid payback periods.			
Install variable-speed switches and controls on any equipment where this is feasible. A variable-speed control can save up to 70 percent of energy used on many installations.			

A typical industrial motor may use 10 times its actual original cost in energy every year. That's like spending $100,000 annually for gas for a $10,000 car. Replace your old electric motors in fans, compressors, and pumps with modern high efficiency motors.			
See if you can downsize any of your business's equipment, including heating and air conditioning, refrigeration, and other systems. Newer, more efficient equipment can often be sized smaller and perform better than older, less efficient machinery.			
Many types of machinery, such as air compressors, turn up to 90 percent of the energy used into waste heat. Investigate methods of using a heat recovery system that allows you to use that waste heat in other areas of your business.			
Switch off any machinery when not in use, or slow down the speed of fans or motors if possible to accomplish without a reduction in efficiency.			
If your building still uses fuel oil, consider switching to cleaner natural gas.			
Better yet, investigate the possibility of installing renewable energy systems on your business property, such as solar thermal heating, solar photovoltaic, wind, or geothermal systems. You might be surprised at the savings possible as fossil fuel energy prices continue to escalate.			
Use all of the energy efficiency measures outlined for travel and transportation (Chapter 9), office equipment and computing (Chapter 10), and building design (Chapter 12), and relating to product and service design (Chapter 13).			
Depending on your particular type of business, there are many more additional energy efficiency measures that you can take for your business. Check all available sources for more energy-saving ideas in Appendix B, on the enclosed CD, and on the Internet.			

Economic Analysis of Energy Efficiency Measures

Simple Cost Payback Analysis

In order to make rational business decisions about which energy efficiency actions to implement, you may wish to run a simple cost payback analysis. In this method, the total initial cost of the improvement is divided by the first-year energy cost savings produced by the improvement. This method yields the number of years required for the improvement to pay for itself. Cost payback analyses can be far more complex and include many other variables. The basics of cost payback analyses were outlined in Chapter 4. Refer to that chapter for more details.

Let's look at the replacement of incandescent lights. If your business currently has, say, 100 incandescent bulbs and wishes to replace them with modern compact fluorescent bulbs, the calculations would be as follows:

100 new compact fluorescent bulbs, at $5/bulb, would cost $500.

Each old incandescent bulb is 100 watt and is on for 18 hours/day for 260 days/year, thus using 468 kilowatt hours of energy (100 X 18 X 260 = 468,000). At an average rate of 10¢ per kWh, this would cost approximately $47/year/bulb in energy. For 100 bulbs then, this amounts to about $470 annually in electric bills.

New compact fluorescent bulbs use only 20 watts of energy for the same time and days, (20 X 18 X 260 = 93,600) thus using only about 94 kilowatts of energy, costing only $9.40 annually or $94 for all 100 bulbs annually.

Thus, if you replace the older less-efficient bulbs, the yearly savings would be $376 ($470 - $94 = $376). If you divide the initial cost of the upgrade by the first year cost savings, your payback period is shown (in years).

Cost of upgrade $500 / Savings per year $376 = 1.33 years payback period.

Thus, the full cost of upgrading all 100 of the incandescent bulbs to energy-efficient compact fluorescent would be paid back in about 16 months. Over a 10-year period, this upgrade would save $3,760 dollars in electricity costs alone. This assumes that the actual costs paid for electricity will not rise. Of course, if the cost for electricity does rise (and no one actually expects the price to go down over the next 10 years), your savings would be even greater. This simple analysis also doesn't take into account that, over that 10-year period, you would not have to replace those new bulbs, nor would you have to spend maintenance time doing such replacements, or disposing of the worn-out incandescent bulbs.

Simple Return on Investment Analysis

Another standard measure of economic feasibility is the *return on investment* formula. This is a measure of the percentage return provided by a particular investment. The standard formula for return on investment (ROI) is:

Net return / capital cost of investment = percentage return on investment

For the net return figure, you need to determine the life of the investment (in years) and multiply it by net annual savings. Use the net annual savings figure that you generated in the cost payback analysis. Then deduct the initial capital cost.

Net annual savings x life of investment - capital cost = net return

Thus, for our example, if we assume a 10-year life for the new bulbs, our Net Return is:

$376 X 10 = $3,760 - $500 capital costs = $3,260 net return

Then, using this net return figure, our return on investment (ROI) is:

$3,260 net return / $500 capital costs = 652 percent ROI =
the return on the investment over a 10-year period.

Then, by dividing that figure by the years of life of the investment, you have a

652 / 10 = 65.2 percent annualized rate of return

These formulas can additionally include calculations to discount the dollar amounts over time and other more sophisticated approaches. For example, full life-cycle cost analyses are a more in-depth alternative to return on investment analyses. This simple approach, however, can provide you with a quick and simple way to compare energy efficiency investments with other business investment choices. In addition, remember that there are many other valuable noneconomic benefits to conserving energy in your business.

On the following page, you will find a simple worksheet to use for cost payback and return on investment calculations. This worksheet is provided on the CD that accompanies this book in a fillable PDF format that will do the necessary calculations for you.

Energy Efficiency Economic Analysis

Capital Costs

	Equipment Costs	$
+	Prep Work Costs	$
+	Installation Costs	$
=	Total Capital Costs	$

Net Annual Savings

	Annual Avoided Disposal Costs	$
+	Annual Avoided Purchase Costs	$
+	Annual Avoided Energy Costs	$
+	Annual Additional Revenue (if any)	$
=	Total Net Annual Savings	$

Simple Payback Period Analysis

	Capital Costs (from above)	$
÷	Net Annual Savings (from above)	$
=	Payback Period in Years	

Simple Return on Investment Analysis

	Net Annual Savings (from above)	$
x	Life of Investment (in years)	
−	Capital Costs (from above)	$
=	Net Return	$
÷	Capital Costs (from above)	$
=	Return on Investment (over life)	
÷	Life of Investment (in years)	
=	Annual Return on Investment Rate	%

These formulas can additionally include calculations to discount the dollar amounts over time and other more sophisticated approaches. Remember that there are many other valuable noneconomic benefits to energy efficiency in your business.

Chapter 7

Green Business Water Use

The efficient use of water is fast becoming a priority for both individuals and businesses across the globe. Every year, as both population and development increase, more demands are placed on the earth's limited supply of fresh water. While usable fresh water levels remain stable at about 1 percent of the total water on the planet, local and regional drought conditions are reaching critical levels. Certain areas around the globe, including the arid U.S. Southwest, and, in recent years, the formerly water-sufficient U.S. Southeast, are realizing that the seemingly endless supply of fresh water is only a mirage. A recent U.S. government survey showed at least 36 states are anticipating local, regional, or statewide water shortages by 2013. Climate change is also altering the rainfall and snow melt patterns around the world, in some cases dramatically altering the availability of water. Accelerating glacier melt in the Andes is posing immediate and dire threats to the water supplies of several major South American cities. The demands for fresh water worldwide are leading to shortages, rising costs, and increasing restrictions on access.

There are immediate and real advantages to companies that strive to become more water efficient. Commercial buildings use close to 20 percent of U.S. drinking water supplies. Reducing total commercial building water consumption by just 10 percent would mean saving well over 2 trillion gallons of water each year. Most businesses can reduce their water use, and its attendant expense, by 30 percent or more. Obviously, reducing water use will result in lower water bills. Unnecessary heating or treating of water can increase energy consumption and energy bills and the reduction of heated water temperature can help lower these costs significantly. Additionally, reducing overall water use can reduce the quantity of wastewater from any facility that may require expensive treatment and disposal. Reducing disposal of water that may be tainted with toxic or hazardous chemicals can also limit a company's exposure to litigation that may stem from the release of such chemicals into the environment. A successful water conservation program can show the public your company's willingness to become an active partner in any community efforts at water efficiency. There is a wide range of water efficiency measures that any company can introduce to control water use within the business—from industrial processes, to office spaces, to landscaping to cafeterias. If a business is in the process of designing a new site, facility, or process, or is redesigning or remodeling a current operation, there are numerous opportunities to incorporate significant water efficiency measures directly into the plans. For large water users or those businesses in arid regions, all of these issues are amplified. Working to maximize the efficiency of current water supplies helps to defer the need to develop new and increasingly more expensive sources of water and their accompanying water treatment facilities. This, in turn, works to prevent the rates paid for water from rising as fast. Finally, conserving our shared water resources is simply the right thing to do.

Business Water Conservation Resources

There are numerous organizations, websites, and resources to assist businesses in their water conservation efforts. The American Water Works Association program, WaterWiser®, is a comprehensive clearinghouse of resources on water conservation, efficiency and demand management for conservation professionals, and the larger water supply community. The site has hundreds of topic-based links to relevant online resources for water efficiency and provides an online marketplace of water conservation products. For information on this program, see: **www.awwa.org/waterwiser**.

The U.S. EPA, through its WaterSense® program, is partnering with manufacturers, retailers and distributors, utilities, water districts, and others to bring water-efficient products to market and spread the word about the need for smart water use. This program helps both consumers and business identify water-efficient products and programs. The WaterSense® label indicates that these products and programs meet water efficiency, and performance criteria. WaterSense® labeled products are selected to perform well, help save money, and encourage innovation in manufacturing. WaterSense® is also partnering with irrigation professionals and irrigation certification programs to promote water-efficient landscape irrigation practices. See **www.epa.gov/watersense**.

You can use also use the U.S. EPA's Portfolio Manager software to track and manage water consumption. The new water tracking features of this program let you track water use and bills for indoor use, outdoor use, and wastewater. This program is available at: **www.energystar.gov/istar/pmpam**. Information regarding other water conservation resources are noted in Appendix B.

Business Water Efficiency Plan

The process to develop and introduce water efficiency measures in any company is a straightforward, four-fold process of Assess, Plan, Analyze, and Implement:

① The first step to improving efficiency in any system is to understand current performance. Conduct a comprehensive water use assessment of your current business practices. For a small business, this may be a simple task. You may only have a single bathroom for yourself or a few employees. For larger companies, this water audit process becomes more complex. There are several worksheets in this chapter that use both a standard data-collection inventory and the process-mapping approach.

Instructions for a Water Use Process Map are provided. Use your own graph or other paper to develop your own water use map. Process-mapping will show you, in graphic fashion, how water flows through your particular business. It can also show where energy is used in the process, where water is actually consumed, where wastes are generated, and where reduction of water use is most cost effective. This map of how water is actually used in your business will provide the basis for a careful examination of which water efficiency methods will be most useful in your particular business.

In addition, a Water Consumption Worksheet is provided to allow you to easily collect your past water use data. A Water Survey Worksheet is also provided to help you make an on-site survey of your business water uses. Your total water use inventory will provide you with measurable data that can be checked periodically to determine the effectiveness of your eventual conservation measures. The conservation plan you develop to reduce water use will only be as good as the information that you compile to develop it.

② On the basis of your water use assessment, you should then formulate and implement a water action plan. A Water Conservation Action Worksheet listing a wide range of water efficiency methods is provided. Choose those actions that are applicable to your business. Your plan should be revisited and, if necessary, revised on at least an annual basis. The plan should include a clear method for monitoring and collecting water and sewer use data. The plan should establish and promote targets for water efficiency throughout the business. Choose the measures on the Water Conservation Action chart that will be most valuable for your company. This chart is available on the enclosed CD as both a PDF form that may be printed out for your use in developing your company's own water conservation Action Plan and also as a text form. The text version of this chart may be used to cut and paste the action steps that you choose into your overall company environmental plan. See Chapter 18 for more details.

③ The third step is to evaluate your possible actions on a sound economic basis over a long term, not just considering the initial cost of investment. Information regarding cost payback and return-on-investment analysis of your water conservation plans is provided at the end of this chapter.

④ The final step in the achievement of water efficiency is to actually implement the plan. Most water efficiency methods are both practical and cost effective and can generally be implemented fairly quickly. Implementation can be done in phases, beginning with the easiest and lowest-cost water conservation methods and progressing to the more expensive or comprehensive steps. Someone in the company should be given the responsibility to implement and oversee the water action plan. Naturally, not all of these water efficiency ideas are not applicable to all businesses.

Water Use Assessment

The goals in this assessment of water use are to develop a water use inventory that is as specific and measurable as possible. This should not be a difficult process, but it will take some time and effort to compile. The result will be a better and more complete understanding of how water is used in your business, where best to implement conservation techniques, and what benefits can be expected from your water efficiency efforts. Initially, your water use assessment will be where your efforts are directed. Once you have the necessary information before you, it will be much easier to develop a list of conservation steps that you wish to take.

Begin by collecting any water use information that already exists. Everyone in your business who uses water should be consulted for his or her input. In larger businesses, operations and maintenance personnel may have the most direct knowledge of water use in your facility.

Use the following to complete the Water Consumption Worksheet:

❑ Water and sewer bills for last two years. For larger and multimeter businesses, it may be easier to set up a simple spreadsheet to record this data.

❑ Typical operating schedules as well as number of employees and/or visitors using any water facilities.

Use these next two items to develop your Water Use Process Map:

❑ Building floor plan

❑ Location of water meters serving your building, if more than one meter is serving your building. For multiple-meter businesses, contact the local water utility for information regarding the types of uses for each meter (i.e., landscape, fire line, etc.). Larger businesses may decide to prepare a simple spreadsheet to record this information.

Finally, complete your Water Survey Worksheet with the following:

❑ List of all water-using equipment and plumbing fixtures with manufacturer's recommended flow rates, where applicable.

Note: Federal Plumbing Fixture Standards are noted at the end of the Water Conservation Action Worksheet.

Water Consumption Worksheet

(Prepare for past 2 years) (Note: CCF on water bills is 100 cubic feet, which equals 748 gallons)

Year:_____	Monthly Water Consumption	Monthly Water Cost	Monthly Sewer Cost	Average Gallons per Workday
January				
February				
March				
April				
May				
June				
July				
August				
September				
October				
November				
December				
Total				
Average (Total divided by 12)				

Prepare a Water Consumption Worksheet for the past two years and then prepare one for every year in the future in order to track the effectiveness of your water conservation measures. If your facility or business is large enough, you may wish to break this information down for each water meter in use at your business. If your business is water-intensive and If you have installed additional submeters, you may be able to monitor water usage much more carefully and evaluate the effectiveness of each conservation measure separately. The installation of submeters in areas of high water use is a cost-effective way to monitor and reduce water use.

Water Survey Worksheet

Completed by:	Date:	Business:
Address:	Phone:	Business Sq. Footage:

Waste water is: ❑ Treated on-site ❑ Sent to city sewer ❑ Other	Recycled water use: ❑ Toilets/urinals ❑ Cooling towers ❑ Irrigation	Main water use: ❑ Bathrooms ❑ Industrial ❑ Irrigation
Number of employees _____	Number of visitors/ customers: _____	Total average occupancy _____
Occupancy Schedule:	Weekdays: _____am to _____pm	Weekends: _____am to _____pm

Existing Plumbing/Water Use Equipment

Location	Equipment	Type	# Units	Make/ Model	Flow rate (gpf)	Uses/ week	Comments

Areas of High Water Use	Location	Usages

You should prepare this Business Water Survey Worksheet initially and then annually if your business is subject to change or expansion. By using the flow rate and usage information compiled with this worksheet, you will be better able to develop a plan that minimizes water use for each item of water-use equipment or fixture.

Water Use Process Map
of Water Inputs, Outputs, and Treatment

Refer to Chapter 4 regarding process mapping and then draw your own simple diagram to help you better understand where your water is used and how it is disposed of. If you have on-site treatment of water or other more complex uses of water, your map will also need to include extensive energy use details. Your Water Use Process Map should included the following details:

• Location of building water meters

• All areas where water is used in your business

• Water and sewer pipe and drainage systems

• Any water treatment methods and/or areas

• Estimates of percentage of water consumption per area

• Estimate of percentage of sewer discharges per area

• Any areas where hazardous products mix with water

• Areas where cost savings might be found

• Areas where accidents or problems may occur

Water Conservation Action Worksheet

	Already Doing	Should Do	Doesn't Apply
Building Water Use			
Prepare a Water Consumption Worksheet to track business water use and expense. Update this information on a regular basis to monitor results of water conservation actions.			
Prepare a Water Survey Worksheet and Water Use Process Map to outline the main water uses in your business and help identify the best areas for conservation efforts.			
Check for water efficiency products and practices on the U.S. EPAs website at: **www.epa.gov/watersense**.			
Check for water efficiency information at the website for the American Water Works Association at: **www.awwa.org/waterwiser**.			
Read water meters regularly and record data. Consider installing additional submeters to better monitor water use in high volume areas.			
Shut off water to any unused areas and/or remove any water faucets that are not necessary.			
Install pressure reducing valves if necessary to reduce high water pressure. This can reduce water use when high-pressure water is unnecessary for a particular use.			
Check your facility carefully for any water leaks. If feasible, shut off all water-using outlets and monitor your water meter. If meter is showing water input, you have leaks in your system. Locate and repair any such leaks.			
Repair or replace any leaking pipes, faucets, or other water-using appliances. Replace seals regularly.			
Eliminate unnecessary wash-downs or cleaning.			
Instruct employees to look for ways to conserve water and eliminate waste.			

Install additional water metering equipment in areas of high water use in order to monitor and maximize efficiency measures. For example, submeters should be installed for cooling towers. (This can earn a LEED point for existing buildings. See Chapter 12 on Green Building Design.)			
Use hot water reuse systems when possible.			
Use air cooling rather than water-based cooling if feasible.			
Determine quantities, qualities, and locations of any possible reusable water sources, including rain water and rinse water.			
Reuse treated wastewater whenever feasible. Verify that reuse of such water does not harm fixtures or pipes.			
Handle any waste products or materials in a dry state only. Drain any water from waste prior to disposal.			
If drain water contains hazardous or toxic chemicals, be certain that it is disposed of properly.			
Verify that all sources of hazardous chemicals that may be entering waste water have been eliminated.			
Adjust valves, nozzles, solenoids, and other water use equipment to minimize water use.			
Replace existing low-efficiency water equipment with the most efficient available. (The reduction of water use below minimum efficiency standards can earn LEED points for both existing and new building construction. See Chapter 12.)			
Install low-flow showers, faucets, toilets, urinals, hose valves, etc. (Zero-water urinals, 1 gpf toilets, and .5 gmp faucets are all readily available. See, for example: **www.zeroflush.com**).			
Install spring-loaded faucets or auto-shutoff faucets.			
Adjust plumbing to use the minimum amount of water necessary for each fixture's use.			
Add non-removable trigger spray grips to any hoses in use.			

Remove overlapping water usages, such as multiple hoses, excess sinks, etc.			
Convert cooling tower systems to closed loop circulation rather than once-through circulation or convert cooling equipment to air-cooled systems.			
Eliminate or downsize cooling towers whereever possible.			
Use nonpotable water source for cooling towers.			
Turn off water-cooled cooling systems whenever not needed.			
Specify a company policy of only purchasing water-efficient appliances or devices.			
Specify a company policy of lowering all water use to the absolute minimum.			
Match the quality of the water used to the actual application. You may not need potable water for all uses. Look for areas where recycled water or rain water may be used instead.			
Use dishwashing or laundry equipment only when needed and always use full loads.			
Use any bleed-off water (for example, from ice making equipment) for cooling uses.			
Use cleaning chemicals that are nontoxic and water-based to avoid water contamination.			
Sweep when mopping is unnecessary. Eliminate hosing-off as a cleaning option.			
Landscape Water Use			
The installation of water meters for landscape irrigation may save significantly on sewer fees if such fees are assessed on the basis of total water use.			
Establish a schedule for landscape watering and use recycled or rainwater if possible.			
Adjust landscape watering schedules seasonally.			
If landscape or other irrigation system is used, convert to carefully scheduled drip irrigation system, if feasible.			

Insure there are no leaks in irrigation system and that water usage is set to minimum requirements.			
Turn off irrigation system when rain is sufficient.			
Use heat- or drought-resistant landscaping and plants whenever possible.			
Limit grassy turf areas as much as possible.			
Investigate xeriscaping (dry landscaping).			
Use mulch around trees and shrubs.			
Mow regularly and leave grass height at 3" or more.			
Use rainwater, gray water, or nonpotable water for landscaping if feasible (A 50 percent reduction in potable water use for landscaping can earn a LEED point for existing buildings; a 75 percent reduction earns an additional point; and the elimination of potable water use for landscaping earns an additional point. See Chapter 12 on Green Building Design.)			
Remember that you don't need to retype any web address: all of the website addresses noted in this book are found, in interactive format, on the BOOK WEB ADDRESSES document that is on the CD that accompanies this book.			

Federal Plumbing Fixture Standards	Residential	Commercial
Toilets—gallons per flush (gpf)	1.6	1.6
Urinals—gallons per flush (gpf)	1.0	1.0
Lavatory Faucets—gallons per minute (gpm)	2.2	.5*
Showerheads—gallons per minute (gpm)	2.5	1.6**

Note: All new fixtures must meet these requirements. Replacement of existing fixtures that do not meet these requirements is not generally required. However, it is usually very cost effective to replace old fixtures with new fixtures that meet or, preferably, exceed these minimum federal requirements.
* Federal standards superseded by UPC and IPC National Plumbing Codes
** Standards for private lavatories in commercial buildings (i.e., hotels, etc.)

Economic Analysis of Water Use Efficiency Measures

Simple Cash Payback Analysis

In order to make rational business decisions about which of your water conservation actions to implement, you may wish to run a simple cost payback analysis. A highly simplified form of cost/benefit analysis is called simple payback. In this method, the total first cost of the improvement is divided by the first-year energy cost savings produced by the improvement. This method yields the number of years required for the improvement to pay for itself. Cost payback analyses can be far more complex and include many other variables. The basics of cost payback analyses were outlined in the Chapter 4.

Let's look at the replacement of a urinal. If your current urinal uses 3 gallons per flush or *gpf* (which is typical for older urinals) and it is used about 30 times per day (also typical) for an average 5-day workweek (260 days per year) and water and sewer usage costs are $4 per 1000 gallons or *mcf* (U.S. average), your annual water costs for one urinal would be as follows:

Fixture	Number in use	Flow rate	Uses per day	Workdays annually	Annual Usage	Cost per mcf	Annual cost
Old urinal	1	3 gpf	30	260	23,400	$4.00	$93.00
New urinal	1	1 gpf	30	260	7,800	$4.00	$31.00

If you replace the older less efficient urinal with a modern low-flow model that uses only 1 gallon per flush, the water cost/year is 1/3 of the older model or $31/year and the yearly savings would be $62.

If replacing the old urinal with a new urinal would cost $250, then to determine your payback period, you would divide the initial cost of the upgrade by the first-year cost savings:

Cost of upgrade $250 / Savings per year $62 = 4.03 years payback period

The bottom line of this analysis is that the upgrade to a more modern and efficient fixture would pay for itself in about four years. Over a ten-year period, this upgrade would save $620 in water and sewer costs alone. This assumes that the actual costs paid for water and sewer services will not rise, an unlikely assumption. Of course, if they do rise, your savings would be even greater. Over a ten-year period, the upgrade for one single urinal would pay for itself and actually save your company an additional $370 in associated water and sewer costs.

Simple Return on Investment Analysis

Let's now take a look at another standard business metric: return on investment. Suppose that the 10 new urinals a business is considering would enable the company to save $620 a year over the lifetime of the fixtures, which would be 10 years. The total savings would thus be $6,200, making for a net return of $3,700 (lifetime return less initial cost). Applying the standard ROI formula of net return divided by cost of investment—or $3,700/$2,500—the ROI for this upgrade is a very attractive 148% over a ten year period or an annualized rate of 14.8%.

Cost of 10 new urinals = $250/urinal X 10 units = $2,500

Lifetime cost savings = $62/year/urinal X 10 units X 10 years = $6,200

Net return = Total savings less upgrade cost = $6,200 - $2,500 = $3,700

Return on Investment (ROI) = $3,700/$2,500 = 148%

Total ROI / life of investment = annual rate of return (148 /10 = 14.8%)

These calculations and formulas can additionally include various amounts to discount the dollar amounts over time and other more sophisticated approaches. You can employ a similar cost payback and return on investment analysis for any of the various water conservation upgrades that you wish to make. You will find that most of the upgrades will pay for themselves over a 10-year or less payback period and provide a very healthy return on investment.

Check your water bill for the cost of water in your locality and be sure to include the cost of sewer use in your calculations. If you are considering an upgrade that would remove a volume of water from sewer disposal and are installing a submeter to measure this, be sure and check with your water provider to make sure that you will be credited on your monthly bill with a rebate for any eliminated sewer usage. The Federal Energy Management Program of the U.S. Department of Energy provides various cost savings calculators for use online or in downloadable program versions. Please see the Appendix for the websites for these DOE cost savings calculators.

On the following page, you will find a simple worksheet to use for cost payback and return on investment calculations. This worksheet is provided on the CD that accompanies this book in a fillable PDF format that will do the necessary calculations for you.

Water Conservation Economic Analysis

Capital Costs

	Equipment Costs	$	
+	Prep Work Costs	$	
+	Installation Costs	$	
=	Total Capital Costs	$	

Net Annual Savings

	Annual Avoided Disposal Costs	$
+	Annual Avoided Purchase Costs	$
+	Annual Avoided Water/Sewer Costs	$
+	Annual Additional Revenue (if any)	$
=	Total Net Annual Savings	$

Simple Payback Period Analysis

	Capital Costs (from above)	$
÷	Net Annual Savings (from above)	$
=	Payback Period in Years	

Simple Return on Investment Analysis

	Net Annual Savings (from above)	$
x	Life of Investment (in years)	
−	Capital Costs (from above)	$
=	Net Return	$
÷	Capital Costs (from above)	$
=	Return on Investment (over life)	
÷	Life of Investment (in years)	
=	Annual Return on Investment Rate	%

These formulas can additionally include calculations to discount the dollar amounts over time and other more sophisticated approaches. Remember that there are many other valuable non-economic benefits to conserving water in your business.

Chapter 8

Green Business Waste and Recycling

Globally, although business provides humanity with a range of products and services that were unimaginable a few short decades ago—from cell phones, to computers, to global transportation, to nearly unlimited consumer choices—we are, as a civilization, dramatically and unnecessarily wasteful. The United States leads the world in generating waste. Each year, 20 tons of basic raw materials are needed to supply the needs of each individual American. At this level of consumption, at least four additional planets' worth of resources would be needed to support the earth's six billion-plus inhabitants. The average North American consumes 10 times as much as the average person living in China and 30 times as much as the average person living in India. Of our insatiable consumption, only 7 percent of the materials "consumed" actually become saleable products—93 percent is waste. Of the 7 percent that actually becomes a usable product, fully 80 percent is discarded after one use and 99 percent becomes waste within six weeks of its purchase by consumers.

Most of us have heard these or similar sobering statistics, but may not have really understood the implications. Modern industrial society is simply not sustainable. Our collective overuse of the natural resources is beginning to have irrevocable impacts on life on earth—including most ominously the alteration of long-term climate patterns. As the 80 percent of the world's population currently without access to the modern attributes of industrial civilization strives to move into the mainstream of development, methods and techniques must rapidly be implemented to dramatically reduce civilization's use of natural resources and raw materials by, at minimum, an order of magnitude—90 percent. Business can lead this effort. By designing new and better ways to produce the products that humanity requires, business can guide society to a sustainable future. Later in this book, we will look at design techniques that business can employ for dramatically reducing material use—both in product design and in building design. But the low-hanging fruit of achieving sustainability is to radically reduce the waste that our society produces. Business can lead the way in this effort as well by developing comprehensive waste management plans that address every possible aspect of waste reduction. The ultimate goal in waste reduction is to reach a point where all waste is either reused by the business itself or fully recycled—zero waste.

The first priority of any business waste management plan should be to aggressively reduce waste as much as possible at the source. If less material enters the waste stream of a business, raw materials are immediately saved. Less waste at the source also directly reduces the expense of waste disposal, waste treatment, and the cost and liability of handling and disposing of hazardous and toxic waste. Reuse of waste products is another way to reduce the amount of material actually entering the waste stream. The most effort in any business waste reduction plans should be applied to eliminating waste before it even enters the waste stream and reusing materials, if possible, before they become waste.

The next priority should be to recycle as much of the generated waste as possible. Recycling is generally a less desirable usage than reuse because recycling most often results in a less valuable product. Additionally, a business has to incur a twofold cost for any waste that is recycled. First, the material being recycled was purchased in the first place and, second, the business must pay for the cost of handling the recycled waste. However, recycling is far superior to the disposal of waste.

Treatment of waste is the third priority and generally involves hazardous or toxic waste. This might include incineration of solid waste (preferably to include energy recovery), treatment of sewer discharges to remove hazardous chemicals, and chemical treatment of waste to lessen toxicity. Dealing with hazardous waste often requires the business to enter into the world of environmental regulation, at best an expensive and time-consuming venture. It is far better to examine where any hazardous or toxic waste is being generated in your business and strive to eliminate its creation entirely than to burden your business with the expense, difficulty, liability, and red tape involved in the safe disposal of the waste products. Zero hazardous or toxic waste is the ideal to strive for in your business.

The final, and lowest, priority is actual disposal of waste. This is, by far, the most expensive way for a business to use materials and is the most damaging use of our common natural resources. Every material that is eventually disposed of was paid for, often as a virgin raw material. Its entry into a landfill is an abject failure to extract all of the potential benefits from the material. This is where your business should seek zero as its goal—zero disposal of any waste at all.

There are a number of direct and immediate benefits to a company that concentrates on the first two priorities of waste management. Reduced operating costs are an obvious benefit, as less wasteful operations will lead directly to lower disposal costs, reduced materials costs, and improved operating efficiency. Better waste management also reduces a company's regulatory burden and may entirely eliminate the need for permits, monitoring, and the requisite reporting of waste management activities.

By reducing waste, particularly hazardous and toxic waste, businesses can also dramatically reduce their exposure to legal liability. Civil and criminal liability for proper use and disposal of hazardous chemicals can stretch far into the future and hamper a company's efforts to expand. As more chemicals are undergoing increased scrutiny with advanced analytical techniques, this can be true for materials that are not yet even currently regulated as hazardous. Reducing waste will have an immediate and positive effect on the health of your employees and the safety of your workplace. The streamlining of production processes to eliminate waste nearly always also results in often dramatic improvements in productivity. Waste is expensive and nearly always unnecessary. By adopting an aggressive program to eliminate every aspect of waste, businesses can profitably lead society on the road to a sustainable future.

Where can you find waste in your business? Using the general outline of operating a lean business, there are six areas that you can examine in depth to eliminate the major sources of waste in a business. Not all will apply to every business, but this outline should point you in the right direction for locating waste in your business.

The first area to examine is the overproduction of products. When a business overproduces, more raw materials and energy are consumed in making the unnecessary products. Before they are used or sold, the extra products may spoil or become obsolete, requiring disposal. Finally, extra hazardous materials used in the production of unnecessary overproduction results in extra emissions, waste disposal, worker exposure, and other wasteful actions. The elimination of overproduction is a key to reducing waste in any business that produces products.

Related to overproduction is unnecessary inventory. By keeping unneeded inventory, a business wastes matter and energy in many ways. More packaging is required to store the unnecessary inventory. Waste is generated from deterioration or damage to the stored products or materials. This leads to the need for more materials to replace any damaged inventory, and, finally, more energy is necessary to heat, cool, and light the inventory space.

Transportation and the moving of materials are other major sources of waste in business. The most obvious source of waste is that more energy must be used for any unnecessary transportation, leading to increased emissions from the transport end of the business. If you are unnecessarily moving materials or products around, your business will require more space, directly increasing your lighting, heating, and cooling demand and energy consumption. Unneeded shifting or movement of materials will require more packaging to protect components during movement. Additionally, unnecessary movement will increase the incidence of damage and spills during transportation. Finally, any transportation of hazardous materials requires special shipping and packaging to prevent risk during accidents, taking more money from your business's bottom line.

The elimination of defects in production of any type can reduce waste dramatically. Better production techniques or processes can reduce the amount of raw materials and energy consumed in making defective products. Any defective components will require recycling or disposal, another added expense. And more business space will be required for rework and repair of any defective products, increasing energy use for heating, cooling, and lighting.

Another overlooked area where waste can be reduced is in the unnecessary overprocessing of materials. This leads to the unnecessary use of more parts and raw materials consumed per unit of production. Unnecessary processing also increases wastes, energy use, and emissions associated with the products eventually produced.

A final place to look for waste reduction is waiting. Waiting encompasses a whole range of inefficiency, from employees waiting for parts or materials to office workers waiting for older computers to handle increasingly complex tasks. No one really likes to wait, and waiting in a business can increase expenses in ways that are hard to see—unless you look for them. Some of the impacts are the potential for material spoilage or component damage caused by waiting. Time lost (and paid for anyway) is another important cost of waiting. Finally, there is a whole range of wasted energy from heating, cooling, and lighting during production downtime.

A close examination of all of the potential sources of waste in a business can bring dramatic improvements to your bottom line. Waste costs money. Wasteful practices increase a business's costs across the board—in time, materials, and energy use. Identifying and eliminating waste in a business can bring immediate cost savings and streamline the efficiency of all of the processes and operations of a business. Finally, by reducing waste in every possible way, you will also be reducing your company's greenhouse gas emissions that are related to the wasteful operations or practices.

Waste Reduction Measurement Tool

The Waste Reduction Model (WARM) was created by the U.S. EPA to help companies estimate greenhouse gas emission reductions from several different waste management practices. WARM is available in a Web-based calculator format and as a Microsoft Excel spreadsheet. WARM calculates greenhouse gas emissions for current and alternative waste management practices, including source reduction, recycling, combustion, composting, and landfilling. The model calculates emissions across a wide range of material types commonly found in municipal solid waste. In addition, the model calculates energy use for each of the options. The user can construct various scenarios by simply entering data on the amount of waste handled by material type and by management practice. WARM then automatically applies material-specific emission factors specific for each management practice to calculate the greenhouse gas emissions and energy savings of each scenario. This tool can be used to calculate the net environmental benefits of an alternative scenario versus a business-as-usual scenario. The WARM tool is based on a life-cycle approach, which reflects emissions and avoided emissions upstream and downstream from the point of use. Before using WARM, you first need to know how many tons of waste were handled (or will be handled) for a given time period by material type and by waste management practice. The various material types recognized by the WARM tool are:

Aluminum Cans	Branches	Carpet
Clay Bricks	Concrete	Copper Wire
Corrugated Cardboard	Dimensional Lumber	Fly Ash
Food Scraps	Glass	Grass
HPDE (#2 Plastic)	LDPE (#4 Plastic)	Leaves
Magazines/3rd-Class Mail	Fiberboard	Mixed Metals
Mixed Solid Waste	Mixed Organics	Mixed Paper
Mixed Plastics	Mixed Recyclables	Newspaper
Office Paper	Personal Computers	PET (#1 Plastic)
Phonebooks	Steel Cans	Textbooks
Tires	Yard Trimmings	

You can find both the online tool and the Excel spreadsheet version at: **www.epa.gov/climatechange/wycd/waste/calculators/Warm_home.html**.

For more information on lean business practices that can help you identify and eliminate waste, two U.S. EPA guides are included on the CD that accompanies this book: *The Lean and Environment Toolkit* and *Lean Manufacturing and the Environment*. Additional resources on waste reduction techniques are also included in Appendix B of this book.

Business Waste Reduction Plan

The development and introduction of waste reduction measures for your business is a four-step process of Assess, Plan, Analyze, and Implement:

① Conduct a comprehensive waste assessment of your current business practices. For a very small business, this may be relatively easy. You may only have a single trash can. As a company's size increases, the waste it generates becomes more complex and the audit process becomes increasingly complicated. There are several worksheets in this chapter that use both a standard data-collection inventory and the process-mapping approach. Process mapping will show you, in graphic fashion, how waste is generated in your particular business. It can also show where energy is consumed in the process, where the most hazardous wastes are generated, and where reduction of waste would be most cost effective. In addition, a Waste Expense Worksheet is provided to allow you to easily collect your past waste disposal expense data. A Waste Survey Worksheet is also provided to help you make an on-site survey of your business waste practices. Your total waste inventory will provide you with measurable data that can be checked periodically to determine the effectiveness of your eventual waste reduction measures.

② The next step is to develop a waste reduction plan. The information collected in your waste assessment now can be used to evaluate, list, and choose appropriate waste reduction measures for your company. Using your waste assessment findings, review the Waste and Recycling Actions Chart that is provided and note all the possible waste prevention, recycling, composting, materials exchange, and purchasing measures that might be effective for your business.

During your waste assessment, you may have noted purchasing changes that could help reduce waste, from buying supplies with reduced packaging to careful inventory control to avoid over-ordering and possibly throwing away perishable items. In addition, the need for favoring products made with recycled content also may have become evident. In any business, many opportunities exist to use the company's buying power to reduce waste and encourage the growth of recycling markets. Check with other suppliers, as well, to see what they may be able to offer. After you have identified opportunities to purchase recycled products and products that can help you reduce waste, each item should be evaluated in terms of availability and cost. Reduced waste and recycled products do not necessarily cost more than other products. For example, although paper made from recycled fibers was once considerably more expensive than virgin paper, the price of paper with recovered content today is competitive with traditional paper. In addition, be sure to compare recycled or reduced-waste products to other products on the basis of long-term costs, rather than purchasing costs alone. For example, while benches and picnic tables made from recycled plastic may initially cost more than their wooden counterparts, they last up to four times longer and do not require maintenance. Similarly, while reusable products may cost more to purchase initially, they often save money over time by avoiding frequent purchases of single-use items. We'll look more at purchasing decisions in Chapter 11.

③ Once a list of waste reduction options has been identified, you can use the Cost Payback and Return on Investment analyses explained at the end of this chapter to decide which options are the most appropriate for your business. While you may be inclined to disregard a particular option with large start-up costs, the measure may end up yielding impressive savings over several years. However, mere cost effectiveness should not always be the overriding criterion. Other criteria, such as improved environmental awareness, employee morale, and community relations, may be equally important. You should also consider the following when deciding which measures to implement and in which order:

- Effects on product or service quality and product marketing
- Compatibility with existing operations
- Equipment requirements
- Space and storage requirements
- Operation and maintenance requirements
- Staffing, training, and education requirements
- Implementation time
- Effects on employee morale, environmental awareness, and community relations
- The long-term economic feasibility of an option

Some options might not require extensive analysis. For example, if your facility already has a copy machine with the ability to make two-sided copies efficiently, then a policy mandating double-sided copying usually can be implemented easily. On the other hand, you will want to carefully analyze complex options that require a significant change in operations or large capital investments. For instance, a food service considering a switch from disposable to reusable serviceware needs to assess factors ranging from the cost of new equipment and added labor expenses to the savings from reduced waste removal costs and the avoided purchase of disposable serviceware. The health and sanitation aspects of such a switch also should be considered.

④ Having determined the initial waste reduction measures to adopt, you should now begin to implement the measures. Implementation can be done in phases, beginning with the easiest and lowest-cost measures and progressing to the more expensive or comprehensive steps. Naturally, all of these waste reduction ideas are not applicable to all businesses. Read through the worksheet to determine which of the measures are valuable for your company. This worksheet is available on the enclosed CD as both a PDF form that may be printed out for your use in developing your water conservation Action Plan and also as a text form. The text version of this chart may be used to cut and paste the action steps that you choose into your overall company environmental plan.

It is essential that all employees be informed about the program and the importance of their cooperation and involvement. Be sure to update employees regarding the options being implemented, changes in work patterns or equipment, expected benefits, and their roles and responsibilities. Some companies can effectively reach all their employees by circulating email memos or holding informal meetings. Larger businesses might need to conduct a full-scale education or training campaign to be sure their entire company is aware of and involved in the program. These outreach techniques also should be used to keep staff up to date on the program's successes and problems. Employees will feel a greater stake in the program if they receive frequent updates on the quantity of waste being reduced, reused, or recycled; the recycled products being purchased; and the cost savings that have resulted. Another method of sustaining employee interest is to encourage them to submit new ideas for increasing the efficiency of company operations.

Monitoring and evaluating the program waste reduction is a dynamic process. Once the program is underway, you will need to evaluate its effectiveness to see if preliminary goals and targets are being met. In addition, once the potential for reducing waste in the company becomes better understood, consider establishing long-term goals for the program. It is important to evaluate the program periodically to:

- Keep track of program success and to build on that success (e.g., waste reduced, recycling rates achieved, money saved).
- Identify new ideas for waste reduction.
- Identify areas needing improvement.
- Document compliance with state or local regulations.

- Determine the effect of any new additions to the program.
- Keep employees informed and motivated.

The best way to assess and monitor program operations is through continued documentation. Use both the Waste Expense Worksheet and the Waste Survey Worksheet periodically to help analyze and record the effectiveness of your waste reduction program over time. Perform your first evaluation after the program has been in place long enough to have an effect on your company's waste generation rate, usually about one year. In addition, you should conduct additional periodic waste assessments to determine the need for further changes in your company's waste management.

Waste Assessment

The goals in this assessment are to develop a waste inventory that is as specific and measurable as possible. This should not be a difficult process but will take some time and effort. The result will be a better and more complete understanding of how waste—in all its manifestations—is generated in your business, where best to implement waste minimization techniques, and what benefits can be expected from your efforts.

Gather Waste Information

Begin by collecting any waste generation information that already exists. Everyone in your business should be consulted for his or her input. In larger businesses, operations and maintenance personnel may have the most direct knowledge of waste generation in your facilities. First, identify each of your key business operations. Then, for each key operation, identify the products and materials used or waste generated in the largest quantities. These are the materials that should be evaluated first for waste prevention opportunities.

Use the following to complete the Waste Expense Worksheet:

❑ Waste disposal invoices for last two years. For larger businesses and businesses with multiple disposal contracts, it may be easier to set up a simple spreadsheet to record this data.

Use the following to complete the Waste Survey Worksheet:

❑ An on-site inspection of your business facility. You will need to check your entire operation and determine where the waste is being generated, what type of materials make up the waste stream, how the waste is being generated, and how, at present, the waste is disposed of or handled.

❑ You may need to assess every waste receptacle in your business over a short period of time to determine what type of waste is being generated. You may need to actually become a "dumpster diver" in order to truly understand the exact makeup of your company's waste stream.

Use these three items to develop your Waste Process Map:

❑ Building floor plan.

❑ List of all materials that are coming into your business—your inputs. These are the items that may eventually become waste. Larger businesses may decide to prepare a simple spreadsheet to record this information.

❑ List of areas or sites where waste is generated and/or collected in your business—your waste outputs.

Waste Expense Worksheet
(Prepare for past 2 years)

Year:_____	Monthly Solid Waste Volume	Monthly Solid Waste Disposal Cost	Monthly Liquid Waste Volume	Monthly Liquid Waste Treatment or Disposal Cost
January				
February				
March				
April				
May				
June				
July				
August				
September				
October				
November				
December				
Annual Total				
Average (Total divided by 12)				
Average Cost of Solid Waste Disposal Per Ton	$			
Average Cost of Liquid Waste Disposal or Treatment Per 1000 Gallons	$			

Prepare a Waste Expense Worksheet for the past two years and then prepare one for every year in the future in order to track the effectiveness of your waste reduction measures. If your facility or business is large enough, you may wish to break this information down for each area where waste is generated in your business or input this data to a simple spreadsheet.

Waste Survey Worksheet

Completed by:	Date:	Business:
Address:	Phone:	Business Sq. Footage:

Waste water is: ❑ Treated on-site ❑ Sent to city sewer ❑ Other _____	Solid waste is: ❑ Sent to landfill ___ percent ❑ Recycled _____ percent ❑ Other _____ percent	Current Waste Contractor Company _____ Contact _____ Phone _____

Existing Types and Volumes of Waste

Type of Waste	Location Where Generated	Amount per Month (# or Gallons)	By-product of What?	Disposal Method	Recycling Rate	Cost of Disposal/ Month

Areas of Highest Waste Generation	Type of Waste	Disposal

You should prepare this Waste Survey Worksheet initially and then annually if your business Is subject to change or expansion. By understanding where your business waste is generated, you will be better able to develop a plan which minimizes (or, preferably, eliminates) waste generation at its source and provides for higher levels of recycling and/or sale of waste products.

Waste Generation Process Map

Refer to Chapter 4 regarding process mapping and then draw your own simple diagram to help you better understand where your waste is generated and how it is disposed of. If you have on-site treatment of waste water or other more complex waste treatment operations, your map will need to also include extensive energy-use details. Your Waste Generation Process Map should included the following details:

• All areas where waste of any kind is generated in your business

• Types of waste products generated in your business

• Any waste collection areas or containers

• The direction of standard waste flows in your business

• Estimates of percentage of waste generation per area

• Estimate of percentage of types of waste per area

• Any areas where hazardous waste products are generated

• Any areas where hazardous waste products are treated

• Any areas where hazardous waste products are stored

• Areas where immediate reductions might be found

• Areas where accidents or problems may occur

Waste Reduction Actions

To stay competitive, companies must continually find new ways to improve efficiency and cut costs. But where do you find the biggest savings for your company? The reduction or elimination of waste can provide dramatic cost savings. Depending on the type of company, the greatest cost savings are generally found in the following areas: shipping and receiving (reducing transport packaging), office operations (reducing paper that is mailed or used internally), and manufacturing (reducing process waste or the amount of material used in a product). The greatest waste prevention savings often accrue from avoided purchasing costs. This means that for any of the above areas, purchasing records can be an important key for identifying major purchases so they can be evaluated for waste prevention potential. Here are a few general ideas to begin your considerations of waste reduction in your business:

- Work with purchasing agents and records to identify major purchases that could be reduced. Then work with suppliers to reduce their packaging or to consolidate orders to reduce freight expenses.

- If purchase orders and other papers are stacked high, could we use the Internet to reduce paper purchase orders and other forms?

- Employees can be your best resource for identifying efficiencies and cost saving opportunities. Solicit their ideas on ways to reduce office waste.

- Copier paper is a significant expense. Is there a way to encourage more double-sided copying? Perhaps with educational posters near copy machines?

- Does this long report really need to be printed? Perhaps employees could view it online and only print essential pages? Perhaps we could shorten the report? Eliminate it altogether?

- Is there a way to reduce these corrugated boxes before they are recycled? Perhaps we could switch to reusable containers or reduce the box size?

- Could these pallets be repaired or the wood reused for another purpose? Can they be recycled? Or sold?

- Could our product packaging use less or lighter-weight material?

- Could our products be redesigned to use less material? Or to create less waste material during manufacture?

- A lot of excess material is generated by the production process—is the equipment as efficient as possible? Could the excess material be reduced through changes in operator practices or materials?

Every single type of waste should be examined and considered for elimination, reuse, or recycling. In terms of cost effectiveness, the elimination of waste at its source is, by far, the best choice. One of the keys to the elimination of waste is to simply begin to measure it. By beginning with simple efforts to measure its waste, IBM has reduced its hazardous waste output by over 80 percent. Sunoco, within just five years of implementing a plan to measure its hazardous waste, managed to reduce it by 85 percent. Waste of all types is money down the drain (or in the dump, as the case may be). Eliminating waste at its source is the best way to avoid the costs and expenses of waste management. The main expense of waste is not its disposal but the fact that your business has paid for the material that is being disposed of. Producing waste is not why anyone goes into business. It is not a valid business activity. It is, in fact, just plain dumb. We'll take a closer look at product design as a way to minimize waste in Chapter 13.

The following chart of waste and recycling actions is separated into three areas: Waste Reduction, Reuse of Waste, and Recycling.

Following this worksheet is a section for dealing with recycling at your business and also information on dealing with any hazardous waste that can not be eliminated, reused, or recycled. (Remember that you don't need to retype any web address: all of the website addresses noted in this book are found, in interactive format, on the BOOK WEB ADDRESSES document that is on the CD that accompanies this book.) At the end of this chapter is information for determining the economic feasibility of your waste reduction measures.

Waste and Recycling Action Worksheet

	Already Doing	Should Do	Doesn't Apply
Waste Reduction			
Office and Equipment Waste Reduction			
Prepare a Waste Expense Worksheet, Waste Survey Worksheet, and Waste Generation Process Map for your business.			
Using your waste assessment tools, examine every type of waste produced by your business and investigate how each type may be eliminated or radically reduced. Brainstorm with the employees who are involved in the generation of the waste for fresh ideas.			
Establish a company-wide double-sided copying policy, and be sure that all future copiers purchased by your company have double-sided capability.			
Reuse envelopes or use two-way ("send-and-return") envelopes.			
Keep mailing lists current to avoid duplication.			
Circulate (rather than copy) memos, documents, periodicals, and reports.			
Reduce the amount of advertising mail you receive by signing up online with: **www.dmachoice.org** (Direct Marketing Association).			
Reduce the number of catalogs that you receive by signing up online at **www.CatalogChoice.org**.			
Use outdated letterhead for in-house memos.			
Put company bulletins on voice or email or post on a central bulletin board.			
Save documents on hard drives or CDs instead of making paper copies.			
Proof documents carefully on the computer screen before printing.			

Eliminate all unnecessary reports.			
Purchase remanufactured office equipment.			
Reformat fax machines to eliminate a cover page.			
Establish a regular maintenance routine to prolong the life of equipment like copiers, computers, and heavy tools.			
Use rechargeable batteries where practical.			
Install reusable furnace and air conditioner filters.			
Reclaim usable parts from old equipment.			
Rent equipment that is used only occasionally.			
Recharge fax and printer cartridges or return them to the supplier for remanufacture.			
Where appropriate, order supplies in bulk to reduce excess packaging.			
Avoid ordering excess supplies that may never be used.			
Implement an improved inventory system (such as systems based on optical scanners) to provide more precise control over supplies.			
Substitute less toxic or nontoxic products for products such as inks, paints, and cleaning solvents.			
Use and sell products that promote waste reduction (products that are more durable, of higher quality, recyclable, reusable).			
Teach your customers about the importance of reducing waste.			
Offer customers waste reducing choices, such as Items in bulk or concentrate form.			
Design and develop more products that are durable, repairable or returnable. (See Chapter 13).			
Consider offering services rather than products in your business, if feasible. (See Chapter 13).			

Packaging Waste Reduction			
Using your waste assessment, examine all of the packaging waste that is generated in your business (including packaging that is passed on to your customers and will become waste). Look for all possible ways to minimize or eliminate it.			
Redesign your own packaging to eliminate or minimize the use of raw materials.			
Order materials for production in greater bulk.			
Purchase products with minimal packaging and/or in concentrated form.			
Work with suppliers to minimize the packaging used to protect their products.			
Establish a system for returning cardboard boxes to suppliers for reuse.			
Develop a company policy that all incoming and outgoing deliveries be shipped in returnable and/or recyclable containers.			
Use reusable and/or recyclable containers for shipping all of your products.			
Repair and reuse pallets or return them to your suppliers.			
Reuse newspaper and shredded paper for packaging.			
Reuse foam packing peanuts, bubblewrap, and cardboard boxes, or donate to another organization. See also **www.loosefillpackaging.com** for a database of locations to drop off packing peanuts.			
Develop a company policy that all incoming packaging not contain nonrecyclable packing materials (peanuts or bubblewrap, etc.) and inform your suppliers.			
Assess your company's storage to see where packaging during storage can be eliminated.			

Organic Waste Reduction			
Compost yard trimmings or ask your landscape contractor to compost them.			
If unable to compost on-site, investigate participating in a municipal composting program.			
Redesign landscape to a design that needs low maintenance.			
Use a worm bin to convert nonfatty food wastes into potting soil (called vermi-compost).			
Use a mulching lawnmower (or request that your landscape contractor use one) and leave grass clippings on the lawn.			
Reuse of Waste			
Examine all waste generated by your business and look for ways any current waste products can be reused on-site or by other businesses.			
Look for ways to alter your waste generation so that the waste produced can be reused.			
Set up an area in your business for employees to exchange used items.			
Advertise surplus and reusable waste items through a materials exchange. See **www.govlink.org/ hazwaste/business/imex** for information. Also note that many states provide industrial materials exchanges. Type your state name and "materials exchange" into your preferred search engine for information.			
Donate surplus produce or food to food banks, if still edible.			
Sell or give old furniture and office equipment to other businesses, local charitable organizations, or employees.			
Donate old magazines and journals to hospitals, clinics, or libraries.			

Recycling

Develop a company policy to recycle every possible material, including glass, paper, scrap metal, phone books, cardboard, aluminum, batteries, plastic bottles, light bulbs, computers and peripherals, ink and toner cartridges, and pallets.			
If you generate over 1,000 used cardboard boxes of a single type, you may be able to resell them through an innovative program. See **www.UsedCardboardBoxes.com**.			
If you have equipment or other items that may not be traditionally recyclable, you may want to list them on **www.freecycle.org**, a localized listserv network for giving away used items.			
Investigate selling used business items on your local Craigslist. See **www.craigslist.com**.			
Investigate opportunities to join other businesses to pool your recycled materials. This may offer better market pricing and better hauling rates.			
Place clearly marked recycling collection bins in easily accessible areas of your business.			
Provide different types of containers for differing types of waste to avoid mixing incompatible materials.			
Every employee should have a recycling bin at his or her desk or work area.			
If feasible, compost any and all nonfat food scraps and landscaping waste materials that can not be eliminated from your waste stream.			
Encourage reuse of shopping bags by offering customers the choice of buying their own bag, and providing a financial incentive for reuse.			
Offer customers a rebate when they reuse grocery bags, containers, mugs, or cups.			
Provide reusable mugs, glassware, plates, and utensils for employee use in cafeteria or breakrooms.			

Dealing with Recycling

Next, evaluate the recycling options you have identified to better manage the waste that cannot be prevented. Before implementing any recycling option, you will need to consider the marketability of the materials to be collected. To locate potential buyers, contact local recycling companies. Consult the Internet, the Yellow Pages (under "recycling"), trade associations, chambers of commerce, and state or local government recycling offices for assistance. When meeting with recycling companies interested in purchasing your collected materials, there are a number of issues you should discuss, including:

- What types of recyclables will the company accept and how must they be prepared? Recycling companies might request that the material be baled, compacted, shredded, granulated, or loose. Generally, recyclers will offer a better price for compacted or baled material. Compacting materials before transporting also can be a cost-effective method of lowering hauling costs for the buyer.

- What contract terms will the buyer require? Discuss the length of the potential contract with the buyer, Shorter contracts provide greater flexibility to take advantage of rising prices, while longer contracts provide more security in an unsteady market. Often, buyers favor long-term contracts to help ensure a consistent supply of materials. The terms of payment should be discussed as well, since some buyers pay after delivery of each load, while others set up a periodic schedule. Also, ask whether the buyer would be willing to allow changes to the contract over time, The buyer might want some flexibility as well; in many cases, the buyer will be willing to pay a higher rate in return for a stable supply of quality materials.

- Who provides transportation? If transportation services are not provided by the buyer, you will need to locate a hauler to transport materials to the buyer. The Yellow Pages, local waste haulers, and state or local waste management authorities can help provide this information.

- What is the schedule of collections? If the recycling company offers to provide transportation, check on the frequency of collections. Some businesses might prefer to have the hauler be on call, picking up recyclables when a certain weight or volume has been reached. Larger companies might generate enough recyclable material to warrant a set schedule of collections.

- What are the maximum allowable contaminant levels and what is the procedure for dealing with rejected loads? Inquire what the buyer has established as maximum allowable levels for food, chemicals, or other contaminants. If these requirements are not met, the buyer might reject a contaminated load and send it back to your company. The buyer also might dispose of a contaminated load in a landfill, which can result in your company incurring additional costs.

- Are there minimum quantity requirements? Find out whether the buyer requires a minimum weight or volume before accepting delivery. If a buyer's minimum quantity requirements are difficult to meet, consider working with neighboring offices or retail spaces. By working together it might be possible to collect recyclables in central storage containers and thereby meet the buyer's requirements.

- Where will the waste be weighed? Ask where the material will be weighed, and at what point copies of the weight slips will be available. Weighing the material before it is transported will eliminate the problem of lost weight slips and confirm the accuracy of the weight recorded by the buyer.

- Who will provide containers for recyclables? Buyers should be asked whether they will provide containers in which to collect, store, and transport the material, and whether there is a fee for this service. Can escape clauses be included in the contract? Such clauses establish the right of a company to be released from the terms of the contract under conditions of noncompliance by the buyer. Obtain and thoroughly check the buyer's references with existing contract holders, asking these companies specifically whether their buyer is fulfilling all contract specifications.

Recycling programs, especially more ambitious efforts, often require purchases of equipment like containers, compactors, and balers. Additional labor also might be required. Moreover, steps might be necessary to ensure that contamination of collected materials is minimized. Some companies also may have to pay a fee to have their collected recyclable material removed. In many cases, however, the savings and revenues (such as reduced removal costs and revenues from selling collected materials) will offset these costs. In addition, consider whether the new recycling program will affect current purchasing practices. For instance, your company might want to begin buying exclusively white legal pads instead of yellow ones to take advantage of the strong market for white office paper. Also examine the extent to which internal collection, transfer, and storage systems are needed and whether these new systems will be compatible with existing operations.

If you discover that yard trimmings or other organic matter make up a significant percentage of your company's waste, evaluate the feasibility of leaving landscaping cuttings in place or composting. Most companies can benefit by leaving cut grass on the lawn, where it will decompose quickly and help add nutrients that improve the quality of the lawn.

If your company has available outdoor space, on-site composting can be used. Companies with composting programs usually find them to be a cost-effective method for turning lawn trimmings into a product that may then be sold or used on company grounds. You can design a program to collect all types of organic materials into piles for composting, or a simpler program designed to compost just yard trimmings might be used. If the local municipal government operates or participates in a composting project, offsite composting also may be an option. A program can be designed to collect and store organic materials and, if necessary, haul them to the composting facility. Even when hauling is necessary, however, these programs also tend to be cost effective.

You should investigate the possibility of chipping other ground debris, like branches, into mulch, The mulch can be used on company property to reduce weeds and conserve moisture around plantings. Other options include planting low-maintenance plants. Slow-growing species and evergreen trees generally do not create large amounts of debris.

Eliminating waste at its source is the best way to avoid the costs and expenses of waste management. The main expense of waste is not its disposal but the fact that your business has paid for the material that is being disposed of.

Although reducing or eliminating waste at its source is the preferable method, recycling those materials that can not be reduced or reused can be used to wring the last utility out of them. Purchasing recycled products for your business should be the other end of this equation. Purchasing is examined in Chapter 11. Additional resources regarding recycling are found in Appendix B.

Dealing with Hazardous Waste

Does your business generate hazardous waste? Many small businesses do so without realizing it. The easiest and most cost-effective way of managing any type of waste is not to generate it in the first place. Zero hazardous waste generation should be your ultimate goal. You can begin to decrease the amount of hazardous waste your business produces by developing a few good business habits.

- Do not mix wastes. Do not mix nonhazardous waste with hazardous waste. Once you mix anything with hazardous waste, the whole batch becomes hazardous. Mixing waste can also make recycling very difficult, if not impossible. A typical example of mixing wastes would be putting nonhazardous cleaning agents in a container of used hazardous solvents.

- Change the materials you use, or the manufacturing processes you use, or both. Businesses can save money and increase efficiency by replacing a material or a process with another that produces less waste. For example, you could use plastic blast media for paint stripping of metal parts rather than conventional solvent stripping.

- Recycle and reuse manufacturing materials. Many companies routinely put useful components back into productive use rather than disposing of them. Items such as oil, solvents, acids, and metals are commonly recycled and used again. In addition, some companies have taken waste minimization actions such as using fewer solvents to do the same job, using solvents that are less toxic, or switching to a detergent solution.

- Safely store hazardous products and containers. You can avoid creating more hazardous waste by preventing spills or leaks. Store hazardous products and waste containers in secure areas, and inspect them frequently for leaks. When leaks or spills occur, materials used to clean them also become hazardous waste.

U. S. Federal Regulation of Hazardous Waste

Federal hazardous waste management regulations apply to most businesses that generate hazardous waste. State regulations may also apply and may, in fact, be more stringent than the federal rules. You should contact your state environmental protection agency for your state regulations. For the address or phone number for your state agency, please check **www.epa.gov/osw**. We'll also take another look at federal environmental regulations governing hazardous waste in Chapter 17.

Determining Whether Your Business Generates Hazardous Waste

To determine whether federal regulations apply to your business, you must first determine whether you even generate hazardous waste. A waste is any solid, liquid, or contained gaseous material that is discarded by being disposed of, burned or incinerated, or recycled. It can be the by-product of a manufacturing process or simply a commercial product that you use in your business—such as a cleaning fluid or battery acid—that is being disposed of. Even materials that are recyclable or can be reused in some way (such as burning solvents for fuel) might be considered waste. Hazardous waste can be one of two types, either *listed waste* or *characteristic waste*.

Listed waste: Your waste is considered hazardous, in the United States, if it appears on one of four lists published in the Code of Federal Regulations (40 CFR Part 261). Currently, hundreds of wastes are listed. Wastes are listed as hazardous because they are known to be harmful to human health and the environment when not managed properly. Even when managed properly, some listed wastes are so dangerous that they are called *acutely* hazardous wastes. Examples of acutely hazardous wastes include wastes generated from some pesticides and those that can be fatal to humans even in low doses. A chart outlining the typical hazardous wastes produced by small businesses is found later in this chapter. This will provide you with some general ideas of the types of hazardous wastes that are commonly generated by small businesses. In addition, a copy of the latest EPA waste listings are included on the CD that accompanies this book. It is titled: *EPA Hazardous Waste Listings* and was released in March, 2008.

Characteristic waste: If your waste does not appear on one of the hazardous waste lists, it still might be considered hazardous if it demonstrates one or more of the following characteristics:

- It catches fire under certain conditions. This is known as an ignitable waste. Examples are paints and certain degreasers and solvents.

- It corrodes metals or has a very high or low pH. This is known as a corrosive waste. Examples are rust removers, acid or alkaline cleaning fluids, and battery acid.

- It is unstable and explodes or produces toxic fumes, gases, and vapors when mixed with water or under other conditions such as heat or pressure. This is known as a reactive waste. Examples are certain cyanides or sulfide-bearing wastes.

- It is harmful or fatal when ingested or absorbed, or it leaches toxic chemicals into the soil or groundwater when disposed of on land. This is known as a toxic waste. Examples are wastes that contain high concentrations of heavy metals, such as cadmium, lead, or mercury. You can determine whether your waste is toxic by having it tested, using a test known as the Toxicity Characteristic Leaching Procedure (TCLP).

If your waste falls into one or more of these *characteristic* hazardous waste categories, it is a regulated waste. Another way to help determine whether your waste exhibits any of the characteristics that would make it hazardous is to check the Material Safety Data Sheet (MSDS) that comes with all products containing hazardous materials (check: **www.msdsonline.com** for information). In addition, your national trade association might be able to help you.

Determining Your Category for Compliance

Once you know that you generate hazardous waste, you need to measure the amount of waste you produce per month. The amount of hazardous waste that your business generates determines the level of your regulatory compliance requirements. This is based on what is termed your *generator category*. The U.S. EPA has set three levels of compliance requirements based on how much hazardous waste you produce. (Note: Here we begin to get heavily into some of the typical bureaucratic acronym-based legalese that is, unfortunately, somewhat prevalent in regulatory agencies).

CESQGs: Conditionally Exempt Small Quantity Generators: You are considered a CESQG if you generate less than 220 pounds per month of hazardous waste. You are exempt from hazardous waste management regulations, provided that you comply with the basic CESQG requirements described later in this chapter. If you are a CESQG and you generate no more than 2.2 pounds of *acutely* hazardous waste (or 220 pounds of acutely hazardous waste spill residues) in a calendar month, and *never* store more than that amount for any period of time, you may manage the acutely hazardous waste according to the CESQG requirements. If you generate or store more than 2.2 pounds of acutely hazardous waste on-site, you must manage it according to the LQG requirements (see later in chapter).

SQGs: Small Quantity Generators: You are considered an SQG if you generate between 220 and 2,200 pounds per month of hazardous waste. SQGs must comply with EPA requirements for managing hazardous waste described later.

LQGs: Large Quantity Generators: You are considered an LQG if you generate more than 2,200 pounds per month of hazardous waste. LQGs must comply with more extensive hazardous waste rules summarized later in this chapter.

Measuring Your Hazardous Waste

To accurately determine your correct category, you will need to measure the hazardous wastes produced by your business. Many hazardous wastes are liquids and are measured in gallons—not pounds. In order to measure your liquid wastes, you will need to convert from gallons to pounds. To do this, you must know the density of the liquid. A rough guide is that 30 gallons (about half of a 55-gallon drum) of waste with a density similar to water weighs about 220 pounds; 300 gallons of a waste with a density similar to water weighs about 2,200 pounds.

You will need to measure all quantities of listed and characteristic hazardous wastes in your business operations that are:

- Accumulated on the property for any period of time before disposal or recycling. (Drycleaners, for example, must count any residue removed from machines, as well as spent cartridge filters.)

- Packaged and transported away from your business.

- Placed directly in a regulated treatment or disposal unit at your place of business.

- Generated as still bottoms or sludges and removed from product storage tanks.

You do NOT need to measure hazardous wastes that are:

- Specifically exempted from counting. Examples include lead-acid batteries that will be reclaimed, scrap metal that will be recycled, used oil managed under the EPA used-oil provisions, and universal wastes (e.g., batteries, pesticides, thermostats, and lamps—see discussion following).

- Might be left in the bottom of containers that have been thoroughly emptied through conventional means such as pouring or pumping.

- Are left as residue in the bottom of tanks storing products, if the residue is not removed from the product tank.

- Are reclaimed continuously on-site without storing prior to reclamation, such as drycleaning solvents.

- Are managed in a container designed to neutralize corrosive waste, a totally enclosed treatment unit, or a wastewater treatment unit, without being stored first.

- Are discharged directly to publicly owned treatment works without being stored or accumulated first. This discharge must comply with the Clean Water Act. Public treatment works are public utilities, usually owned by the city, county, or state, that treat industrial and domestic sewage for disposal.

- Have already been counted once during the calendar month, and are treated on-site or reclaimed in some manner, and used again.

- Are regulated under the universal waste rule or have other special requirements. Federal regulations contain special, limited requirements for managing certain commonly generated wastes. These wastes can be managed following the less burdensome requirements listed below instead of the usual hazardous waste requirements. Check with your state agency to determine whether your state has similar regulations.

Universal Wastes

The *Universal Waste Rule* was developed to streamline environmental regulations for wastes generated by large numbers of businesses in relatively small quantities. It is designed to reduce the amount of hazardous waste disposed of in municipal solid waste, encourage the recycling and proper disposal of certain common hazardous wastes, and reduce the regulatory burden for businesses that generate these wastes. Universal wastes are items commonly thrown into the trash by households and small businesses. Although handlers of universal wastes can meet less stringent standards for storing, transporting, and collecting these wastes, handlers must still comply with the full hazardous waste requirements for final recycling, treatment, or disposal. Universal wastes include:

- Batteries, such as nickel-cadmium (Ni-Cad) and small sealed lead-acid batteries, which are found in many common items, including electronic equipment, cell phones, portable computers, and emergency backup lighting.

- Agricultural pesticides that have been recalled or banned from use, are obsolete, have become damaged, or are no longer needed due to changes in cropping patterns or other factors. They often are stored for long periods of time in sheds or barns.

- Thermostats, which can contain as much as 3 grams of liquid mercury and are located in almost any building, including commercial, industrial, agricultural, community, and household buildings.

- Lamps, which typically contain mercury and sometimes lead, and are found in businesses and households. Examples include fluorescent, high-intensity discharge (HID), neon, mercury vapor, high-pressure sodium, and metal halide lamps.

The Universal Waste Rule also encourages communities and businesses to establish collection programs or participate in manufacturer take-back programs required by a number of states. Many large manufacturers and trade associations have national and regional collection programs for their universal waste products. Materials are continually added to the Universal Waste list. Check the following website for the latest information: **www.epa.gov/epaoswer/hazwaste/id/ univwast.htm**.

Rules for CESQGs: Conditionally Exempt Small Quantity Generators

If you generate no more than 220 pounds of hazardous waste per month, you are a Conditionally Exempt Small Quantity Generator (CESQG). You must comply with three basic waste management requirements to remain exempt from the full hazardous waste regulations that apply to generators of larger quantities. (Note: there are different quantity limits for acutely hazardous waste: you must generate no more than 2.2 pounds of *acutely* hazardous waste (or 220 pounds of acutely hazardous waste spill residues), in a calendar month, and *never* store more than that amount for any period of time.)

First, you must clearly and comprehensively identify all of the hazardous wastes that your business generates.

Second, you may not store more than 2,200 pounds of hazardous waste on your business site at any time.

Finally, you must either

*   Ensure the delivery of your hazardous waste to an off-site disposal treatment or disposal facility that is a state or federally regulated hazardous waste management facility, a facility that legitimately recycles or reuses the waste, or a universal waste handler, or

*   Actually be a state or federally regulated hazardous waste management facility, a facility that legitimately recycles or reuses the waste, or a universal waste handler.

Note also that some states have additional requirements.

Rules for SQGs: Small Quantity Generators

If your business generates between 220 and 2,200 pounds per month of hazardous waste, you must adhere to additional requirements. (Note: if you generate no more than 2.2 pounds of *acutely* hazardous waste (or 220 pounds of acutely hazardous waste spill residues), in a calendar month, and *never* store more than that amount for any period of time, you may manage the acutely hazardous waste according to the SQG requirements. If you generate or store more than 2.2 pounds of acutely hazardous waste on-site, you must manage it according to the much more stringent LQG requirements.)

First, you must obtain and use an EPA Identification Number that you will use when you send your hazardous waste off site to be managed or treated. These 12-digit numbers are used to monitor and track hazardous waste activities.

To obtain your EPA Identification Number, you should call or write your state hazardous waste management agency or the hazardous waste division of your EPA Regional office and ask for a copy of EPA Form 8700-12, "Notification of Hazardous Waste Activity." You can also download the form and an instruction booklet at: **www.epa.gov/epaoswer/hazwaste/data/form8700/forms.htm**.

You must also accumulate no more than 13,228 pounds (6,000 kg) of hazardous waste on-site for up to 180 days without a permit. You can accumulate this amount of waste for up to 270 days if you must transport it more than 200 miles away for recovery, treatment, or disposal. (Note: Different quantity limits apply to acutely hazardous wastes.) SQGs must accumulate waste in tanks or containers, such as 55-gallon drums, and the containers must be in good condition, properly labeled as "Hazardous Waste" with the date generated noted on the container. If you exceed these limits, you are considered a Toxic Substance Disposal Facility (TSDF) and must comply with more extensive regulations.

Rules for LQGs: Large Quantity Generators

If your company generates more than 2,200 pounds per month of hazardous materials, you must comply with a detailed and comprehensive set of hazardous waste regulations. The table in the next page summarizes the federal LQG requirements. This is only a summary and does not include all of the LQG requirements. For more details, contact the RCRA Call Center at 800 424-9346 or see the Code of Federal Regulations, Chapter 40, Part 262. Be sure to check with your state as well, because certain states have additional or more stringent requirements than the federal government. Finally, we will look at some design methods and techniques to eliminate the use of toxic and hazardous chemicals in your business in Chapter 13.

Hazardous Waste Regulations for Large Quantity Generators

Summary of Requirements	Federal Regulation
Identify all hazardous wastes you generate. Measure the amount of hazardous waste you generate per month to determine your generator category (e.g., LQG).	Hazardous Waste Determination (40 CFR Part 262.10) Generator Category Determination (40 CFR Part 262.10 (b) and 261.5 (b) and (c))
Obtain a copy of EPA Form 8700-12, fill out the form, and send it to the contact listed with the form. An EPA identification number will be returned to you for your location.	EPA Identification Numbers (40 CFR 262.12)
Package, label, mark, and placard wastes following Department of Transportation requirements. Ship waste using hazardous waste transporter.	Prepare Hazardous Waste for Shipment Off Site (40 CFR Parts 262.30 - 262.33)
Ship waste to hazardous waste treatment, storage, disposal, or recycling facility. Ship hazardous waste off-site using the manifest system (EPA Form 8700-22) or state equivalent.	The Manifest (40 CFR Parts 262.20 - 262.23, 262.42)
Accumulate waste for no more than 90 days without a permit. Accumulate waste in containers, tanks, drip pads, or containment buildings. Comply with specified technical standards for each unit type.	Managing Hazardous Waste On Site (40 CFR Part 262.34)
Retain specified records for 3 years. Submit biennial report by March 1 of even-numbered years covering generator activities for the previous year.	Recordkeeping and Biennial Report (40 CFR Parts 262.40 - 262.41)
Ensure that wastes meet treatment standards prior to land disposal. Send notifications and certifications to TSDF as required. Maintain waste analysis plan if treating on site.	Comply with Land Disposal Restrictions (40 CFR 268)
Follow requirements for exports and imports, including notification of intent to export and acknowledgement of consent from receiving country.	Export/Import Requirements (40 CFR Subparts E and F)
If applicable, use various monitoring and control mechanisms to: • Control volatile organic compound (VOC) emissions from hazardous waste management activities. • Reduce organic emissions from process vents associated with certain recycling activities and equipment that is in contact with hazardous waste that has significant organic content. • Control VOCs from hazardous waste tanks, surface impoundments, and containers, using fixed roofs, floating roofs, or closed-vent systems routed to control devices.	Air Emissions (40 CFR Part 265, Subpart CC)
Decontaminate and remove all contaminated equipment, structures, and soil, and minimize the need for further maintenance of your site. Meet unit-specific closure standards for tanks, containment buildings, and drip pads.	Closure (40 CFR Parts 265.111 and 265.114)

Typical Hazardous Wastes Generated by Small Businesses

Type of Business	How Generated	Typical Wastes
Drycleaning and Laundry Plants	Commercial drycleaning processes	Still residues from solvent distillation, spent filter cartridges, cooked powder residue, spent solvents, unused perchloroethylene
Furniture/Wood Manufacturing and Refinishing	Wood cleaning and wax removal, refinishing/stripping, staining, painting, finishing, brush cleaning, and spray brush cleaning	Ignitable wastes, toxic wastes, solvent wastes, paint wastes
Construction	Paint preparation and painting, carpentry and floor work, other specialty contracting activities, heavy construction, wrecking and demolition, vehicle and equipment maintenance for construction activities	Ignitable wastes, toxic wastes, solvent wastes, paint wastes, used oil, acids/bases
Laboratories	Diagnostic and other laboratory testing	Spent solvents, unused reagents, reaction products, testing samples, contaminated materials
Vehicle Maintenance	Degreasing, rust removal, paint preparation, spray booth, spray guns, brush cleaning, paint removal, tank cleanout, installing lead-acid batteries, oil and fluid replacement	Acids/bases, solvents, ignitable wastes, toxic wastes, paint wastes, batteries, used oil, unused cleaning chemicals
Printing and Allied Industries	Plate preparation, stencil preparation for screen printing, photoprocessing, printing, cleanup	Acids/bases, heavy metal wastes, solvents, toxic wastes, ink, unused chemicals
Equipment Repair	Degreasing, equipment cleaning, rust removal, paint preparation, painting, paint removal, spray booth, spray guns, and brush cleaning	Acids/bases, toxic wastes, ignitable wastes, paint wastes, solvents
Pesticide End Users/ Application Services	Pesticide application and cleanup	Used/unused pesticides, solvent wastes, ignitable wastes, contaminated soil (from spills), contaminated rinsewater, empty containers
Educational and Vocational Shops	Automobile engine and body repair, metalworking, graphic arts-plate preparation, woodworking	Ignitable wastes, solvent wastes, acids/bases, paint wastes
Photo Processing	Processing and developing negatives/ prints, stabilization system cleaning	Acid regenerants, cleaners, ignitable wastes, silver
Leather Manufacturing	Hair removal, bating, soaking, tanning, buffing, and dyeing	Acids/bases, ignitables wastes, toxic wastes, solvent wastes, unused chemicals

Economic Analysis of Waste Reduction Measures

Simple Cost Payback Analysis

In order to make rational business decisions about which of your waste reduction actions to implement, you may wish to run a simple cost payback analysis. A highly simplified form of cost/benefit analysis is called simple payback. In this method, the total first cost of the improvement is divided by the first-year cost savings produced by the improvement. This method yields the number of years required for the improvement to pay for itself. Cost payback analyses can be far more complex and include many other variables.

You will need to have determined the actual *capital costs* necessary to implement the measure. This would include any equipment that might need to be purchased (for example, balers, recycling containers, etc.), any prep work necessary (such as grading a site for composting or construction of storage areas, etc.), and the cost of installation and utility hookup, if necessary. Thus, your capital costs formula would be:

Equipment needed + prep work cost + installation cost = capital cost

You will also need to know the *net annual savings* from the action. To determine this you will need to determine the *avoided removal costs*. This is calculated as the amount of waste that will be removed from your waste stream annually by the action multiplied by the amount by the current cost of disposal and/or treatment. Your waste reduction measures might have additional economic benefits as well. By implementing measures that would reduce the amount of supplies or materials used, you would also have *avoided purchase costs*. If your measures result in recycled materials that you can sell as product or recycling, you would have *additional annual revenues*. Either of these two additional amounts should be determined and taken into consideration in determining your net annual savings. Your net annual savings formula would be:

Avoided removal costs (annual amount of waste eliminated in tons or gallons x cost per ton or gallon to dispose of or treat such waste)

+ Avoided purchase costs (the annual amount of avoided purchase costs stemming from the measure), and

+ Additional annual revenue (the amount of additional revenue attributable to the measure, such as from recycling revenues)

= Net annual savings

Greening Your Business

To calculate the cost payback period for a particular waste reduction measure, use the following formula:

Capital costs / net annual savings = payback period (in years)

For example, if you decide to install a system that reuses material that would normally be waste, and it costs $2,000 to purchase and install the necessary equipment, your capital costs are $2,000.

If the system saves your business from disposing of 10,000 pounds of waste annually at a cost of $50/ton:

Your avoided removal costs are $250. (10,000 / 2,000 X $250).

If you also do not need to purchase $500 of additional materials:

Your avoided purchase costs are $500.

Using the reused material provides your company now with product worth $500 annually as additional annual revenue. Thus:

Your total net annual savings would be: $1,250 ($250 + $500 + $500 = $1,250).

Finally, your payback period would be calculated as:

$2,000 / $1,250 = 1.6 years

This would indicate that this particular investment was an excellent choice. Don't forget that there are numerous additional noneconomic benefits that you will get from your aggressive waste reduction efforts, such as reducing liability for spills or accidents, reducing the time necessary to handle, store, and dispose of waste, and improving health and safety for your employees, and, of course, the satisfaction that you are lessening your company's environmental footprint.

Simple Return on Investment Analysis

Another standard measure of economic feasibility is the *Return on Investment* formula. This is a measure of the percentage return provided by a particular investment. The standard formula for Return on Investment (ROI) is:

Net return / capital cost of investment = percentage return on investment

For the net return figure, you need to determine the life of the investment (in years) and multiply it by net annual savings. Use the net annual savings figure that you generated in the cost payback analysis. Then deduct the initial capital cost.

Net annual savings x life of investment - capital cost = net return

Thus, for our example, if we assume a 10-year life for the additional equipment, our net return is:

$1,250 X 10 = $12,500 - $2,000 capital costs = $10,500 net return

Then, using this net return figure, our return on investment (ROI) over a 10-year period, is:

$10,500 net return / $2,000 capital costs = 525 percent

And, finally the annual return on investment would be:

Total ROI / life of investment = annual rate of return (525 / 10 = 52.5 percent)

These formulas can additionally include calculations to discount the dollar amounts over time and other more sophisticated approaches. Waste reduction measures are often surprisingly cost effective. If you analyze each of your potential waste reduction measures, you can then prioritize their implementation. Remember, however, that there are many other valuable noneconomic benefits to achieving zero waste in your business.

On the following page, you will find a simple worksheet to use for cost payback and return on investment calculations. This worksheet is provided on the CD that accompanies this book in a fillable PDF format that will do the necessary calculations for you.

Waste Reduction Economic Analysis

Capital Costs

	Equipment Costs	$
+	Prep Work Costs	$
+	Installation Costs	$
=	Total Capital Costs	$

Net Annual Savings

	Annual Avoided Disposal Costs	$
+	Annual Avoided Purchase Costs	$
+	Annual Avoided Costs (handling, etc.)	$
+	Annual Additional Revenue (if any)	$
=	Total Net Annual Savings	$

Simple Payback Period Analysis

	Capital Costs (from above)	$
÷	Net Annual Savings (from above)	$
=	Payback Period in Years	

Simple Return on Investment Analysis

	Net Annual Savings (from above)	$
x	Life of Investment (in years)	
−	Capital Costs (from above)	$
=	Net Return	$
÷	Capital Costs (from above)	$
=	Return on Investment (over life)	
÷	Life of Investment (in years)	
=	Annual Return on Investment Rate	%

These formulas can additionally include calculations to discount the dollar amounts over time and other more sophisticated approaches. Remember that there are many other valuable non-economic benefits to eliminating waste in your business. Please see Appendix B for additional waste reduction resources.

Chapter 9

Green Business Travel and Transportation

Transportation and travel are some of the most energy-intensive and polluting industries on Earth. Air travel, in particular, is nearly impossible to make eco-friendly. Vehicles of all kinds emit about one-third of all volatile organic compounds and half of the nitrogen oxides and air pollution that contribute to poor air quality. They also contribute more than half of the known ozone-forming pollutants, aggravating asthma and other respiratory ailments. Transportation is also one of the main contributors of carbon dioxide, the most wide spread greenhouse gas and the most powerful driver of global climate change.

Greening business travel and transportation can save money and energy for both the business and its employees. A quick example: if the business upgrades one company vehicle from a 20 mpg version to a 30 mpg version, in five years the money saved on fuel costs would be $2,500, assuming 15,000 miles traveled and $3.50/gallon gas. The carbon footprint of this simple change would also be lessened by over 30 percent. (Note: gas prices may never see $3.50/gallon again.)

As we saw in Chapter 6 regarding a company's overall energy use, measuring the carbon footprint of a business is quickly becoming a standard yardstick by which to compare different companies' commitments to energy efficiency. In early 2008, eleven large multi-national corporations, including Hewlett-Packard, Pepsico, Dell Computer, and Proctor & Gamble, agreed to calculate their total carbon footprint. These companies will release the results of their calculations through the Carbon Disclosure Project, a nonprofit organization set up to coordinate carbon disclosure efforts on behalf of institutional investors, such as Goldman Sachs and Merrill Lynch, with over $40 trillion in investments. Each of these multinationals will in turn look to as many as 50 additional suppliers in their supply chains to determine their overall carbon footprint. Carbon footprinting is the first step in addressing carbon emissions prior to managing and then reducing the carbon output of businesses. Business carbon footprint calculations are generally based on three sources of carbon emission: *direct emissions* from sources actually owned by a business (such as the use of an on-site diesel electric generator owned by the business); *indirect sources* from emissions from the use of electricity or natural gas used by the business (this was covered in Chapter 6 on green business energy use) and business transportation emissions; and finally *other indirect sources* of emission such as various upstream or downstream emissions from suppliers of components or raw materials or from customers use of a product.

There are many ways that your business can lessen the environmental impact of its own and its employees' transportation. Travel habits are some of the most difficult to change. Many people avoid anything other than commuting by car because of the difficulties associated with changing one's mode of transportation. By providing amenities that foster and facilitate your employee's use of public transportation, carpooling, biking, or walking, a business can positively impact the environment far beyond its own operations. Introducing telecommuting can provide savings in energy (less or no employee commuting and less on-site business office heating, air conditioning, lighting, and equipment energy expenses), time (no time spent in vehicle commuting), and space (less office space required and fewer or even no parking spaces necessary). With a few simple incentives, many employees will be happy to improve their own transportation choices.

Your business most likely uses transportation in many ways that can be made more efficient and cost effective. Travel of employees for business purposes is an excellent place to look to reduce your transportation expenses and energy use. While many businesses rely on direct face-to-face contact, the Internet and modern communication have provided methods that can reduce or even eliminate much employee travel. Audio and video conferencing has become a highly sophisticated tool that can be used very effectively in many standard business situations.

If your business operates its own trucks, one of the simplest and most immediate steps that you can take to increase efficiency is to eliminate truck idling whenever possible. It is not necessary for drivers to idle their trucks at the end of the work day to avoid engine damage. Simply cutting idling time in half will generally increase fuel efficiency by nearly 15 percent. Wal-Mart equipped their enormous trucking fleet with small separate generators (called *alternative power units*) for heating and cooling the cabs and realized a reduction of 15 percent in fuel expenses. Their goal is to double their fleet's fuel efficiency by using better tires, redesigned trucks, and various other efficiency measures. As the price of fuel continues to escalate, every business stands to save money and energy by implementing such measures.

Business shipping costs are also a prime source of savings in transportation. By reducing your overall shipping expenses, your business will save money and energy, while simultaneously reducing its transportation carbon footprint. If your company ships products or is itself a truck or rail company that delivers these products, look into the U.S. EPA SmartWay Transport Partnership. This is an innovative collaboration between EPA and the freight industry to increase energy efficiency while significantly reducing greenhouse gases and air pollution. Hundreds of businesses are benefitting from this program, particularly companies that ship products and the truck and rail companies that deliver these products. This program is open to any company that would like to improve the environmental performance of their freight operations. Companies commit to measure and improve the efficiency of their freight operations, using EPA-developed tools that quantify the benefits of a number of fuel-saving strategies.

The SmartWay program also is working with states, banks, and other organizations to develop innovative financing options that help companies purchase devices that save fuel and reduce emissions. You can use the online SmartWay Technology Package Savings Calculator to calculate how your company can reduce emissions and save money. This program is also establishing idle-free corridors nationwide to reduce unnecessary truck engine idling by developing a nationwide network of idle-reduction options along major transportation corridors—truck stops, travel centers, distribution hubs, rail switch yards, borders, ports, and even along the side of the road. Finally, this program is trying to develop easier methods for businesses to use rail transport effectively. Ton-mile for ton-mile, rail is a very efficient mode of transportation. If you are interested in this program, please see: **www.epa.gov/smartway**.

Business Travel and Transportation Efficiency Plan

Once again, the process of greening your travel and transportation is a simple four-step process of Assess, Plan, Analyze, and Implement.

① Conduct a comprehensive assessment of your current business practices. This chapter provides a Business Transportation Carbon Footprint Worksheet to help you begin the process of measuring your company's carbon emissions from transportation. This basic carbon footprint calculator can provide you with a baseline from which to build your company efforts to reduce its overall carbon emissions. Reducing carbon means reducing the fossil fuel costs associated with the emissions. By reducing your business expenses related to fuel use, you will be strengthening your bottom line as well as preparing your business for the coming inevitable regulation of carbon.

If you wish to use a more detailed business carbon footprint calculator, two are available free online at: **www.carbontrust.co.uk/solutions/ CarbonFootprinting/FootprintCalculators** or **www.carbonfootprint.com/ businessregister.aspx.** There is also a useful general travel carbon footprint calculator available at: **www.nativeenergy.com/pages/travel_calculator/ 30.php**.

Finally, some very sophisticated, but easy-to-use, Excel® spreadsheets for calculating emissions from both business and employee transportation are available on the CD that accompanies this book. Prior to their use, you should make sure that you have the most recent available version of these spreadsheets at: **www.ghgprotocol.org/calculation-tools**.

② On the basis of your carbon footprint assessment, you should then formulate a transportation action plan. The Travel and Transportation Action Worksheet that is provided outlines a wide range of ways to lessen the transportation portion of your business's environmental footprint. This worksheet is divided into two main areas: employee commuting and business shipping/travel actions. Incorporate as many as possible into your overall business environmental plan. Choose those actions that are applicable to your business. Your plan should be revisited and, if necessary, revised at least on an annual basis. (Remember that you don't need to retype any web address: all of the website addresses noted in this book are found, in interactive format, on the BOOK WEB ADDRESSES document that is on the CD that accompanies this book.)

③ Evaluate your possible actions on a sound economic basis over a long term, not simply by considering the initial cost of investment, but the entire life cycle of the investment. Information regarding cost payback and return-on-investment analysis of your transportation plans is provided at the end of this chapter.

④ The final step is to actually implement the plan. Someone in the company should be given the responsibility to implement and oversee your new travel and transportation plan. The following worksheets are available on the enclosed CD as both a PDF form that may be printed out for your use in developing your company's own green travel and transportation action plan and also as a text form. The text version of this chart may be used to cut and paste the action steps that you choose into your overall company environmental plan. See Chapter 18 for more details. Additional green travel and transportation resources are found in Appendix B.

Business Transportation Carbon Footprint Worksheet

Completed by:		Date:		Business:	
Address:				Phone:	

Company-Owned Vehicles

Vehicle Make/Model/Year	MPG rating	Miles/month	Average gallons of fuel/ month (Miles/mpg)	Carbon Footprint (lbs CO_2) (# gallons x 25 lbs)	Alternatives
Total Company Vehicle Carbon Footprint					

Employee Commuting

Vehicle Make/Model/Year	MPG rating	Miles/month	Average gallons of fuel/ month (Miles/mpg)	Carbon Footprint (lbs CO_2) (# gallons x 25 lbs)	Alternatives
Total Employee Commuting Carbon Footprint					

Company Air Travel

Reason for travel	Round trip distance	Number of employees	Total person miles (# persons X miles)	Carbon Footprint (lbs CO_2) (Person-miles X .5 lbs)	Carbon Offset?
Total Company Air Travel Carbon Footprint					

Company Shipping (In and Out-bound)

Reason for shipping	Average trip distance	% of full load (in whole numbers)	Carrier	Carbon Footprint CO_2) (Miles X 25 lbs X percent of full load—whole numbers)	Carbon Offset?
Total Company Shipping Carbon Footprint					

Total Monthly Travel & Transportation Carbon Footprint (Add all footprints)	
Total Annual Travel & Transportation Carbon Footprint (Multiply by 12)	

Note: Your total company travel/transportation footprint is calculated in pounds of CO_2 equivalent and is based generally on the emissions methodology developed by the Carbon Trust. See www.carbontrust.co.uk for more details. Review and redo your calculations quarterly and work to implement methods that will lessen your overall business carbon footprint.

Travel and Transportation Action Worksheet

	Already Doing	Should Do	Doesn't Apply
Employee Commuting			
Complete the employee commuting portion of the Company Transportation Carbon Footprint Worksheet.			
Provide incentives to employees for carpooling and the use of public transportation—incentives might include privileged parking locations for vans, vehicles for ride-sharing, and bus passes (which are often provided at volume discounts by bus systems to large employers).			
Promote carpooling (ride-sharing) for employees. Check out **www.carpoolworld.com** or **www.erideshare.com.**			
You may wish to provide disincentives to lower the number of employees arriving in single-occupancy vehicles by charging a parking fee for single-occupant cars or trucks.			
Work with the local municipality to provide safe pedestrian crossings on adjacent streets, and on routes leading to and from public transportation stops or facilities.			
Coordinate your employees' hours to coincide with public transportation timetables.			
Lower the number of employees arriving in single-occupancy vehicles by encouraging other modes of transportation, particularly public transportation, walking, or biking.			
Provide premium parking locations for hybrid or electric vehicles that also ride-share.			
For pedestrians, provide safe and clearly defined pathways across and around the business, including all entrances.			
For bike riders, provide designated on-site bicycling routes that are user-friendly.			

Provide easily accessible bike racks, sheltered from the weather, if possible.			
Provide shower and locker facilities for bicycle and pedestrian commuters.			
Provide pedestrian-friendly access to public transportation. If your company is big enough this might include all-weather shelters and well-lighted, secure routes.			
Try to eliminate or minimize your parking lots and convert them to grasslands, wetlands, or other uses that require minimal or no landscaping, if possible.			
If your company is big enough, provide shuttle service to and from airports, train stations, light rail stops, and even bus stops.			
Whenever possible, allow employees to telecommute (work from home over the Internet or other network). This one step, if used aggressively, can reduce your employee commuting carbon footprint to zero. There are many telecommuting resources provided in Appendix B of this book.			
Encourage audio or video conferencing whenever possible. This saves time, travel costs, and the associated emissions.			
Allow flex-time work hours for your employees. A compressed work week of four 10-hour days will reduce commuting costs and emissions by 20 percent.			
Business Shipping and Travel			
Complete the Business Transportation Carbon Footprint Worksheet and evaluate any immediate areas where transportation use and expenses may be decreased or eliminated.			
Use a travel carbon calculator to determine your carbon footprint for auto, airline, rail, or bus travel. See **www.nativeenergy.com/pages/travel_ calculator/30.php**.			
If your business has company-owned cars or a fleet of vehicles, specify that all vehicles will be hybrid, whenever possible. Check **www.hybridcenter.org** for the latest information on hybrid vehicles.			

If your company ships products or is a truck or rail company that delivers these products, look into the EPA SmartWay Transport Partnership. This is an innovative collaboration between EPA and the freight industry to increase energy efficiency while significantly reducing greenhouse gases and air pollution. Hundreds of businesses are benefitting from this partnership. See **www.epa.gov/smartway**.			
Develop a company-wide policy to eliminate unnecessary idling of truck engines. One way is by installing auxiliary power units that will heat or cool the truck when stopped, allowing the main engine to be shut down. Wal-Mart installed auxiliary power units on its 6,845 semi tractors and saved $22 million in 16 months			
Coordinate your shipping and freight to use full loads whenever possible. Try to work with your shippers to assure full loads in both directions whenever possible.			
Remove all excess weight from company vehicles. Mandate observance of speed limits for company vehicles. Request that employees use cruise control and overdrive whenever possible to increase fuel efficiency.			
Whenever possible, book your travel accommodations at "green" hotels. See **www.greenhotels.com**.			
During any necessary hotel stays, let management know that it is not necessary to change your towels and sheets every day, and turn off the AC/heat, lights, and TV whenever you leave the room.			
Whenever possible, use a hotel van instead of renting a car and use public transportation in your destination city.			
If you must rent a car, consider renting a hybrid vehicle. See **www.evrental.com** for rentals in California and Arizona. Also check with Avis, Budget, and Enterprise car rentals, which are beginning to provide hybrid rentals.			

Consider carbon offsetting for required travel. This concept is designed to reduce overall carbon by off-setting carbon-intensive uses (such as airline travel) with carbon-neutral uses (such as windpower). See **www.nativeenergy.com** for one of the best offset programs. It finances wind energy projects on native American reservations.			
If you must use air travel, patronize airlines that provide carbon offsetting. Many airlines such as American, British Airways, Continental, Delta, Quantas and several online travel booking sites such as Travelocity and Expedia are either offsetting carbon emissions or allowing passengers to purchase carbon offsets.			

Economic Analysis of Travel and Transportation Measures

Simple Cost Pay Back Analysis

To make rational business decisions about which of your travel and transportation changes your company should implement, it's wise to run a simple cost payback analysis and a return on investment analysis. A highly simplified form of cost/benefit analysis is called simple payback. In this method, the total first cost of the improvement is divided by the first-year energy cost savings produced by the improvement. This method yields the number of years required for the improvement to pay for itself. Cost payback analyses can be far more complex and include many other variables. Return on investment analyses can show you how a particular investment compares to other ways of using your company's money.

Let's look at a simple example. Your company currently uses a nice big SUV for as its main company vehicle, for running errands, delivering packages to the post office or FedEx, and picking up supplies. This vehicle gets roughly 15 mpg for its in-town driving, which is about average. Maybe it's time to upgrade. Besides the obvious environmental and climate implications, perhaps a hybrid car would serve your company's purposes just as well. But is this a good, sound, pragmatic economic decision?

A Toyota Prius costs about $20,000 list. (Note: although the federal tax credit for buying Prii has expired, there are still many tax incentives available at the state level to help offset this cost.) The EPA estimates the Prius has in-town mileage of 48 mpg.

If you drive your company vehicle about 15,000 miles per year (about average) and fuel costs are $4 per gallon (U.S. average at press time), your annual gasoline costs would be as follows:

Vehicle	Number in use	Cost/ gallon	MPG	Mile/year	Gallons/ year	Annual cost of fuel
SUV	1	$4.00	15	15,000	1000	$4,000
Hybrid	1	$4.00	48	15,000	312.5	$1,250

If you replace your SUV with the hybrid, the yearly savings in fuel alone would be $2,750. Of course, there would be many other benefits that stem from buying a hybrid vehicle, such as lower insurance premiums, customer appreciation, employee satisfaction, lower maintenance costs, etc.

If replacing the SUV with a new hybrid would cost $20,000, then to determine your payback period you would divide the initial cost of the upgrade by the first year cost savings:

Cost of upgrade $20,000 / savings per year $2,750 = 7.27 years payback period

OK, so 7+ years looks like a pretty long payback period and you're now climbing right back into your SUV. Hold on there a minute, the actual payback should be based on the savings per year and the cost differential between purchasing a new SUV and purchasing a new hybrid. This turns this equation upside down because the hybrid actually costs *less* than virtually any new SUV. If a new hybrid costs $20,000 and a new SUV costs $30,000 (a pretty basic SUV) and the life of the vehicle is 10 years, you actually have an annual cost savings of an additional $1,000 over the vehicle's life. So, our new figures are:

Cost of upgrade $20,000 / savings per year $3,750 = 5.33 years payback period

The cost of gas is extremely likely to be higher than our estimated $4/gallon over the next ten years. Consider finally that vehicles seldom have a positive payback at all. In this case however, if you save money on the actual cost of the upgrade itself and also on your yearly fuel bill *and* the vehicle will actually pay for itself in the savings generated over its the first half of its useful life and generate an additional $2,750 savings for 5 years after payback, what are you waiting for?

Simple Return on Investment Analysis

Another standard measure of economic feasibility is the return on investment formula. This is a measure of the percentage return provided by a particular investment. The standard formula for return on investment (roi) is:

Net return / capital cost of investment = percentage return on investment

For the net return figure, you need to determine the life of the investment (in years) and multiply it by net annual savings. Use the net annual savings figure that you generated in the cost payback analysis. Then deduct the initial capital cost.

Net annual savings x life of investment - capital cost = net return

Let's take a quick look at how your hybrid stacks up using return on investment. Thus, for our example, if we assume a 10-year life for the Prius, our net return is:

$3,750 X 10 = $37,500 - $20,000 capital costs = $17,500 net return

Then, using this net return figure, our return on investment (ROI) is:

$17,500 Net return / $20,000 capital costs

= 87.5 percent ROI or return on the investment over a ten-year period.

Then, by dividing that figure by the years of life of the investment, you have a

87.5 / 10 = 8.75 percent annualized rate of return

Thus, we show a very respectable annualized return of 8.75 percent on buying a hybrid vehicle instead of a new SUV. Since most vehicles provide no actual return on their investments, buying an energy efficient vehicle in times of high energy costs is, in fact, a wise business choice.

These formulas can additionally include calculations to discount the dollar amounts over time and other more sophisticated approaches. For example, full life-cycle cost analyses are a more in-depth alternative to return on investment analyses. This simple approach, however, can provide you with a quick and simple way to compare energy efficiency investments with other business investment choices. In addition, remember that there are many other valuable noneconomic benefits to conserving energy in your business.

On the following page, you will find a simple worksheet to use for cost payback and return on investment calculations. This worksheet is provided on the CD that accompanies this book in a fillable PDF format that will do the necessary calculations for you.

Travel and Transportation Economic Analysis

Capital Costs

		Item	Value
		Equipment Purchase Costs	$
	+	Prep Work Costs	$
	+	Implementation Costs	$
	=	Total Capital Costs	$

Net Annual Savings

		Annual Avoided Fuel or Other Costs	$
	+	Annual Avoided Purchase Costs	$
	+	Annual Additional Revenue (if any)	$
	=	Total Net Annual Savings	$

Simple Payback Period Analysis

		Capital Costs (from above)	$
	÷	Net Annual Savings (from above)	$
	=	Payback Period in Years	

Simple Return on Investment Analysis

		Item	Value
		Net Annual Savings (from above)	$
	x	Life of Investment (in years)	
	−	Capital Costs (from above)	$
	=	Net Return	$
	÷	Capital Costs (from above)	$
	=	Return on Investment (over life)	
	÷	Life of Investment (in years)	
	=	Annual Return on Investment Rate	%

These formulas can additionally include calculations to discount the dollar amounts over time and other more sophisticated approaches. Remember that there are many other valuable noneconomic benefits to greening your business travel and transportation.

Chapter 10

Green Business Office Equipment and Computing

Computers and other electronic office equipment have ushered in an age of enormous productivity. By 2008, over 1 billion computers had been put into use around the world and, fueled by the rapid expansion in computer use in China, that amount is expected to double by 2015. This tremendous amount of computing power has allowed humanity to vastly increase its economic prowess. But with the tremendous gains brought about by the use of computers have come significant environmental problems. Computer and electronic use devours colossal amounts of electricity. Whereas a generation ago, a small six-person office, with perhaps an electric typewriter and a copy machine, might have used 600 watts of power, today that same size office typically has a connected load of over 7,000 watts powering individual computers, monitors, printers, faxes, scanners, and other electronics. More, and more powerful, equipment is being added to offices every year.

The actual production and manufacture of computers worldwide also consumes enormous amounts of energy. According to a recent United Nations report, the amount of fossil fuels necessary to manufacture one desktop computer is over 500 pounds—equal to over ten times the weight of the computer itself. A wide range of toxic chemicals and materials, including lead, mercury, cadmium, and chromium, is used in the production of electronic equipment, leading to probable long-term health effects on workers, families, and communities due to chemical exposure and emissions from electronics manufacturing. But, perhaps the main risks may be from the millions of computers that have been dumped indiscriminately in landfills and from unhealthy and environmentally unsafe recycling processes that are common in the developing world. At least 12 million computers and over 100 million cell phones end up in U.S. landfills every year, and 80% of U.S. electronic waste is exported to developing countries. Both of these numbers are growing rapidly.

One of the main recommendations stemming from the comprehensive U.N. report on computing was to increase the upgradability of computers. On the average, a computer is used for three years. Businesses spend enormous amounts of money replacing out moded computers and peripherals annually. In many cases, the computers can be successfully updated with minor changes. Prompt resale of used computers was also noted as a viable and important measure to prevent computers from being disposed of prematurely. In addition to the need for upgrades and resale of older computers, energy-efficient use of computers has the potential to save vast amounts of electricity. Experts estimate that 65% of computer energy consumption is used (read wasted) when the computers are entirely idle. IBM estimates that it saves over $15 million annually by simply encouraging employees to turn off their computers when not in use and overnight. The purchase of more energy-efficient equipment is also an important consideration.

In the United States, the EPA Energy Star program provides strict standards for energy-efficient computers. Beginning on July 20, 2007, Energy Star's new specifications for computers and electronics went into effect. The new specifications apply to a variety of products, including desktop and notebook (or laptop) computers, game consoles, integrated computer systems, desktop-derived servers, and workstations. Since computers are in use many more hours per day than in the past, Energy Star has strengthened its requirements to better save energy. Qualified products must now meet energy use guidelines in three distinct operating modes: standby, sleep mode, and while computers are being used. This approach ensures energy savings when a computer is active and performing a range of tasks, as well as when it is simply standing by. Newly qualified computers must also include a more efficient internal power supply. By requiring efficiency savings across operating modes, the new computer specifications are expected to save consumers and businesses more than $1.8 billion in energy costs over the next 5 years and prevent greenhouse gas emissions equal to the annual emissions of 2.7 million vehicles.

The U.S. EPA has also developed an easy-to-use, online tool to help select and compare environmentally safe electronic products: EPEAT (Electronic Product Environmental Assessment Tool) rates computer desktops, laptops, and monitors based on their environmental attributes. EPEAT-certified products have reduced levels of cadmium, lead, and mercury to better protect human health, and are easier to upgrade and recycle, in addition to meeting the government's Energy Star guidelines for energy efficiency. This tool is found at: **www.epeat.net**.

An additional source of information for purchasing energy-efficient computers is provided by the U.S. Department of Energy's Federal Energy Management Program at **www1.eere.energy.gov/femp/procurement/eep_computer.html**.

If your business operates a data center, the U.S. Department of Energy has developed a new software tool, DC Pro, designed to allow a comprehensive assessment of data center energy-efficiency opportunities. The final release date for this program is slated for September 2008. Data centers are among the fastest growing industries in the United States. The Department of Energy has identified them as a main key to increasing energy efficiency, reducing load on the electricity grid, and enhancing data center reliability. Last year, data centers were estimated to have used 61 billion kilowatt-hours, or 1.5 percent of electricity in the United States, and that use is projected to grow 12 percent per year through 2011. This new software is part of a suite of tools backed with a training curriculum, energy assessment protocols, best-in-class guidelines, and a process to certify data center energy experts. The Department of Energy is considering working with industry on a voluntary certification process that will validate any data center's continual improvement in energy efficiency. After September 2008, the software should be available from the Department of Energy. Please see the Energy Efficiency and Renewable Energy, Industrial Technology Program website at **www1.eere.energy.gov/industry/bestpractices/software.html**.

In the European Union, the groundbreaking Waste Electrical and Electronic Equipment legislation allows consumers to return their used equipment to the manufacturer free of charge. This legislation also requires the substitution of various heavy metals (lead, mercury, cadmium, and hexavalent chromium) and brominated flame retardants (polybrominated biphenyls [PBB] or polybrominated diphenyl ethers [PBDE]) in new electrical and electronic equipment put on the market in Europe after July of 2006.

Before you consider recycling any of your computer or electronic products, check locally to see if any churches, nonprofit, or community organizations can use them. Reuse is always a better choice than recycling. If you can't find any organizations to reuse your castoffs, there are lots of recycling options:

In the U.S., Dell Computer will accept any Dell computer back for free recycling, even if you aren't buying a new one. You ship it to them and they reimburse you for the shipping. In addition, if you buy a Dell computer or printer, they will accept for recycling any other manufacturer's product. See **www.dell.com/recycling** for more details. For larger businesses, see **www.dell.com/assetrecovery**.

IBM has an extensive program to purchase eligible used computers and equipment regardless of manufacturer. They have an online instant-quote tool that will give you the price they will pay for the used products. They will also arrange for recycling if the products are not eligible for purchase. See **www-03.ibm.com/financing/us/recovery/small/buyback.html**.

Apple Computer also offers a free take-back and recycling program for computers and monitors if you purchase a new Mac product. In addition, they will accept for recycling Ipods or cell phones from any manufacturer. See **www.apple.com/ environment/recycling** for more information.

Hewlett-Packard accepts its products back for recycling, but you have to pay for this service unless you're buying a new HP product (in which case you get an e-coupon for shipping costs). HP may also pay you for equipment with remaining resale value, regardless of manufacturer. See **www.hp.com** for further details.

There are many electronics recycling programs around the country that will accept nearly every type of electronic product. The Electronic Industries Alliance, a national trade organization that includes electronic and high-tech associations and companies, has developed a comprehensive website to allow you to find reuse, recycling, and donation programs across the country for your electronic products You'll find their user-friendly listings at: **www.eiae.org.** Be sure to also check your choice of electronics recycler to be certain that they have agreed not to ship their electronics overseas to developing countries for environmentally and human health-damaging recycling. See **www.ban.org** to make this determination.

Cellphones are used, on average, for only 24 months. If you want to recycle your business's cellphones, you should contact the aptly-named Good Deed Foundation: **www.gooddeedfoundation.org/recycle**. Some of the phones that they receive will be resold and the proceeds used to support climate change initiatives or to support programs to alleviate poverty for women and children, and others will be provided to seniors for making free 911 calls. You have three choices in how to participate in this great program: They'll send you a free postage-paid envelope that will hold up to seven recycled cellphones; or they'll ship you a box for collecting used cellphones from your employees or customers; or they'll let you print out a postage-paid shipping label right from their website if you want to ship multiple phones and accessories.

Office Equipment and Computing Efficiency Plan

This chapter provides a look at other ways that your business can green its computer and electronics use and save energy and money in the process. You should begin with a quick survey of your computer and electronics use, then review the various action steps, analyze them, and finally implement your green equipment business plan.

① Conduct a comprehensive computer and electronics assessment of your current business practices. Do a walk-through of your business and note every computer and peripheral (monitor, printer, scanner, fax machine, etc.) in use. A Electronics Survey Worksheet is provided to help you make an on-site assessment. An Electronics Process Map can also help you note the locations of all of your electronics. No instructions are included for this map—just get some paper and draw a simple diagram of your electronics in use.

② Read through the Equipment and Computer Action Worksheet (that follows the Survey worksheet) to determine which of the measures are valuable for your company. This chart is available on the enclosed CD as a PDF form that may be printed out for your use in developing your overall plan and also as a text form. On the basis of your survey and worksheet, you should then formulate and implement a computer and electronics action plan. This plan should be revisited and, if necessary, revised at least on an annual basis. The plan should establish and promote more efficient computer and electronics use throughout the business and sound disposal practices.

③ Although it is difficult to separate energy efficiency savings from other benefits stemming from faster and more efficient computers and electronics, this equipment should be evaluated for energy efficiency. No worksheets are provided for cost payback analysis or return on investment, but there is a very useful online tool for evaluating the dollar value of energy saved by implementing various computer power management techniques. This tool is at: **www.energystar.gov/index.cfm?c=power_mgt.pr_power_mgt_users**. You can also use a power meter to calculate your actual power use and savings from individual efficiency measures.

In general, the implementation of computer energy efficiency and power management techniques is estimated to save up to $60 per year per computer in energy expenses. The techniques that follow are all easily employable and readily adaptable to any size business. The use of more energy-efficient equipment can also increase these savings dramatically.

④ The final step in the achievement of computer and electronics efficiency is to actually implement the plan. It will take a conscious effort to educate all employees involved in purchasing, using, and disposing of electronic equipment to insure that they all understand your new company policies. Every employee should be updated regularly on the company's efforts to green their electronics and computer use. Employees can also be encouraged to take many of these ideas home and implement them on their home computer and electronics systems.

Equipment and Computer Survey

Completed by:		Date:			Business:		
Address:					Phone:		

Existing Computers and Office Equipment

Location	Equipment	# Units	Make/ Model	Date of Manufacture	Energy Star®?	Hours on/week	Comments

Equipment and Computer Action Worksheet

	Already Doing	Should Do	Doesn't Apply
Equipment and Computer Purchasing and Recycling			
Prepare a Computer and Electronics Survey Worksheet for your business.			
Prior to purchasing any new electronics, repair or upgrade your current machines whenever possible.			
Prior to purchasing any new electronics, consider purchasing used or refurbished equipment. See **www.dell.com/outle**t for refurbished PCs. Also see **www.refurbdepot.com** for factory direct office equipment of all kinds.			
If you need to upgrade your monitors, replace your old cathode ray tube (CRT) monitors with newer, more energy-efficient flat screen monitors. Be sure to recycle, rather than landfill, any CRT monitors, as they contain up to 5 pounds of lead.			
Before you recycle any electronics equipment or computers, consider donating your machines to a local church, school, or nonprofit organization. They may be able to get many more productive years out of the product before it is ultimately recycled.			
If you must recycle your products, check the manufacturer. Dell, Apple, IBM, and HP all have electronics recycling programs. Sony has a television take-back program. Check their respective websites for more information. Also check the Electronics Industry Alliance at: **www.eiaa.org**. Be sure to choose a recycler that has pledged to not export the e-waste to developing countries. See **www.ban.org**.			
If your company is in California or Massachusetts, check with your waste management provider. These states have banned CRT monitors and televisions from landfills.			
New computer and electronics purchases should be free of brominated flame retardants (BFRs), mercury, and polyvinyl chloride (PVCs) if possible.			

Choose copy machines that are Energy Star®-certified and that have duplexing (double-side) capabilities. Turn off copiers when not in use.			
If you need to purchase new computers or electronics, purchase Energy Star- or EPEAT-compliant models. Energy Star products consume up to 70% less energy than noncompliant models, and EPEAT products are energy-efficient and also contain far less toxic materials. See **www.energystar.gov** and **www.epeat.net**.			
Reuse any peripherals, like keyboards, monitors, or mice, with any new computers that are purchased.			
Consider using laptops as desktop computers. Laptops are far more energy efficient and can consume up to 80% less energy than equivalent desktops.			
Inkjet printers use 75 to 90 percent less energy than laser printers. Consider the use of inkjet printers for draft documents or when speed and print quality are not as important. If you need to purchase laser printers, pick Energy Star ones, as they will automatically power down when not used for a certain time period.			
Consider using a fax modem so that your computer becomes your fax machine. This will allow for paperless faxing and electronic storage of faxes, while eliminating another piece of equipment.			
If you need to purchase new equipment, buy equipment that is durable and can be easily upgraded. Consider whether the product has online manuals that reduce the need for printed manuals, and also whether the equipment is recyclable or whether the manufacturer has a take-back policy.			
Investigate the leasing of computers and other office equipment. IBM has focused on lease programs and will help companies by purchasing or arranging for the proper recycling of old equipment. See **www.ibm.com**.			
Investigate the packaging of electronics products before you buy them. Insist that manufacturers ship their products in a reusable, or at the minimum, easily recyclable, shipping containers.			

Computer and Electronics Efficiency During Use			
Turn your computers off when they are not needed. It does not harm modern computers to be turned on and off repeatedly. This is the most important action that you can take to reduce computer and peripheral energy use.			
Turn down the brightness on your monitor. The brightest setting on a monitor consumes twice the power used by the dimmest setting.			
Turn off your monitors when not in use. Monitors account for around 50% of a computer's energy use.			
Turn off all peripherals such as printers, scanners, and speakers when not in use.			
Prevent shadow energy use. Connect your equipment to power strips that can be easily turned on and off. Turn all equipment off (except perhaps your fax machine) at night and on weekends.			
Consider using simple timer devices to shut off equipment at night and on weekends. These can easily be set to shut off your power strips, and thus shut off multiple pieces of equipment.			
Consider using energy-efficient surge protectors or power strips. The Belkin Conserve Surge Protector works with a remote control. See **www.belkin.com**. The Smart Strip Power Strip automatically cuts power to peripherals (like monitors, speakers, printers, etc.) when your computer is shut down. See: **www.bitsltd.net/consumerproducts**. The Isole Plug Load controller combines a surge protector with a motion detector shut-off. See: **www.wattstopper.com**.			
Turn off your screen savers. Screen savers do not save energy and are not necessary on any modern computer screens. The use of screen savers can prevent more efficient power management settings from taking effect on your computer.			
Set up local area networks within your business to share printers, scanners, and even computers. The fewer electronic devices needed, the less your energy bills will be.			

Computer Power Management			
Consider the use of a power meter to find out how much energy your computer actually consumes and to calculate your actual savings from each measure.			
Enable power management modes on your computer. These features allow computers to go into lower-energy modes after a certain amount of time. Sleep modes can save up to 90% of the energy consumed.			
Even for PCs with a low-power sleep mode, you can save more energy and possibly extend your computer's lifetime if you manually shut it off completely at night, on weekends, and during long periods of non-use during the day.			
If your networked computer(s) must stay on and connected at night for file backup or other purposes, make sure the monitor is shut off.			
Look for network features that provide a timed shut-down, automatic shutdown after file backup, or, alternatively, auto-boot-up before backup. Using sleep and off modes will not shorten your PC's lifetime.			
Plug-in power supplies for laptop PCs typically use 15 watts or less but cannot be shut off completely. To save energy, unplug your power supply after the laptop battery is charged, or use a power-strip with an on-off switch.			
Many laptop PCs (and some desktops) offer a "hibernate" or "bookmark" feature, which saves active programs and files before shutting off, then restores the same status when the PC is turned on. This added convenience encourages users to shut off their computers when not in use.			
On Windows XP systems, under Control Panel, go to Power Options and select the most efficient settings. The recommended energy efficiency settings: Turn off monitor/sleep mode: 15 minutes or less Turn off hard drives/sleep mode: 15 minutes or less System standby/sleep: after 30 minutes or less.			

For Windows Vista, there are even more options for power management: a power button on the Start menu that encourages the use of power-saving modes, restrictions on the ability of applications to interrupt computers in sleep mode, a new user interface for managing applications that are blocking shutdown, and a simpler presentation of power management settings (you can use three preset power management plans: balanced, energy-saving, or performance-oriented, or you can create your own settings). You can access Vista power management under Control Panel, then System and Maintenance, then under Power Options.			
For Apple Mac computers, on the Apple menu, select System Preferences, then Show All, then select Energy Saver under the Hardware section, then Show Details, then select settings for Power Adapter. Use the settings noted above under Windows XP and select "Put the Hard Drive to sleep when possible" for the best power-saving results.			
If you are not sure about activating power management features yourself, there is an easy-to-use tool available from the Energy Star program. EZ Wizard is a simple software tool that automatically activates power management features for you and will help you decide the right power management settings. It is online at (hold on this is a long one): **www.energystar.gov/index.cfm?c=power_ mgt.pr_power_mgt_ez_wiz.** (Remember that you don't need to retype that address: all of the website addresses in this book are found, in interactive format, on the BOOK WEB ADDRESSES document that is on the CD that accompanies this book.)			
If you must leave a computer on overnight (to operate as a fax or answering machine, for example), it might as well also be doing some valuable work for the environment. Investigate allowing your always-on computers to run climate modeling software in the background. Oxford University operates a network that uses the computing power of dormant computers to test complex climate models. See **www.climateprediction.net** for more details.			

Chapter 11

Green Business Supply Chains and Purchasing

Every year, more businesses are beginning to examine their supply chains and procurement processes in an effort to measure and lessen their overall environmental impacts. Large corporations, under pressure from customers and shareholders alike, are increasingly putting direct pressure on their suppliers to operate in more environmentally sound ways. *Supply Chain Magazine* identified the greening of supply chains as its number one trend in 2007. Beginning in 2008, the world's largest retailer, Wal-Mart, will begin rating the packaging of all of its suppliers. The Wal-Mart supply-chain "scorecards" will assess the type of material used, the amount of packaging, recycled content, and other factors in an attempt to influence these suppliers to lessen packaging waste. Wal-Mart will also introduce a comprehensive supply chain scorecard for all of its electronics suppliers. The results of these supply chain assessments will be made available to consumers via the Internet and will clearly influence buying decisions, both at the corporate and individual consumer level. While it is doubtful whether "big box" retailers can ever be truly sustainable, the move by Wal-Mart and other large retailers to identify problems in their supply chains heralds a very positive step in the right direction.

Most businesses are both suppliers and customers to some extent. You obtain products or supplies from other companies and you sell your products or services either directly to consumers or to other businesses. Whether you operate a company with a long chain of suppliers or a business that is itself a supplier, you need to begin to examine the impacts of your niche in the supply chain and modify your procurement efforts to make them as sustainable as possible. Improving the quality and environmental impact of your suppliers can only help improve the overall performance of your business itself. Lee Scott, CEO of Wal-Mart, explained the rationale behind the Wal-Mart efforts to green their supply chain, even if such efforts increase Wal-Mart's short-term costs: "Paying more in the short term for quality will mean paying less in the long term as a company. Higher quality products will mean better value, fewer problems, fewer returns, and greater trust with our customers."

Purchasing decisions are often made in companies large and small with little regard to environmental, social, or labor standards. Cost and quality are the most common factors that are considered. Adding environmental and social responsibility concerns to purchasing decisions can provide your company with real and substantial benefits. If your suppliers become more energy conscious, those savings can be passed on to its customers. Better and less packaging will lower overall costs associated with employee time to remove and handle packaging, eventual waste disposal of any excess packaging, and shipping costs stemming from unnecessary packaging. Greener products are generally more durable and their use in your business will lead to fewer losses from damage or returns from customers. Efforts to source your purchasing from companies that use innovative materials can dramatically reduce the amounts of hazardous or toxic chemicals that your company must handle or dispose. This can, in turn, reduce insurance rates, disposal and treatment expenses, and legal liability while simultaneously increasing customer satisfaction and employee health and safety.

Today's consumers are demanding that companies become accountable for the overall impacts of their products and services, whether environmental or social. As this consumer pressure is applied at the retail level, retail providers, worried about their image and brand names, will increasingly pass this pressure along to their suppliers, and on up the supply chain to the raw material level. Working closely with suppliers and, in fact, with your supplier's suppliers, will help improve the products and services that your business ultimately supplies to its own customers. Redesigning packaging or products to eliminate waste and increase the use of recycled content will ultimately make your company a leaner operation, with both improvements in profits and savings to customers made possible. The greatest benefits can be found by extending your focus both upstream to your raw materials suppliers, and then downstream to your ultimate customers, and finally back again to your company as the products are recycled or disposed of.

Retailers and consumers are exerting more and more control over the supply chain process and demanding accountability from every level. Ask Kathy Lee Gifford and Nike about the damage that lack of attention to supply chain management can wreak on a product line. Reports of the use of child labor to produce Ms. Gifford's Global Fusion line of clothing ignited a firestorm of negative publicity. Nike also learned the hard way to pay attention to its supply chain after highly damaging reports that its Asian factories were paying wages of pennies per hour for the manufacture of $100+ sneakers. Both of these instances led to greater disclosure and transparency in supply chain logistics. Nike eventually released the names and locations of all of its suppliers so that they could be monitored by independent third-party groups. Ms. Gifford's quick response to the damaging disclosures led other apparel manufacturers to quickly examine their own suppliers, and she herself went on to work on the White House Apparel Industry Partnership Task Force to end sweatshop labor use in the clothing industry.

Shifts in retailer purchasing policies can have an enormous impact up and down a supply chain. Again, using Wal-Mart as an example, both the organic food and wild-caught seafood industries received major positive boosts when Wal-Mart announced their decisions to dramatically increase the retail presence of both product lines in their stores. Conversely, the repercussions were felt throughout the nonorganic food and farmed-seafood industries. In today's networked world, every business and industry is under increasing scrutiny because of the global nature of communications. The Internet and 24-hour news provide near-immediate disclosure of unsustainable practices by business. Those businesses that begin now to examine their entire supply chain will be well poised to prevent future events from disrupting their businesses. Those companies that ignore the greening of their supply chains will begin to suffer the consequences in the increasingly connected and environmentally conscious marketplace.

The overall benefits of being a part of a sustainable supply chain are being realized by businesses up and down those chains, from the beginning, where the commodities or raw materials are produced, to the middle of the chain, where the commodities are turned into retail products and distributed around the globe, and ultimately to the retail or service end of the supply chain. Better market appeal to consumers, more efficient operations, less risk of negative impacts or liability, and a positive influence on your company's reputation are all enhanced by closer attention to your supply and procurement chain.

Part of your efforts to green your supply chain should be to develop a company purchasing policy that incorporates environmental issues into the mix of purchasing decisions. Many state governments and federal agencies have instituted programs in recent years to purchase "environmentally preferable" products or services, or products or services that have a lesser or reduced effect on human health and the environment when compared with competing products or services that serve the same purpose. This comparison may consider raw materials acquisition, production, manufacturing, packaging, distribution, reuse, operation, maintenance, or disposal of the product or service. These agencies have found that their efforts in preventing waste and pollution have been enhanced by considering environmental impacts, along with price, performance, and other traditional selection factors, when making purchasing decisions. In fact, federal agencies are required to consider the following factors in acquisition planning for all procurements and in the evaluation and award of contracts: "elimination of virgin material requirements; use of biobased products; use of recovered materials; reuse of product; life-cycle cost; recyclability; use of environmentally preferable products; waste prevention (including toxicity reduction or elimination); and ultimate disposal." In addition, the U.S. EPA has developed its own internal guidelines for green purchasing. These require the agency to:

- Include environmental considerations as part of the normal purchasing process

- Emphasize pollution prevention as part of the purchasing process and examine multiple environmental attributes throughout the product or service's life cycle

- Compare environmental impacts when selecting products and services

- Collect accurate and meaningful information about the environmental performance of products and services

The U.S. EPA also operates a Database of Environmental Information for Products and Services. This very useful database contains over 130 local, state, and federal contract and policy specifications, 523 product environmental performance standards/guidelines, 25 lists of products identified as "green" by other organizations, and 155 links to additional useful environmental information on products and/or services. You can access this database at **http:// yosemite1.epa.gov/oppt/eppstand2.nsf**. Additionally, the CD that accompanies this book includes two useful U.S. EPA documents: *Integrating Green Purchasing Into Your Environmental Management System (EMS)* and *Promoting Green Purchasing: Tools and Resources to Quantify the Benefits of Environmentally Preferable Purchasing.* Next, you will find information on newly developed software that can help your business make both purchasing decisions and product life-cycle assessments. These tools and other considerations should help as you develop your own company's green purchasing guidelines.

Life-Cycle Assessment Software

To make environmentally sound purchasing decisions, it is necessary to understand the life cycle of the products or materials that you will need to purchase. Likewise, it is useful for companies to understand the full life cycles of the products that they themselves sell. Small and medium-sized businesses and even many Fortune 500 companies lack the time, money, and expertise to conduct traditional life-cycle analyses on their own products, much less on those of their supply chains. Without a life-cycle analysis of products and materials they use, companies that are asked to improve their environmental performance have a difficult time making the correct decisions. They may spend extensive resources on an initiative that produces little return while ignoring easier targets. Purchasers who want to reward good performers are also left with no means of comparing one product with another. A joint government/business/academic project aims to put user-friendly life-cycle analysis tools in the hands of all companies, along with the tools to market the environmental performance of their own products and allow comparison shopping based on these life-cycle analyses.

The Life-Cycle Assessment Tool

The U.S. EPA and the state of Texas combined to fund the University of New Hampshire and the industrial ecology company, Sylvatica, to create a purchasing prioritization tool based on life-cycle assessment principles. The Life-Cycle Assessment Tool was developed on a commercial software platform developed by Lumina Decision Systems, called Analytica. This innovative software has been used worldwide to see how much a company's decisions reduce greenhouse gas emissions, or to evaluate all the energy, environmental, and economic costs and benefits of many commercial decisions. Users can run the Life-Cycle Assessment Tool using the demonstration version of Analytica, which is free and yet allows full analysis capability with the tool. Advanced users can pay for a version of Analytica that allows them to add features and data to the tool. The free version of Analytica is available at **www.lumina.com/ana/player.htm**. The assessment tool itself is provided by **www.earthster.org**. The Earthster platform is now a prototype in development, and you can test-drive it for free. Simply create an organization profile (which can be hypothetical) by joining the member directory, and do a life-cycle assessment on products.

This tool makes life-cycle assessment more accessible to all users worldwide. In addition to offering the benefits of life-cycle assessment without a lot of capital or time investment, companies have the option of reporting their own current environmental performance, their year-to-year improvement, or both.

The tool is built around easy step-by-step instructions. First, the user decides how he or she wants to use the tool: to find the most important purchases for reducing impacts; or to compare two different purchasing scenarios—shifting transportation from truck to rail, for example. Data can be entered according to the user's commodity list or according to other standards. The user specifies only the dollars spent per commodity, allowing analysis of a company, a product line, or a specific product. The data itself comes from the U.S. Input-Output database so is based on U.S. manufacturing. This database includes cradle-to-gate materials and emissions data, so, for example, when a user selects the amount of gasoline purchased for its corporate fleet, the data will include the emissions to get the petroleum out of the ground, processed into gasoline, and delivered to the pump, but will not include the emissions from the cars themselves. It is important to consider these emissions as part of the decision-making process.

Earthster.org has also joined forces with the OPEN LCA project to make life-cycle assessment a free and open tool using open-source software and the Internet. The OPEN LCA project is hard at work developing modular software for life-cycle analysis and sustainability assessments. The software will be available as open source, and will be available for free. For more information on this project or to join, please see **www.openlca.org**.

The Recycled Content Tool

The Recycled Content (ReCon) Tool was created by the U.S. EPA to help companies and individuals estimate life-cycle greenhouse gas emissions and energy impacts from purchasing or manufacturing materials with varying degrees of post-consumer recycled content. The ReCon Tool calculates greenhouse gas emissions and energy consumption related to purchasing and manufacturing activities using analyses of baseline and alternative recycled-content scenarios. Emissions and energy units are calculated using a life-cycle perspective (what impacts will this purchasing or manufacturing decision have on emissions and energy use throughout all stages of this product's life-cycle?). The model calculates emissions in metric tons of carbon equivalent, and energy consumption in British thermal units (Btus) for several material types. The user can construct various scenarios by entering the amount of materials purchased or manufactured and the recycled content of the types of materials. The ReCon Tool then applies material-specific greenhouse gas emissions and energy factors to calculate the emissions and energy consumption for each scenario and the benefit of choosing one scenario over another. The ReCon Tool provides two outputs, one for greenhouse gas emissions and another for energy consumption. The greenhouse gas output provides an estimate of the total emissions (based on manufacturing processes, carbon sequestration, and avoided disposal) related to the manufacture of the materials with recycled content. The energy output provides an estimate of the total energy consumed (based on manufacturing processes and avoided disposal) related to the manufacture of materials with recycled content. This tool can be either used online or as an Excel spreadsheet and is located at **http://epa.gov/climatechange/wycd/waste/calculators/ReCon_Home.html**.

There are other life-cycle assessment tools available and these are noted in Appendix B of this book. Some of these tools are very sophisticated and complex and require an extensive learning curve. A very basic and simplified limited life-cycle assessment worksheet is provided in Chapter 13 on green product design.

Green Business Purchasing Plan

The steps in building a more sustainable and greener supply chain are fourfold: Assess, Plan, Analyze, and Implement.

① First, you need to understand your current supply chain and its impacts. This will require two activities. First, you need to examine what your supply chain actually consists of. What are your supplies and where do they come from? You probably know this part of your business quite well, but it is a valuable exercise to look at supply chain logistics from a new, environmental perspective. The process-mapping technique is well suited to helping you do this. This chapter supplies an outline of the information that you will need to develop your own Supply Chain Process Map.

② You will then need to develop an approach to purchasing that will incorporate environmental concerns into the criteria. To assist in this process, a Supply Chain and Purchasing Action Worksheet is provided. Part of the process of greening your supply chain is consulting with your suppliers on their efforts. For this, a sample basic Supply Chain and Purchasing Questionnaire for your suppliers is shown. For small businesses, particularly at the retail end of the chain, this may, at first, seem a bit presumptuous. However, even the smallest of businesses are coming under increasing pressure and scrutiny from consumers, investors, and others to make certain that their products and services meet the highest standards.

③ In your analysis process, you need to actually identify the impacts of each product in your supply chain. A careful consideration of the attributes of each item in your supply list will help you focus on how best to lessen the environmental impact of each supply. A Supply Chain Worksheet is provided for this purpose. To complete your Supply Chain Worksheet for each of your suppliers, you will need the this additional information:

- Whether the product's raw materials are produced in a sustainable manner. Various certification programs may help in this effort. See Chapter 14 for more information on certification programs.

- Whether the product or material contains hazardous or toxic chemicals. See Chapter 8 for more information on dealing with hazardous or toxic chemicals.

- Whether the product or material is packaged in reusable or recyclable packing.

- Whether and to what extent the product itself contains recycled content.

- Whether the product or material is produced under verifiable fair labor standards.

- Whether the product or material is traceable to its source with a barcode or other label.

- Whether and to what extent the product or material is produced with renewable energy.

- What measures, if any, have been taken to assure that the product will be reused or recycled at the end of its product life.

④ Finally, you will need to actually implement the actions that you have decided upon. This will mean developing a set of purchasing guidelines, contacting various suppliers and requesting that they complete your Supply Chain and Purchasing Questionnaire, and beginning to make company purchases based on your new green purchasing perspective.

Supply Chain Process Map

Refer to Chapter 4 regarding process mapping and then draw your own simple diagram to help you better understand where basic supplies are coming from. Your Supply Chain Process Map should included the following details:

- All of the inputs to your business

- Where in your business those inputs are used

- Who is the supplier of each of the inputs

- Estimate of the amounts of each of those inputs used per period (monthly, quarterly, or annually, as appropriate)

- Estimates of any waste produced from the inputs (recycled or disposed of)

Supply Chain Worksheet

Completed by:		Date:		Supplier:				
Product Supplied:				Amount:				

Are raw materials sustainable?	Contains hazardous or toxic material?	Packed in reusable or recyclable material?	Contains recycled content? What %?	Produced with fair labor standards?	Traceable with barcode or labels?	Produced with renewable energy?	Shipped with energy efficiency?	End of product life

Prepare a Supply Chain Worksheet for every supplier in your supply chain and then update each one every fiscal quarter in the future in order to track the effectiveness of your company's supply chain measures.

Supply Chain and Purchasing Action Worksheet

	Already Doing	Should Do	Doesn't Apply
Prepare a Supply Chain and Purchasing Process Map of your company's supplier list.			
Complete a Supply Chain Worksheet for each product that your company uses in its operations.			
Develop a set of purchasing guidelines relating to those qualifications that you feel are most important for your suppliers to adhere to.			
Part of your purchasing guidelines should be to give a pricing preference of some type to environmentally preferable products.			
Make a concerted and measurable effort to purchase recycled-content products whenever possible.			
Review any contracts with suppliers to ascertain any current purchasing requirements that could be strengthened to be more environmentally sensitive.			
Attempt to eliminate all materials and products from your supply chain that contain hazardous or toxic chemicals or that produce toxins when manufactured or disposed of.			
Incorporate green specifications into bid or quote requirements where appropriate. For example, you can specify that products contain no hazardous chemicals, that they do contain post-consumer recycled content, or that all plastic components are not painted or varnished, or that all electronics equipment be Energy Star certified.			
Incorporate environmental safety requirements into any maintenance or janitorial contracts. For example you can specify that all cleaning products contain no hazardous or toxic chemicals that might be harmful.			
Develop a Supply Chain Questionnaire and request that all suppliers complete one. Encourage suppliers to inform you, in detail, why their products are sustainable. See sample at the end of this chapter.			

Investigate the use of ISO 14001, SA 8000, or other environmental management systems to help identify the origin of raw materials and resources. See Chapters 15 and 16 for more information.			
Use the EPA Database of Environmental Information for Products and Services to investigate products in your supply chain. See the website at **http://yosemite1.epa.gov/oppt/eppstand2.nsf**.			
Use product assessment software to evaluate and identify the products and producers that meet your new environmental purchasing goals. See **www.earthster.org** and **www.openLca.org**.			
Investigate whether your business can influence changes in product design up your supply chain that will eliminate environmental issues later in the chain.			
Check for more supply chain, purchasing, and life-cycle assessment resources in Appendix B.			
Remember that you don't need to retype any web address: all of the website addresses noted in this book are found, in interactive format, on the BOOK WEB ADDRESSES document that is on the CD that accompanies this book.			

Supply Chain and Purchasing Questionnaire	
Our company is undertaking a review of our supply chain and procurement policies. We ask that you please complete this questionnaire to help us determine our suppliers, compliance with minimum supply chain requirements. This information may be necessary for our customers, shareholders, investors, or other partners in our supply chain.	Yes/No
Does your company have an environmental and/or sustainability policy or environmental management system? If so, please share a copy with us.	
Does your company have a product stewardship or extended product responsibility policy? If so, please share a copy with us.	
Are your any of your products certified by a 3rd-party certification program (such as Energy Star®, Green Seal, or others)? If so, please provide us with details.	
Does your company follow an industry Code of Conduct or set of standards? If so, please provide us with details.	
Is there any external verification of your adherence to the standards? If so, please provide us with details.	
Can you track your products or materials back through a chain of custody to their raw material source? If so, please provide us with details.	
Do you have packaging guidelines that reinforce the need for recycled materials in all packaging? If so, please provide us with details.	
Do you and your suppliers comply with local, state, national, and international labor standards, including ILO (International Labor Organization) standards? If so, please provide us with details.	
Can you certify that all products or materials have been produced without child or forced labor? If so, please provide us with details.	
Can you certify that your company complies with all existing local, state and national environmental regulations? If so, please provide us with details.	
Do all of your materials or products comply with all hazardous substance regulations, including the Toxic Release Inventory Act? If so, please provide us with details.	
Can you verify the recycled content levels of all of your products or materials? If so, please provide us with details.	
Does any of your energy use come from renewable sources? If so, please provide us with details.	
Would you be willing to work with our company to reduce the environmental impacts of your products or materials?	

Chapter 12

Green Business Building Design

According to the U.S. Department of Energy, there are over 81 million buildings in the United States, and the energy used to heat and power America's buildings consumes enormous amounts of fossil fuels, which, in turn, generates vast amounts of carbon dioxide, the most widespread greenhouse gas. In fact, U.S. buildings consume more energy than any other segment of the economy, including all of our industry and all of our transportation. Buildings are responsible for nearly half (48 percent) of all U.S. greenhouse gas emissions annually, according to the U.S. Energy Information Administration. Incredibly, 76 percent of all electricity generated by U.S. power plants goes to supply the energy needs of buildings, which amounts to over 40 percent of *all* the energy used in America. Beyond the buildings themselves, the construction of buildings is responsible for the release of greenhouse gases in other ways—for example, from construction and demolition debris that degrades in landfills and generates methane, and from the extraction and manufacture of building materials that also generates greenhouse gas emissions. Reducing the energy use and greenhouse gas emissions produced by buildings and their construction is therefore fundamental to the effort to slow the pace of global climate change. Buildings are one of the most important areas to apply green business techniques and find green business opportunities.

Any type of building has the potential to become a green or sustainable building. New buildings—which may be in place for the next 50 to 100 years—can be designed, built, and operated as green buildings from their very start. Existing buildings—many of which are extremely inefficient in their use of energy and ripe for upgrades—can become green through remodeling, retrofitting, and improved operations. Green construction methods can be integrated into buildings at any stage—from design and construction, through to renovation, and eventual demolition (and hopefully, even through the reuse of its materials).

By greening your business's building, whether by remodeling and upgrading or by expanding into a new building, you'll find that there are many significant potential benefits. Green buildings provide a wide range of environmental advantages. They can enhance and protect biodiversity and ecosystems in which they are located, actually improving air and water quality of their communities. Their design can reduce waste and conserve and restore natural resources by careful planning to insure that they are built with every possible green characteristic in mind. Green building design can bring significant economic benefits as well by reducing a building's operating costs, improving the productivity and health of all of its occupants, and optimizing the entire life-cycle economic performance of the building and the businesses that it holds. In addition to the satisfaction of contributing toward a better environment, a healthier workplace, and an improved community, commercial structures that are built green can bring financial rewards.

Obviously, green business buildings are better for the environment. But what's becoming more and more apparent is that they're significantly better for the bottom line. Carbon emissions are one of the most important environmental impacts of a building. These impacts include on-site emissions that result from burning fuel and off-site emissions at the power plant as a consequence of generating the electricity used in the building. Although the impact on the environment from constructing a building can be significant, the accumulated environmental impact of energy consumption, which repeats year after year throughout the lifetime of the building, usually adds up to several times the consequences of its initial construction. On average, about 84 percent of a building's total energy use is consumed during the "use" phase of its life. Office buildings, in particular, consume energy voraciously. In fact, office building energy bills are the highest of any commercial building type. While heating, ventilation, air conditioning, and lighting are still the big power consumers in office buildings, modern office equipment now accounts for almost 16 percent of an office building's energy use. By using the latest design strategies, a 50 percent reduction in energy consumption can become standard practice for a new generation of green buildings. Leading-edge buildings demonstrate that even greater reductions in energy consumption are both possible and cost effective.

Energy efficiency is an excellent reason to build greener, but greater workforce productivity is proving to have an even more significant effect on company profits. In addition to cutting operating costs, green buildings can actually enhance the comfort and performance of workers and boost productivity. Many of the same measures that improve a building's energy performance also make it a more comfortable place to work. Employees benefit from the use of daylighting and nontoxic chemicals, plus better temperature control, ventilation, and indoor air quality. With the high cost of labor, payback on energy features is shortened even further when savings from reduced absenteeism are combined with energy cost savings. Energy-efficient building features also help building owners attract and retain tenants. A green building can dramatically enhance the overall quality of life for everyone connected to the building. Simply put, green buildings are cleaner, fresher, and more comfortable—as well as being energy and cost efficient.

Unfortunately, however, there is a pervasive, but mistaken, assumption that building green will cost significantly more than traditional construction techniques—both when renovating older buildings and constructing new ones. The belief is that introducing green building concepts will simply not provide a healthy return on investment. However, a world-wide survey of 1,400 building professionals, conducted in 2007 by the World Business Council for Sustainable Development, found that the actual costs of building green are vastly overestimated by the building industry.

The average building professional estimated that using green building practices would add, on average, 17 percent to the cost of a building project. The actual average is only 5 percent. In fact, the latest report from the U.N. Intergovernmental Panel on Climate Change estimates that CO_2 emissions from buildings could be reduced by 29 percent over the next 12 years at *no additional cost* over standard building practices. A review of 33 of the most energy-efficient buildings constructed over the last few years in the U.S. found that the cost of including green attributes in the buildings actually averaged only 1.8 percent over traditional construction. And this is just a consideration of the initial cost. Most of the savings attributed to green buildings are in their dramatically lower operating costs and higher occupant productivity. The potential value of health and productivity gains in green building alone is estimated to be as high as $170 billion annually.

At the heart of high performance commercial building is the need to integrate green parameters at all stages of development—from concept and design through construction and occupancy. Green buildings incorporate efficient lighting and daylighting systems, as well as advanced windows, roofing, insulation, and mechanical and ventilation systems. These high-performance building designs also consider the use of renewable energy systems, water conservation features, recycling and waste management systems, and environmentally sensitive building products and systems.

In existing buildings, renovations that replace older systems with more efficient technology can easily yield savings of up to 30 percent, with the same positive impact on building costs and comfort. A quick way to realize savings of 10 percent or more—at little or no cost—is to effectively operate and maintain existing systems. Energy-efficient behavior, such as turning off lights when leaving a room, helps reduce energy use. Automated controls like occupancy sensors and programmable thermostats ensure reduced energy use in unoccupied offices or infrequently used areas like conference rooms. By implementing all of the energy-efficiency concepts that were outlined in Chapter 6, energy use and operating costs of existing buildings can be dramatically reduced, often by much more than 30 percent.

Whether you are planning a new building or upgrading an older one, the use of green building practices and techniques will prove to be an excellent investment that will continue to reap financial, productivity, health, and environmental benefits far into the future.

Green Building Incentive Programs

Offsetting the small initial cost premiums that green building may entail are a host of private and government incentives. Utility companies often give cash incentives to encourage energy and water efficiency, and different levels of government offer tax, financial, and other incentives, such as fast-tracking the building approval process or waiving building permit fees. The State of California, for example, offers up to $300,000 per project to spur the construction of high-performance nonresidential buildings. Cities such as New York, Chicago, and many others offer tax incentives for energy-efficient buildings. And the federal government, for now at least, offers a 10 percent tax credit for commercial solar applications. An overview of a few state's incentive programs shows the range of incentives available.

New York
Available from the New York State Energy Research and Development Authority (**www.nyserda.org**) are technical assistance, loans, and incentives to help offset the initial cost of energy-saving designs and equipment. The state is also in the process of developing a tax credit program for sustainable design. Information on the program is available at **www.dec.state.ny.us**.

New Jersey
New Jersey sponsors the SmartStart Building Program and the New Jersey Clean Energy Program. Both programs were set up by the Board of Public Utilities to encourage the use of energy-efficient equipment and renewable resources. The SmartStart Building Program (**www.njcleanenergy.com/commercial-industrial/ programs/nj-smartstart-buildings**) offers equipment rebates and design assistance and is administered by the local utility company. The Clean Energy program (**www.njcleanenergy.com**) provides rebates for renewable and low emission equipment such as wind, photovoltaics, and fuel cells.

Pennsylvania

Pennsylvania supports green design through the Governor's Green Government Council (**www.gggc.state.pa.us**). The purpose of this program is to facilitate the incorporation of environmentally sustainable practices into state projects. In addition, under electricity deregulation, individual utilities were each required to set up "Sustainable Energy Funds" to promote energy conservation and the use of clean and renewable energy.

Connecticut

Connecticut offers grants and other support for renewable energy technologies through the Connecticut Clean Energy Fund (**www.ctcleanenergy.com**). Eligible technologies include solar, wind, biomass, and fuel cells. It also offers numerous property, sales, and use tax exemptions for renewable energy use.

Oregon

Oregon's Business Energy Tax Credit, administered by the State Office of Energy, provides a tax credit of 50 percent of the eligible project costs for high-efficiency combined heat and power or renewable energy projects; and a credit of 35 percent of the eligible project costs—the initial cost of the system or equipment that's beyond standard practice—for all other green building practices and upgrades. Please see **www.oregon.gov/energy/cons/bus/betc.shtml**.

Nearly all states offer some type of assistance for green building technologies. In recent years, such legislation has been at the forefront of government efforts to encourage energy conservation and efficiency. These very valuable incentives can often more than offset any additional costs for upgrading new or existing construction for greater efficiency. For information on other various state and federal tax and other energy efficiency incentives, please see the Database for State Incentives for Renewables and Efficiency at **www.dsireusa.org**.

Green Building Rating Programs

In recent years, the development of systematic methods to measure the green building attributes of both new construction and building renovation have offered builders and designers a set of clear guidelines to follow. To date, 15 states have passed legislation regarding the use of green building rating systems, primarily for state-funded construction projects. Two of the most commonly used green building rating systems in the United States are the Green Building Initiative's (GBI) Green Globes program and the U.S. Green Building Council's Leadership in Energy and Environmental Design (LEED) program. The Greenguard Environmental Institute and others also offer green building certification programs (see Appendix B).

The Green Building Initiative Green Globes™ Program

The Green Globes system is a relatively new rating system in America, having been introduced in the United States in 2004. It was adapted from a Canadian protocol of the same name. The Green Globes system is a green management tool that includes an assessment protocol, rating system, and a guide for integrating environmentally friendly design into commercial buildings. It also facilitates recognition of the project through third-party review and assessment. Designed for use on building projects of any size, the Green Globes system is suitable for everything from large and small offices and multifamily structures, to institutional buildings such as schools, universities, and libraries. The Green Globes system is an online, questionnaire-driven program. At each stage of the design process, users are walked through a logical sequence of questions that guide their next steps and provide guidance for integrating important elements of sustainability. The construction documents questionnaire is the basis for the rating system, however, buildings cannot be promoted as having achieved a Green Globes rating until a GBI-authorized assessment takes place. This third-party assessment process takes place in two stages. The first stage includes a review of the construction documents developed through the design process. The second stage includes a walk-through of the building post-construction. The online self-assessment is priced at $500 per self-assessment, which is, at least initially, less expensive than other rating systems. To have a building third-party verified at the walk-through stage costs an additional average of $4,000 to $5,000.

Green Globes encourages designers to consider the elements of green design and sustainability early in the project. Because it generates a report written in plain language, Green Globes also promotes interaction between the building designers and client. Among its other attributes, it introduces users to the idea of incorporating life cycle assessments into the decision-making process for resource and material selection, and encourages the use of EPA's EnergyStar Target Finder for developing building energy benchmarks. Because of its flexibility, the Green Globes program is easy to apply to smaller, lower budget buildings—smaller projects that can't justify an expensive complete assessment. You can also perform the assessment in-house (or anywhere there's Internet access), allowing you to try several schematics to see which offers the best results. Depending on the region, building a structure to comply with Green Globes normally adds only between 1 and 2 percent more to the design and construction costs for most projects. This innovative system has been recommended through laws passed in Arkansas and Maryland, which recommend either LEED or Green Globes, and other states which recommend using either LEED or another equally rigorous standard—which includes Green Globes. For more information on the Green Building Initiative and Green Globes rating system, please see **www.thegbi.org/commercial**.

U.S. Green Building Council LEED® Program

One of the most widespread and accepted sustainability frameworks for buildings is called Leadership in Energy and Environmental Design or LEED. Developed by the U.S. Green Building Council, LEED is a voluntary, consensus-based rating system that awards different levels of green building certification based on total credit points earned. It is a certification system that deals with the environmental performance of buildings based on overall characteristics of the project and gives credits for incorporating specific sustainable design strategies into a building's overall design and construction.

The various design-strategy categories for this system include sustainable sites; water efficiency; energy and atmosphere considerations; materials and resources; indoor environmental quality; and the innovation and design process. The LEED system can be applied to every building type and phase of a building life cycle. Commercial buildings, as defined by standard building codes, are eligible for certification under the LEED for New Construction, LEED for Existing Buildings, LEED for Commercial Interiors, LEED for Retail, LEED for Schools, and LEED for Core & Shell rating systems. Building types include offices, retail and service establishments, institutional buildings (such as libraries, schools, museums, and religious institutions), hotels and residential buildings of four or more habitable stories. Every type of business-oriented building in the U.S. is eligible to be assessed and certified as a LEED project. Many of the most cutting-edge environmentally sound building projects in the U.S. are seeking LEED certification, and hundreds of commercial buildings have already achieved it.

The LEED system is a performance-oriented rating system where building projects earn points for satisfying criteria designed to address specific environmental impacts inherent in the design, construction, operations, and management of a building. The program provides ratings that can award a building with a LEED-certified, Silver, Gold, or Platinum rating, depending on the overall efficiency of the design and construction. LEED-Online allows projects to submit all of their documentation online. The cost for LEED certification at around $2,250 for new construction of under 50,000 square feet.

The LEED program has set the standard for green building certification in the U.S. and has established green building design and construction as a central aspect for all future building construction. Later in this chapter, you will use a Green Building Action Worksheet that is based, in part, on many of the standards that are used in the LEED green building certification process. For more information on the LEED certification program and for downloadable checklists regarding the various rating programs for different building types, please see **www.usgbc.org**.

New Green Building Construction

If you are considering a new building for your business, you have a choice of building or leasing. If you decide that leasing is the better alternative, the greening of your leased property is discussed later in this chapter. Should you decide that your business needs an entirely new home, the best time to begin thinking about energy, water, and transportation efficiencies for the new building is well before you have even thought of the design. Whatever the size of your new building, you can incorporate the latest green concepts and technologies into your plans at little or no initial cost over traditional building, and you will be reaping the rewards for the entire life of the building. The sooner that you begin your planning, the easier and cheaper it will be to incorporate green techniques into your overall plans.

Initially, you will need to set a scope and budget for your new green construction plan. Seeking certification for your building from the start will help you understand the savings that green buildings can achieve. The LEED program has downloadable checklists for new building construction that will provide you with a clear overview of the various practices that are considered in the ratings certification process. The Green Globes program provides for free use of their assessment program for 30 days to evaluate your building design. See their respective websites for more details. Additionally, it is wise to perform a cost analysis for any green building project that will allow you to look at various building scenarios and evaluate the costs and benefits of each. You will most likely be pleasantly surprised to see, in real terms, the overall cost and energy benefits that can be obtained by using green building techniques for your new construction project. Tools to assist you in this regard are outlined later in this chapter.

Whole Building Green Design

A key strategy in green building is to consider your building as a whole system. Most people, including most building and design professionals, are not used to considering a building as an entire working system. They generally look at each individual component of a building as a separate unit—such as the roofing, walls, floors, heating and air conditioning system, etc.—and, in doing so, miss the enormous potential synergies that can be realized by viewing the building as an whole. Designing the building as an entire integrated system from the very start offers the best opportunities for efficiencies and cost savings. Additionally, by examining the entire life cycle of a building, designers are finding it easier to maximize the potential of individual green technologies and innovations. Buildings embody tremendous amounts of energy, from their construction through their choice of materials. By using an integrated whole-system approach from the very beginning, you will be better able to secure the most benefits from green building.

Site Selection and Development

The choice of where to locate a new building can have a major effect on its long-term environmental impacts. The overall building efficiencies can be entirely offset if the building's site is causing harm to the environment. Construction that interferes with water flows, displaces wetlands, damages local biodiversity, or requires extensive paving can counter all of the other green characteristics that a building provides. Poor construction practices that allow extensive erosion and runoff into the local watershed can also cancel many of the green benefits of sustainable building. Design of the building landscaping is also important for insuring that the site's overall impact on the local environment is minimized. Selection of a building site that has access to natural light and shade can also lower the long-term energy costs for the building. This phase of the design process should also take community and transportation needs into consideration. How the building impacts its environment, community, and region are important concerns for maximizing potential benefits.

Materials Use

The selection of which building materials to use for the construction and, in fact, where to obtain them can also have an enormous impact on the overall environmental footprint of a new building. Construction that uses recycled or renewable resources is more sustainable than projects that do not. The use of materials that are found and generated locally can also lower the overall environmental impact, and often, the cost of the building. The use of the least harmful and most nontoxic materials available is also a basic consideration in green building. The health and safety of employees and occupants are directly related to the choice of materials that go into the construction of the building. By choosing the materials wisely and considering their long-term use from the start of the project, you can ensure that the environmental impacts will be the least possible for your green building. The Greenguard Environmental Institute operates an extensive building products certification program for interior products, particularly products with low emissions of toxic or hazardous chemicals. For more on this program, see **www.greenguard.org**.

Building Systems

Advance planning of your building's various systems—lighting, heat/air conditioning, plumbing, electrical, and mechanical—to be certain that they incorporate the latest green design attributes and technologies will help ensure that your building will be efficient well into the future. Consideration of how these various building systems will be integrated into the total overall design of the building will help maximize their potential efficiency. For example, clever use of daylighting techniques (the use of natural light from windows and skylights) can have a dramatic impact on how your lighting systems will be designed. By lowering your overall lighting needs and intensity, and thus lowering heat gains associated with the lighting, you will be able to downsize your air conditioning system. Lowering your cooling needs can save energy and, for water-cooled systems, dramatically lower your water and sewer costs. By applying a holistic approach to both the exterior and interior design of your building, you can reap additional savings that are lost in the traditional design process.

Energy Efficiency

The area where some of the most important savings can be found in green design and building are in saving energy and lowering a building's emissions. As noted in Chapter 6, the costs of carbon emissions will be increasing, perhaps dramatically, in the coming years as the world begins to come to grips with the need to halt CO_2 buildup in the atmosphere. Businesses of all sizes will begin to feel both governmental and consumer pressure to pay attention to their carbon emissions and energy consumption. Rapidly rising energy costs also provide a direct incentive to design and build any new structures using the most advanced techniques available. Buildings are, today, being built that are effectively energy and carbon neutral, both by incorporating advanced energy efficiency technologies into the original design and construction of the building and by using on-site solar and wind technologies to provide direct renewable energy for the building.

Using Green Building Professionals

In order to reap the most benefits from any green building project, you should locate and rely upon building industry professionals who are up-to-date on the most valuable and advanced techniques and technologies. Engineers, architects, consultants, and construction professionals around the country are beginning to specialize in green building. One good source for locating professionals who are accredited in green building techniques is the Green Building Certification Institute. This program provides a searchable database of over 50,000 professionals who have passed a rigorous examination process on green building techniques, particularly focused on the LEED program. Over 10,000 architects, 3,500 engineers, and 2,000 project managers around the country have been certified by this organization. For more information, see **www.gbci.org**.

Green Building Remodeling

Many of the same considerations that apply to new building also apply if you are planning to renovate an existing building to incorporate green building concepts. Green remodeling and renovation can save and actually make money for your business. Naturally, there will be significant long-term energy savings, but the cost to implement green features into your project is often even less than conventional construction. Green upgrades also significantly increase the resale value of your property, generally far more than the cost of the upgrade itself. Installing energy-efficient upgrades that save money or energy-producing equipment that generates renewable energy for your business is very cheap insurance against the increasingly rapid escalation of energy prices. The value of increased occupant productivity is also a direct and often immediate benefit to your green building remodeling projects.

By rebuilding or renovating older buildings, you will also be minimizing the environmental costs associated with providing all of the new materials necessary to construct a new building. Your community will benefit, too, from the redevelopment and improvement of its commercial building stock. Upgrading the efficiency of older buildings provides an immediate reduction in the carbon emissions associated with that building. Moving to a new building and building it with green principles in mind—while certainly a distinct improvement over conventional building—leaves the former building in place, with all of its inefficient characteristics intact.

Although site selection is not a consideration (unless you are moving to a building to be renovated), the same careful whole-systems design process should be used in any green renovation project. The retrofitting of energy and water efficiency equipment into existing building has been previously covered in Chapters 6 and 7 of this book. You should seek certification of your building renovation plans if they are extensive, and you should certainly consider the retention of qualified green building planning personnel from the very beginning of the planning stage of your project. Later in this chapter you will find an overview of the various tools that are available to assist you in evaluating the costs and benefits of various green building upgrades and remodeling scenarios. Also later in this chapter you will find a Green Building Action Worksheet that outlines an array of ideas and practices that can be effectively incorporated into any of your green renovation projects. In addition, Appendix B provides many additional resources for green building.

Greening Your Leased Property

Even if the building you are occupying is leased, green building actions can be taken during the development and negotiation of the lease as well as after it is signed. These actions can affect the outfitting of the building and furnishing of the leased space as well as operations and maintenance procedures after occupancy. It is best to introduce green concepts during the earliest stages of building selection and lease negotiation. The range of actions that can be taken by building managers may be limited by lease agreements, but, even with these constraints, many operations and maintenance practices can be implemented to improve the environmental performance of leased buildings. The issues relating to the ongoing operation and maintenance of leased buildings are virtually identical to those of owned buildings. The difference lies in who has the responsibility to tackle these issues. As the lessee of a building and the one who is responsible for the energy bills, you have the greatest incentive to insist on green building performance.

Reducing energy use and costs in a leased space can be challenging, particularly since workers and tenants are often unaware of actual building expenses. It is becoming increasingly feasible to require green elements in building leases. The U.S. Green Building Council has developed a LEED rating system for Commercial Interiors and Renovations that will be helpful in guiding lease negotiations and building upgrade designs.

Even before you sign the lease there are positive steps that you can take to ensure that you will have the maximum opportunities for green improvements. For example, before leasing a building, you can conduct a detailed survey of all energy and environmental issues to select a building that is—or can become—an energy-efficient building. You can, in advance, plan and identify strategies for greening the facility. If you are searching for a building, you can include a preference for buildings having the Energy Star, Green Globe, or LEED certification as part of the selection criteria for acquiring leased buildings. If you are in a build-to-suit lease situation, the lease can contain criteria encouraging sustainable design and development, energy efficiency, and verification of building performance. Some of the criteria that can be addressed in a commercial lease are:

Indoor Air Quality

One of the greatest contributors to poor indoor environmental quality and poor health is an improperly designed, sized, installed, and maintained HVAC system. Along with addressing equipment selection (if that is an option), a lease should address HVAC maintenance: filter changing, control system inspection, air/water system balancing, etc. Interior finishes can also cause air quality problems. With leased space, look for low-emission materials, especially paints, wall coverings, carpets and carpet padding, adhesives, sealants, varnishes, particleboard, and furnishings. Require low-VOC materials (volatile organic chemicals, such as paints, lacquers, and varnishes) in the lease terms; most are cost-competitive with traditional materials. Other requirements can include timing the construction so that VOC-emitting materials are applied before materials that might absorb the vapors (such as carpet) are installed and thorough cleaning of duct work that might have become contaminated during construction.

Energy Consumption

Depending on the lease provisions, energy consumption of the building can vary greatly. If you are leasing an entire building you may be in a position to require substantial upgrades, including modifications to the heating, ventilation, and air conditioning system, addition of an energy management system, or the installation of improved T-8 or T-5 fluorescent lighting. All of these energy-efficiency upgrades can dramatically affect your operating costs. For example, extensive lighting retrofits or window replacements can significantly reduce your heat or air conditioning loads, enabling equipment to be downsized or operated more efficiently.

Water Use

Older leased buildings probably have old plumbing fixtures that use considerably more water than today's standards. During renovations of restrooms, replace fixtures or valves with low-flow products. When upgrading faucets and urinals, products can be installed that significantly reduce water use. Ensuring that malfunctioning and leaking fixtures are quickly repaired can also greatly reduce water consumption.

Materials

In addition to specifying low-VOC finishes, requirements can include salvage or the recycling of materials being removed during renovation; reuse of certain existing materials (such as ceiling grid systems, doors, and wood flooring); installation of materials with high recycled content (such as carpet and insulation); the use of natural and biobased products (such as natural-fiber upholstery and straw particleboard); and the use of only certified sustainable wood products when wood is specified.

Recycling Programs

Reducing the environmental impacts of buildings, whether leased or owned, can be helped greatly by controlling the generation of waste. Paper waste accounts for the greatest quantity of solid waste generated. The implementation of recycling programs is fairly straightforward, though you'll need to ensure that programs are being successfully carried out and that materials collected for recycling are actually being recycled. If you are leasing, you can work with the building's owners to coordinate your efforts with that of other lessees, perhaps combining your recycled waste to obtain a better market price.

Transportation

Access to public transportation should be considered when selecting a building to lease. Reducing the need for employees to use private automobiles can significantly improve the overall greenness of your chosen building. In negotiating parking spaces in the lease, preferred parking for carpools can be included as well as secure bicycle storage. Consider offering employee incentives to encourage commuting by other than private automobiles and reduce the amount of parking required.

Green Building Cost Analysis

The economic analysis of green building projects can become a very complex process. A number of very valuable tools have been designed to help you effectively evaluate the various aspects of your particular project and even to look at different construction scenarios and choose the one with the most overall benefits.

Building Life-Cycle Cost Software
The Building Life-Cycle Cost software from the National Institute of Standards and Technology can be used to evaluate alternative designs that have higher initial costs but lower operating-related costs over a project life compared with the lowest-initial-cost design. It is especially useful for evaluating the costs and benefits of energy and water conservation and renewable energy projects. The life-cycle costs of two or more alternative designs are computed and compared to determine which has the lowest life-cycle cost and is therefore more economical in the long run. A further discussion of the program is provided in Chapter 6. This software is available at **www1.eere.energy.gov/femp/information/download_blcc.html**.

eBids Database
The Energy Building Investment Decision Support (eBIDS) database is made available by the Carnegie-Mellon University Center for Building Performance and Diagnostics with funding from the U.S. Department of Energy. This web-based tool illustrates the benefits of daylighting, high performance electric lighting, mixed mode HVAC, commissioning, underfloor air, and cool roofs. This free website also provides detailed case study information with return on investment data. You can use this tool at **http://cbpd.arc.cmu.edu/ebids**.

eVALUator
This free software program is available from Energy Design Resources and can be used to calculate the life-cycle benefits of investments that improve building design. It analyzes the financial benefits from buildings that reduce energy cost, raise employee productivity, and enhance tenant satisfaction. This program is available for download at **www.energydesignresources.com/resource/131**.

A number of additional software programs for green building cost analysis are available and are outlined in Appendix B.

Green Building Plan

The process of greening your building, whether you are upgrading an existing building, greening a leased space, or planning the construction of a new building is a four-step process of Assess, Plan, Analyze, and Implement.

①The first step in the process of greening your building is to conduct a comprehensive assessment of your current building. Earlier, in Chapter 6, you prepared a Business Carbon Footprint Worksheet that measured your company's carbon emissions from purchased energy. That basic carbon footprint provided you with a baseline from which to better understand your current building's use of energy. The worksheets that you prepared in Chapters 7 and 8 regarding your current water use and waste reduction practices will also provide you with an awareness of where efficiency efforts can best be applied in those areas. Portions of your business travel and transportation assessments, performed in Chapter 9, will also provide information that can be used in your green building efforts to lower transportation costs and emissions. If you are planning a new building that you wish to have constructed using green building techniques and materials, you should consult the green building certification programs (Green Globe or LEED) and look over their various checklists to determine the elements of sustainable building that you would like to apply to your building.

② On the basis of your various earlier assessments of energy and water use, and waste management and transportation practices, you should then formulate a green building action plan. The Green Building Action Worksheet that is provided outlines a wide range of ways to lessen the building portion of your business's environmental footprint. This worksheet is divided into separate areas for consideration: preliminary considerations, site selection, water efficiency, energy efficiency, materials and resources, business systems, and indoor air quality. Most of these areas apply equally to new construction activities as well as existing building upgrades (with the notable exception of site selection). Many of these ideas also apply to the greening of leased property as well. Incorporate as many as possible of the appropriate actions for your green building project into your overall business environmental plan. Choose those actions that are applicable to your particular building plans. If your plans are for renovations, your plan should be revisited and, if necessary, revised at least on an annual basis. If your project is a new building, be sure that you have considered methods to monitor the energy use, water use, and waste management aspects of your new building to be certain that it is living up to expectations.

③ Evaluate your possible actions on a sound economic basis over a long term, not simply by considering the initial cost of investment, but the entire life cycle of the building investment. A simple economic analysis worksheet for building upgrades is provided at the end of this chapter for an analysis of relatively modest improvements. For more extensive remodeling cost analyses and for cost/benefit analyses of new green building construction, you will need to use much more sophisticated approaches to obtain usable data. Please see the section on green building cost analysis earlier in this chapter for more details. Also check out the various cost evaluation tools that are noted in Appendix B.

④ The final step is to actually implement the plan. Someone in the company should be given the responsibility to implement and oversee your green building plans. The following worksheet is available on the enclosed CD as both a PDF form that may be printed out for your use in developing your company's own green building action plan and also as a text form. The text version of this worksheet may be used to cut and paste the action steps that you choose into your overall company environmental plan. See Chapter 18 for more details. Many additional green building resources are found in Appendix B.

The following Green Building Actions have been compiled from many sources, including, in part, the standards that have been developed by the U.S. Green Building Council for the LEED new construction and existing buildings certification programs.

Green Building Action Worksheet

Preliminary Considerations	Do? Yes/No
Engage accredited green building design professionals from the early stages of the project. See **www.gbci.org** for a list of qualified personnel.	
Make sure that you apply a whole-building design approach to your planning, even if you are simply remodeling or renovating a building.	
You may wish to seek green building certification for your green building project. See LEED, Green Globes, or other certification programs in this chapter or Appendix B.	
Even if you do not seek formal certification, you (or your design and construction team) may wish to use the valuable tools that such green building certification programs make available.	
As your building plans develop, use the various software green building life-cycle analysis and cost evaluation tools that are available to understand the costs and benefits from various approaches to your green building plans and material use.	
Your building plans should strive to create an efficient floor plan that incorporates as many green building attributes as possible while maintaining, and even enhancing, the building's functionality.	
Your green building plans should incorporate the most advanced energy, water, waste, and other green technologies as possible. Remember that you will be paid back many times over for your initial investments in green building upgrades.	
The site and building design should use passive solar systems whenever possible, including building orientation plans.	
Site Selection	Yes/No
All pollution from the building site should be eliminated by steps to control soil erosion, runoff to storm sewers or local waterways, and dust generation.	
The site should not be located on floodplains, prime farmland, habitat for endangered or threatened species, or wetlands.	
New building construction or renovation of an existing building should be on a previously developed site in a medium- or high-density area that has easy pedestrian, public transportation, and bicycle access, as well as access to basic services.	

If possible, any new building should be developed on a site classified as a brownfield under the U.S. EPA's Sustainable Redevelopment of Brownfields Program. See **www.epa.gov/ brownfields/sustain.htm**.	
If possible choose an infill site that will fill in otherwise unused urban property or a *greyfields* site (an economically depressed or outdated property—typically a vacant old shopping center that is surrounded by a greyfiel' of old asphalt parking lots).	
If possible, the building should be located near commuter rail, subways, or bus stops.	
The building should be designed to be pedestrian and bicyclist friendly and include bike racks and a changing or shower room for pedestrians or bikers.	
If your facility is large enough, install an alternative energy filling station on the site (natural gas, hydrogen, electric vehicle charging stations, etc.).	
If your project is the rehabilitation of an existing building, you should not construct any new parking areas, if possible.	
If your project is a new building, you should only construct sufficient parking to meet the minimum local zoning requirements.	
Preferred parking spaces should be designated for vanpool, carpool, and alternative energy vehicles.	
Any disturbance of the building site should strictly limit the amount of earth disturbance and the clearing of any vegetation to the minimum possible area.	
Site development should avoid any unnecessary soil compaction.	
The site development should not disturb any nearby wetlands, soil, or streams.	
Any disturbance of the building site should be restored to its original (or better) condition as soon as possible after construction.	
Prepare a natural resources inventory of your selected site that catalogs the current status of the area.	
Create a construction site protection plan to protect and preserve the natural habitat and biodiversity as much as possible.	
If the project is for new construction, the building site should be developed to provide the highest possible ratio of open space to developed land in order to minimize the building's disturbance of natural habitat.	

The entire project design should limit erosion and the amount of changes to the site's water runoff capabilities by limiting the total amount of area covered by development (building or pavement).	
Any possible heat island effect should be minimized by using the least possible paved area and by providing shade for any open paved areas.	
Any exterior vegetation that is used should be native and compatible with local vegetation.	
Roofing materials that limit heat buildup should also be employed, preferably by using an Energy Star-compliant roof.	
Light pollution from the development of the site should be minimized as much as possible so that no direct illumination leaves the building site.	
Water Efficiency	
Landscape vegetation should be selected to minimize the use of watering.	
If any irrigation is necessary, it should either be highly efficient drip irrigation, use captured rain water, or use water that is otherwise recycled from the site itself.	
The building should be designed to significantly reduce the amount of water necessary for operation.	
Ideally, the water that is used on the site should not exceed the water that falls on or flows through the site. If water needs exceed the water available, the difference should be purchased from sources that have excess water to sell as long as this process has no damaging impact on the natural systems.	
The quality, temperature, and rate of flow of the water both on-site and leaving the site should have no damaging impact on the natural systems of the watershed.	
Use all of the water efficiency actions noted in Chapter 7 in the design and construction of any new building, including the use of Energy Star-certified equipment wherever possible.	
Consider the use of green roofing techniques to maximize the use of rain water, minimize runoff, and provide natural insulation barriers. Green roofs are totally or partially covered with vegetation. For additional information see **www.greenroofs.com**.	
If local codes permit, separate and reuse greywater.	
If local codes permit, consider composting or waterless toilets.	

Energy Efficiency	
The building should be designed to significantly reduce the amount of energy necessary for operation.	
Ideally, all energy sources used should be 100 percent renewable and the amount of energy used should not exceed the amount of solar, wind, and geothermal energy available on the site itself.	
Consider the use of solar thermal heating systems.	
Use passive solar building techniques whenever possible.	
Use active solar panels or solar photovoltaic roofing systems whenever possible.	
Consider using ground-source geothermal heating/air conditioning systems if your area has sufficient resources.	
Consider using wind power to supplement your building's energy use if your area's wind resources are sufficient.	
Use Energy Star building materials whenever available, such as for windows, doors, fans, etc.	
Any cooling or fire suppression equipment should not use any CFC-based refrigerants, HCFCs, or halons whatsoever.	
Use all of the energy efficiency actions noted in Chapter 6 in the design and construction of any new building.	
Specifically, the following systems should be designed for the maximum possible energy efficiency: lighting, motors, chillers, boilers, heating and air conditioning systems, building ventilation systems.	
Purchase renewable energy from a certified green power supplier. See: **www.green-e.org/about.shtml**.	
Use advanced daylighting techniques combined with modern low energy lighting systems to minimize lighting energy use.	
Materials and Resources	
Ideally, all materials used in the construction should be non-persistent, nontoxic, and procured either from reused, recycled, renewable, or abundant-in-nature sources. Abundant-in-nature sources means that human use of the resources is small compared with the amount of resource available. Examples include iron and steel, glass and silica, and aluminum. (Note: this does not take into account the material's embedded energy—the amount of energy needed to make these raw materials into usable products.)	

Use agricultural byproducts for construction materials if possible, such as soy-based insulation, bamboo, or wood-byproduct materials.	
If wood is used, it should be certified as sustainably harvested by credible certified third-party organizations, such as the Forest Stewardship Council.	
Building materials should be obtained from as near to the building site as possible, preferably locally.	
Use building materials that require minimal or no additional finishing actions to complete.	
Use precut, premanufactured, or panelized construction techniques if the available products are available without long shipping distances.	
Use construction materials for both exterior and interior surfaces that are the most durable available and that require the minimum, or preferably no maintenance for upkeep.	
Use materials that are durable and reusable at the end of their life cycle.	
If possible, reuse materials that have been salvaged from other buildings.	
Choose only non-VOC (volatile organic compound) sealants, finishes, adhesives, carpets, and composite wood products.	
Materials that should be avoided include products using CFCs or HCFCs, products using PVC, products using urea formaldehyde, and any products with persistent bioaccumulative toxic chemicals (PBTs) that may be found in paints, varnishes, caulks, electrical switches, thermostats, solders, and vinyl, etc.	
If available, specify the use of Portland cement with at least a 25 percent fly ash content (up to 60 percent is acceptable).	
Use recycled plastics for signs, parking stops, trash receptacles, benches, tables, bike racks, etc.	
Specify high–recycled content rebar whenever possible.	
Consider 100 percent recycled content roofing materials.	
Use recycled content gypsum wallboard. 95 percent post industrial content wallboard is now available.	
90 percent recycled fiberboard and 100 percent recycled content particleboard are available for nonstructural use.	

Many recycled content flooring products are available.	
Properly dispose of any paints, varnishes, or other chemical compounds used in the construction.	
A whole-building waste management plan should be developed and instituted, including during the construction phase.	
Waste should be minimized and should, ideally, be zero by using efficient design and construction techniques.	
All on-site construction debris should be recycled whenever possible. In larger urban areas, nearly all construction debris can be recycled, including wood, cardboard, metals, drywall, plastics, asphalt roofing, concrete blocks, etc.	
Protect the ground from contamination from any construction materials that may be hazardous.	
During remodeling, separate metals and other recyclable and salvageable materials.	
If vegetation, bushes, or trees must be removed during construction, consider replanting or selling any removable vegetation.	
Building Systems and Indoor Air Quality	
All building systems, such as HVAC, electrical, mechanical, and plumbing should be designed to be complementary when possible and use efficiencies gained in one system to assist another system.	
All equipment purchased for building systems should be as technologically efficient as possible. Energy Star–certified equipment is generally the best choice.	
Provide operable windows in sufficient quantities to allow for adequate ventilation, views, and the use of outside air for cooling or heating purposes.	
Provide that all cleaning materials used are non-toxic and non-hazardous in nature.	
Provide adequate controls for all HVAC and lighting systems to allow them to be shut down or controlled by occupants.	
Install sufficient electric monitoring devices to allow occupants to understand how their activities impact the building's energy use.	
Install CO_2 and other monitoring systems to insure that air quality remains at high levels throughout the building's life.	

Economic Analysis of Building Upgrades

Simple Cost Payback Analysis
In order to make rational business decisions about which basic green building upgrades to make, you may wish to run a simple cost payback analysis. For any extensive remodeling or new construction, you should use some type of building economic analysis software that provides adequate life-cycle cost assessments. Some of these programs were discussed earlier in this chapter and others are noted in Appendix B. You may wish to involve a design professional with green building experience to help you assess the economic aspects of any major projects. The simple methods provided in this section are not adequate to provide you with sufficient information to make a sound business decision for large projects.

In this simplified method, which is only adequate for smaller upgrade projects, the total initial cost of the improvement is divided by the first-year cost savings (energy or otherwise) produced by the improvement. This method yields the number of years required for the improvement to pay for itself. Cost payback analyses can be far more complex and include many other variables.

Simple Return on Investment Analysis
Another standard measure of economic feasibility is the Return on Investment formula. This is a measure of the percentage return provided by a particular investment. The standard formula for Return on Investment (ROI) is:

Net Return / capital cost of investment = percentage return on investment

For the net return figure, you need to determine the life of the investment (in years) and multiply it by net annual savings. Use the net annual savings figure that you generated in the cost payback analysis. Then deduct the initial capital cost.

These formulas can additionally include calculations to discount the dollar amounts over time and other more sophisticated approaches. For example, full life-cycle cost analyses are a more in-depth alternative to return on investment analyses. This simple approach, however, can provide you with a quick and simple way to compare energy efficiency investments with other business investment choices. In addition, remember that there are many other valuable noneconomic benefits to conserving energy in your business.

On the following page, you will find a simple worksheet to use for cost payback and return on investment calculations. This worksheet is provided on the CD that accompanies this book in a fillable PDF format that will do the necessary calculations for you.

Building Upgrade Economic Analysis

Capital Costs

	Equipment Costs	$
+	Prep Work Costs	$
+	Installation Costs	$
=	Total Capital Costs	$

Net Annual Savings

	Annual Avoided Disposal Costs	$
+	Annual Avoided Purchase Costs	$
+	Annual Avoided Energy Costs	$
+	Annual Additional Revenue (if any)	$
=	Total Net Annual Savings	$

Simple Payback Period Analysis

	Capital Costs (from above)	$
÷	Net Annual Savings (from above)	$
=	Payback Period in Years	

Simple Return on Investment Analysis

	Net Annual Savings (from above)	$
x	Life of Investment (in years)	
−	Capital Costs (from above)	$
=	Net Return	$
÷	Capital Costs (from above)	$
=	Return on Investment (over life)	
÷	Life of Investment (in years)	
=	Annual Return on Investment Rate	%

These formulas can additionally include calculations to discount the dollar amounts over time and other more sophisticated approaches. Remember that there are many other valuable noneconomic benefits to energy efficiency in your business.

Chapter 13

Green Product and Service Design

Until this point, this book has concentrated on making your existing business processes and operations better—improving energy efficiency, implementing water conservation techniques, reducing waste, developing better transportation and building efficiencies, and implementing other decidedly green improvements. While all of the principles and practices introduced thus far will allow your business to operate in a much cleaner and greener manner and save you considerable money in the process, the path to becoming a truly sustainable business leads directly to reimagining the true purpose of your business. As you rethink the ultimate purpose of your business, you will begin, almost inevitably, to think of better ways to do things and better ways to provide your customers with the goods and services that your company provides. To truly become a green business is to reinvent your business in a way that aligns it with nature, using inspiration from the natural world to redesign, from the bottom up, what your business produces or provides. Whether it is referred to as green design, eco-design, industrial ecology, sustainable design, or design for the environment, the process of totally rethinking the design and delivery of your products and services to your customers is at the heart of creating a sustainable business. We'll use the term *green design* to describe the concept of rethinking your business from a natural perspective.

The process of green design is not one of incremental improvements in efficiency, although these steps are, of course, extremely valuable. Nor is green design limited to only a consideration of where you are in the stream that takes your product or service to its ultimate customers. Green design requires a deep look at the entire life cycle of a product, from raw material to the end of its life, and a search for every possible way to lessen the overall impact of the product or service on the natural world. For green design to be successful, it has to be at the heart of your business—a permanent and integral part of your overall green business strategy.

One of the goals of green design is to dramatically increase the services that we wring out of the natural resources used by our human society. Our industrial civilization wastes tremendous amounts of water, energy, minerals, lumber, soil, and all of the other natural resources upon which modern industrial society is based and upon which our civilization ultimately depends. Massive quantities of both renewable and nonrenewable resources are consumed, and disposed of, in ways that are not sustainable, even in the short term. The damage inflicted on the earth's environment by such wasteful consumption of resources has harmed every system and natural function on the planet—fresh and sea water, soil, plant and animal life, the earth's climate, and the very air that we breathe. Even if every business on earth instituted all of the earlier green ideas and practices outlined thus far in this book, our society, as presently constituted, could not sustain itself in the long run.

Why? Because present-day industrial society simply does not operate using the right set of rules. The economic system that has developed over the past few centuries is based on a very human-centered view of nature—a view that does not take into account the enormous damage that human civilization inflicts on the natural world. Our economic system judges the success of our society by the total value of the goods and services provided, with no differentiation as to the positive or negative impacts resulting from those goods or services. For example, our national system of accounting does not count oil spills as a negative. In fact, the efforts to clean up such a spill and the money that such a cleanup ultimately costs is counted as an economic positive and is simply added to our nation's Gross Domestic Product calculation, seemingly raising the overall value of our society. The money spent on treating and disposing of toxic waste and the health care costs attributable to our dirty air and water are, likewise, counted as positive entries in our national accounting system. Collapsing fisheries and rampant deforestation are all counted as having added to our national wealth. As the late Bobby Kennedy eloquently explained, in words that ring just as true today as when he spoke them over 40 years ago: "Our gross national product—if we should judge America by that—counts air pollution and cigarette advertising, and ambulances to clear our highways of carnage. It counts special locks for our doors and the jails for those who break them. It counts the destruction of our redwoods and the loss of our natural wonder in chaotic sprawl. It counts napalm and the cost of a nuclear warhead, and armored cars for police who fight riots in our streets. It counts Whitman's rifle and Speck's knife, and the television programs which glorify violence in order to sell toys to our children. Yet the gross national product does not allow for the health of our children, the quality of their education, or the joy of their play. It does not include the beauty of our poetry or the strength of our marriages; the intelligence of our public debate or the integrity of our public officials. It measures neither our wit nor our courage; neither our wisdom nor our learning; neither our compassion nor our devotion to our country; it measures everything, in short, except that which makes life worthwhile."

The Concepts Behind Green Design

To achieve a truly sustainable society, we need to operate by an entirely different set of rules—rules that have already been honed to perfection by billions of years of development and refinement—the set of rules that govern nature and life.

Nature knows no waste. The by-products of natural systems serve as the food for other systems. The vast array of life that has blossomed and flourished on our planet is powered by one source of energy—the sun. As Janine Benyus, author of *Biomimicry: Innovation Inspired by Nature,* notes, life itself creates the conditions that are conducive to more life: "What surrounds us is the secret to survival." We need to understand the underlying rules that govern nature and redesign our civilization to live by those rules—without question an enormous task, but, considering the alternative, one well worth undertaking. We looked briefly at some of the basic conceptual frameworks behind green business earlier in Chapter 3. To understand green design requires a more detailed examination of these theories.

The Natural Step

The attempt to understand nature's rules was behind the efforts of Dr. Karl Henrik Robèrt to develop the *Natural Step for Business.* As noted in Chapter 3, he identified four conditions that he believed must be met for any society to be sustainable:

*   The natural world should not be subjected to increased concentrations of substances extracted from the Earth's crust (i.e., minerals, oil, gas, etc.)

*   The natural world should not be subjected to increased concentrations of substances produced by society (such as PCBs, insecticides, nuclear waste, and other chemicals or compounds not found in nature)

*   The natural world should not be subjected to degradation of its capacity for renewal (such as by overfishing the oceans, destroying topsoil, deforestation, mountaintop-removal mining and other similar activities)

*   Humanity should not be subjected to conditions that systematically undermine their capacity to meet their needs (most particularly abject poverty)

How to achieve this ideal is the goal of green design. Instead of merely focusing on the treatment of air and water pollution after it has been created or on the recycling of waste that is already produced, green design encourages a fundamental redesign of the products themselves and the manufacturing processes that create them. Products and services can be redesigned to entirely eliminate the concept of waste. They can be designed to be completely taken apart and reused in order to extend the useful lives of the materials and energy that were necessary to create them, thus reducing and even eliminating the need to extract raw materials in the first place. Likewise, benign chemicals can be effectively substituted for their toxic or hazardous counterparts, eliminating any need to handle or dispose of the toxins and removing the dangers they pose to humans or the environment that we share with the rest of the natural world.

Natural Capitalism

These same conceptual ideas were eloquently advanced by Paul Hawken, Amory Lovins, and L. Hunter Lovins, in the framework that they described as the 'next industrial revolution.' Their four tenets of *Natural Capitalism* meshed elegantly with the Natural Step and further reinforced the idea that there was a different way to view the task of business, a new way to look at the idea of commerce—a way to align business and commerce with the realities and lessons of the natural world. If human capital is regarded as all of the goods and services provided by humanity, then *natural capital* is all of the goods and services that are provided by nature— the fundamental building blocks upon which all life, and by extension, our entire economic system, is built. This natural capital is the vast array of services that nature provides—the photosynthesis that greens plants, the production of oxygen that enhances the atmosphere, the nutrient cycle that enriches the soil, the pollination that fertilizes crops, the natural systems of flood control and protection from soil erosion. Further, it is the myriad natural products themselves—clean water, fresh air, forests and fields, the animals of the land and sea—and all the other attributes of the natural world that are currently given no value in our economic system.

Natural capitalism, then, is a theoretical framework on how the world of human capital could be brought into alignment with the world of natural capital and what that alignment would look like. Their first natural capitalism concept of radically increased resource productivity—how we can do so much more with dramatically less impact on the natural world—was addressed in the earlier chapters of this book regarding energy, materials, and water efficiency, and waste reduction. Eco-efficiency, as this process is sometimes defined, is the first—and an extremely vital—step on the road to sustainability in business. Every ounce of use must be wrung out of every natural resource that we put in service for humanity. Resource productivity can halt the current overuse of resources caused by the failure to understand the foolish inefficiencies of our current systems of production.

Their second natural capitalism concept of biomimicry—harmonizing our industrial systems with biological concepts—is also an integral part of the process of green design. It is a natural extension of their first concept of resource efficiency. By using nature as its guide and teacher, business can begin to develop a fully efficient industrial system—a system that mimics the abundantly successful model that nature has provided. The natural systems of life constantly reuse materials in closed loops with waste being merely a passage into another process in the loop. How to emulate the brilliant designs and systems that nature has provided is the key to the success of this step in the process.

Their third concept of natural capitalism is the innovative idea that perhaps business should deliver services rather than products to fulfill many of the needs of society. Do we really need to own a car, or would the ability to move from one location to another be enough to satisfy our needs? Fully adopting the first two concepts of resource efficiency and biomimicry leads naturally to an approach to commerce that closes the loop of material use and enhances our use of resources. One of the most effective ways to institute a closed-loop system may be to provide customers with services and for business to retain the ownership of the products themselves. Providing services may well be the future of commerce as we begin to prize and protect our natural capital.

Fourth in their framework of natural capitalism is the concept of actual investment in natural capital. The protection and expansion of all of the various processes and services that nature supplies, through restorative investment, is a vital component of the next industrial revolution and the final step in our progress toward sustainability. When humanity finally begins to fully restore and, indeed, expand the natural capital of our world, the future of sustainability may finally be in view.

Cradle-to-Cradle Design and Green Chemistry

The natural world has developed in such a way that materials are endlessly reused in a vast array of processes. Organic material decays and is reused by a panoply of insects and microbes, that, in turn, create a new set of materials to be used by other members of the natural world. At each stage in the natural process, something has developed to exploit the resources that nature provides. In human industry, this same technique can be used to develop products that are endlessly (in human terms, at least) reused. The key is to begin to examine the entire life-cycle of the products of human invention—from their raw materials through the end use—and redesign that life-cycle to be a continuous loop, or in the terms of innovative architect, William McDonough, and green chemist, Michael Braungart, in a *cradle-to-cradle* design. Their concept is that products can be designed with components that are either "biological nutrients" that can easily reenter the natural ecosystem without causing any harm to water, air, or soil; or "technical nutrients" that can circulate continually as valuable components in a technological closed-loop system.

The cradle-to-cradle concept is based, further, on a set of pragmatic principles that identify various steps in the process of designing products for a closed-loop system.

Products should be designed that are free of any and all known chemicals and compounds that are hazardous or toxic. McDonough and Braungart describe this as putting a "filter" into the head of the designer, instead of at the end of a pipe or the top of a smokestack. By using knowledge to filter out problems in advance, many issues related to pollution and contamination can be avoided.

Their next concept explores the idea that we can't know the consequences of all of the various environmental choices that we are called upon to make in the greening of a business. Even the choice of which materials to use in a given product is hampered by our lack of fundamental knowledge regarding many materials that are in common use. We are all called upon to make choices between two less-than-ideal options. But we all must begin somewhere, and the "best" somewhere, according to McDonough and Braungart, is to become informed to the fullest extent possible and then make decisions based on that knowledge, with a respect for the difficulties involved in making such choice, all while retaining a sense of wonder and delight. This may be, at once, one of the most realistic and difficult steps in the process of greening your business.

Another important aspect of green and cradle-to-cradle design is to develop products that are the least harmful to living things and the environment. Modern products contain an enormous array of materials, many of which are composites, compounds, or chemicals not found in the natural world. Many of these human-created materials have caused profound damage to our global ecosystem and its inhabitants. Products and by-products that contain compounds that mimic animal and human hormones, known as endocrine disruptors, are of particular concern as they can inhibit or disrupt the fertility of animals and humans with devastating effects on birth and reproduction. How can toxic, hazardous, and otherwise dangerous chemicals be kept out of our products?

One response to this question has come from chemists themselves, in the guise of *green chemistry*. Green chemistry is the use of chemistry in the design and manufacture of products to reduce or eliminate the use of hazardous substances at their source. A number of green chemistry principles and concepts have been developed to quantify its use. As you can see, the following principles of green chemistry are designed to adhere to the rules that nature has already developed:

- Design chemical processes to prevent and eliminate waste.

- Design chemicals to be safer, fully effective, but with little or no toxicity.

- Design chemical processes to use renewable materials, and than depletable ones.

- Design chemicals to degrade after their use.

- Design chemical processes to run at lower temperatures and pressures.

These and other green chemistry principles can be applied to product design and innovation from the beginning in order to minimize the problems associated with the use of chemicals in the vast assortment of products that are developed daily.

The green chemistry facet of the cradle-to-cradle approach is to develop a set of lists that identify the chemicals and materials that are possible candidates for use in your products. They suggest an "X" list of materials that should never be used; a "gray" list of materials that may, if necessary, be used, but that are not the best choice; and a "P" or "positive" list of materials and chemicals that can be used with confidence. Then work toward actually activating the "P" list in your design process.

Their final step of the cradle-to-cradle approach is to reinvent—to totally rethink what you are trying to accomplish in your design and with your business. By reimagining what we are trying to accomplish, we can begin to better understand how to design, create, and deliver goods and services that fulfill real needs without causing harm. This part of the process will depend on your own and any borrowed creativity that you can muster. Green design is a continual process of learning about sustainability and then attempting to apply that learning to every aspect of your business.

The Basic Rules of Green Design

But how can we apply the ideas developed by all of these innovative thinkers in a practical way to further the design of the products and services of modern society. Braden Allenby, President of the International Society for Industrial Ecology, and professor of environmental ecology, writing in the book *Inventing for the Environment*, attempted to put these rules into a more pragmatic context that can be used by designers and business. His ten rules—the basic rules governing green design—are paraphrased here with additional explanatory phrases added in parentheses:

1. Business operations should be designed to produce no waste (the way that nature operates).

2. Businesses should be designed to be easily adaptable to all foreseeable innovations (the way that nature is).

3. Everything that enters a manufacturing process should leave as a usable product (in the way that processes work in nature).

4. Every bit of energy used in manufacturing should produce a material transformation (in the manner that energy is used in nature).

5. The absolute minimum of materials and energy should be used in all processes (in the way that natural world operates).

6. The materials used should be the least toxic available (in the way that the natural world has developed).

7. Industry should get most of its materials by recycling material already in use or disposed of, rather than from raw materials (in the way that nature operates).

8. Every product should be designed so that it can either be reused itself (by using modular equipment) or used to create other useful products (in the manner that nature recycles matter).

9. Every business should be designed to improve the local habitat and species diversity and to minimize any effects on natural resources (in the manner that nature operates).

10. Close interactions should be developed between suppliers, customers, and competitors to minimize packaging and maximize reuse and recycling (much as nature operates).

In short, a green business needs to produce no waste, be interactive and adaptable to innovation, use the minimum of energy and matter and the least toxic materials possible, and use such materials in such a way that they may be easily reused with no harm to the environment—a definition right out of nature's operating manual.

To utilize these basic rules in redesigning our industry is, by no means, a call to return to a less industrial, less technological time. It is, rather, a call to use our technology to design better products and services—products and services that use less raw material and energy to produce and use, and that have less overall impact on our environment. To achieve this will require technologies that are, in fact, far more sophisticated than current ones in their use of materials and energy, not less. This vision of a vastly more efficient and lower-impact civilization is at the very center of the efforts to seek a sustainable society. To accomplish such a fundamental reengineering of society will require a herculean effort, one that will require our modern industrial society to be in tune with both the rules of the natural world and with the central aspirations of ancient medicine, as first enunciated by the Roman physician Galen: "First, do no harm."

How would such redesign work in actuality? Can we really design products, services, and processes to be in tune with the laws of nature? Let's look at some real-world examples for inspiration:

Innovation inspired by nature is how author Janine Benyus likes to describe *biomimicry*: "looking to nature as our teacher". Instead of asking the typical questions that tend to be asked in business, we should, instead ask how nature performs the task in question. For example, when the question is "how to clean a surface," we need to ask not "what is the best and least toxic detergent?" or "how can we reduce the amount of energy needed to clean the surface?" but rather, we should ask "how does nature stay clean?" Scientists in Germany asked just that question and looked to the lotus plant, which lives in muddy swamps but stays incredibly clean. By looking closely at the surface of lotus leaves, botanists saw that the seemingly smooth surfaces are, in fact, amazingly bumpy. The bumps seem to prevent dirt from adhering to the lotus leaf surface in the first place. Nature, in effect, changes the question from "how do you clean a surface?" to "how to you prevent it from getting dirty in the first place?" A German company has developed a paint, Lotusan, that mimics this natural principle by creating microscopic bumps in the painted surface that inhibit dirt from ever adhering and collecting. Brilliant!— and the answer has been around for millions of years.

Humans tend to design products with little thought to their ultimate disposal. We make plastic bags that are used once, for a few minutes, then disposed of in a landfill where they will remain, unused and unrecycled, for thousands of years. We create products to power our energy systems that will never, in real terms, become safe to be around, and then we struggle to find ways to bury them to prevent them from harming future generations. Even one of our strongest products, steel, takes enormous amounts of energy, raw materials, transportation, heat, and labor to produce. Yet, a spider, in making its web, can produce a product that is, ounce for ounce, five times stronger than steel and far more flexible. And the spider creates this substance from insect parts and water, in a quiet process that operates at room temperature, creates no waste, and produces a biodegradable end product that will be entirely reused by nature. Biomimicry seeks to understand this process.

The ideas behind biomimicry are not meant to be used to farm nature, not to harvest spiders and use them to create new fibers, not to collect plants or bacteria and use them to assist humans. Rather, the idea is to try to understand how nature creates designs—for better surfaces, better structures, better adhesives—to solve real problems that have arisen in the natural world. And then take those natural design innovations and use them to create better human products that will cause less problems for us—and for nature.

Many products have already been created by innovative designers who are taking their inspirations from nature. Natural air conditioning based on termite mounds; fans and propellers based on the natural spirals found in nature, new plastics derived from carbon dioxide inspired by plants, adhesion to surfaces without the use of glue motivated by the feet of geckos, water purification systems inspired by marshes—these and other innovative products are already a reality. By looking to nature for inspiration, green designers are creating new and exciting products that are leading the way into a future when designers and engineers will team up with biologists, botanists, and chemists to fundamentally reinvent human industry.

The Green Design Process

All of the frameworks that have been developed to approach the greening of business provide assistance in formulating a new way to look at the products and services that humanity uses. Using all of these various theoretical approaches, can we develop a systematic way to look at nature for inspiration in the design process? If we combine the concepts, we see a clear pattern emerge.

Consider the Entire Life-Cycle of the Product
All of the various approaches to building a sustainable economy have in common the concept that understanding the entire life-cycle of a product is essential in understanding and lessening its impacts on the environment. Green design can then be used to examine each stage of a product's life cycle and look for ways to minimize the environmental impacts. Recall our definition of green business: it needs to produce no waste, be interactive and adaptable to innovation, use the minimum of energy and matter and the least toxic materials possible, and use such materials in a way that they may be easily reused with no harm to the environment. Green design, then, is applying those basic concepts over the entire life-cycle of a product.

The Raw Material Stage of a Product's Life
Each stage of a product's life introduces opportunities to redesign how a product is created, used, and disposed of or, most preferably, reused in a continual manner. During the raw materials stage of production, a vast array of innovative solutions might be applied. Can the product itself be made from recycled material? Could it be made compostable? Can it be made from the by-products of another process? Can it be made from less toxic or hazardous materials? Can it be made from less hybridized materials (blended materials that are difficult or impossible to separate), but rather from more basic materials that can easily be reused? Can it be created from fewer materials? Using less material? Can the materials used be themselves created solely from natural materials, rather than from petro- or other human-created chemicals?

The Manufacturing Stage of a Product

Turning to the manufacturing process itself we can, again, derive our inspiration from nature. Natural materials are designed to be either very durable—think of obsidian, granite, or teak—or very degradable—think of leaves or animal waste. Human-designed products can use these two different design characteristics to develop basic design principles for human-engineered products, Can the product be used more than once and have a long useful life? Then it should be made as durable as possible. If it will likely be used only once and then discarded, can it be redesigned so that it will be used more than once, to be kept and reused repeatedly? Cloth grocery sacks are an easy replacement for disposable plastic bags. Why aren't they the dominant way that humans carry their food home from market? Until recent times, the idea of an utterly disposable product was, in fact, abhorrent to most of humanity. Comfort and convenience have led to the greater use of disposable, throwaway products, but ultimately such products are the creature of the marketing machinery of modern society. There are, of course, some products that can only be used for a relatively short period of time and should not be durable; those type products need to be designed to be quickly biodegradable or compostable.

Regardless of how durable a product is, ultimately it will reach the end of its intended life. For modern technological products, that life may be much shorter than the durability of the materials used. Trash bags are an example of a product that should not be designed for durability; short-term strength, perhaps, but not long-term durability. For such short-term products, whenever possible, the natural principle of reuse should be a part of the entire design process. How can the initial design of the product optimize the later disassembly and reuse of the component parts or the actual materials used in the product? Can the product be easily disassembled into its biological and technological components? Can this be accomplished in a way that allows them to be reused in a similar or even better use, rather than the normally degraded usage often associated with recycled products. Naturally, the process used to manufacture any product should be designed to use the least amount of materials, operate with most energy efficiency possible, and produce no waste that can not be used in some other manner, or by some other process. By looking at both the materials used in a product and the various processes involved in crafting those materials into a product, we can design harm out of the equation.

The Distribution and Usage Stage of a Product

Part of any product's life-cycle involves how it reaches the customer. This encompasses both its packaging and its transportation and distribution. To reduce the impacts in these areas, we can also look to nature for inspiration. Nature tends to package itself in ways that are easily recycled or reused. From tree bark to egg shells to onion skins—nontoxic, biodegradable, and compostable packaging is a hallmark of nature's products. Can our society's packaging mimic nature's? The ubiquitous use of plastic has come to dominate much of today's packaging. Much of it is unnecessary, most of it is not recyclable, some of it is toxic, and almost none of it is compostable (there are a few soy- and corn-based plastics on the market, some made of polylactic acid). But these negative attributes are not really part of the service we want from our packaging. We generally merely want a way to protect a product during its transport from where it was created to where it will be used. If the product itself is designed to be more durable, with less likelihood of damage in transit, then less packaging becomes an added benefit. If any necessary shipping packaging can be continually reused, so much the better. If there must be individual packaging, it should be recyclable or compostable. These attributes can apply to any and all packaging—regardless of the fears of the marketing and advertising departments.

At the stage in a product's life-cycle when it is in the hands of its ultimate user, there are a whole range of questions that need to be examined. Does the actual final use of the product create potential harm? Can the type or quantity of energy necessary for its ultimate use be altered to reduce its impact? How can the life-cycle of the product be designed to maximize its reuse? Here, we can look to nature and mimic the closed-loop process that is inherent in all of the systems of the natural world.

Providing Services Instead of Products

Closed-loop systems have been difficult to arrange in a complex global economic system. One of the most successful methods for achieving a closed-loop is to not sell a product, but rather, to provide the customer with the service or function that the product supplies. People really don't want to own a copy machine—they want to be able to make copies of documents. They don't want to own a carpet—they just want a durable product to cover their floors. Both of these two examples highlight two of the companies that have successfully pioneered the idea of a service and flow economic model—Xerox and Interface. These two innovative companies provide customers with business services—for example, floor coverings or photocopies—that are created to be part of a process designed so that the products themselves flow back directly to the company to be remanufactured into new products that can be put right back into the customer's hands. Instead of focusing on selling more products—and using more natural resources in the process—these businesses focus on how to supply a service in the most efficient manner possible. Examining ways that any business can prosper by selling the service that its products provide, rather than selling the product itself, can be an integral part of any efforts to rethink and redesign a business.

The End of a Product's Life

Finally, every product must seemingly come to the end of its useful life. In nature, however, every end is a new beginning and all waste is simply food for the next stage in the life of a nature's products. The goal for human production should also be the design of products made of materials that can easily separated into basic raw materials to be used again; or components that can be continually reused, recycled, disassembled, and remanufactured; or, if necessary, of materials that are ultimately degradable into matter that can quickly and safely reenter the natural ecosystem without harm. To create such products that will be an integral part of a closed-loop system, either biological or technological, will involve an investigation of the return portion of the product's supply chain, a section not often considered in product design. Can the product be designed to be more easily returned to the manufacturer? Can it be manufactured to be disassembled by others and the component parts reused? Can it be designed to be ultimately degradable in a manner that will cause no harm to the air, water, soil, or biodiversity of the earth?

Whenever a product is in its design stage, its eventual ecological and carbon footprint can be reduced in the most profound ways. The basic ecological attributes of any product are essentially set during its design stage. This is when the most meaningful steps can be taken to align the product or its services with the rules of nature. In a few pages, you will find a Green Product Design Worksheet to help you incorporate these basic green design principles into your own efforts to redesign your enterprise as a sustainable business. Use this worksheet to first take a comprehensive look at every product that you produce, use, or sell in your business.

Even if your business is not involved in the actual manufacture of the product to be analyzed, working through the questions relating to its actual design will help you assess any product's attributes from a sustainability point of view. If you are selling products or providing services that use certain products—whatever they may be—a careful look at every product's basic characteristics can help you appraise whether other, less harmful, products or merchandise can be substituted, used, or sold in their place. For many products, it will be very useful to have conducted a detailed life-cycle assessment of the entire life of the product—from raw materials to end of life—prior to completing this worksheet. Tools to conduct life-cycle assessments are discussed in Chapters 4 and 11, and life-cycle assessment resources are provided in Appendix B of this book. If you don't have the time or resources to conduct a deep life-cycle assessment of each product, a basic Limited Life Cycle Assessment Worksheet is provided to assist you in understanding the process and materials that may have been used to create and ultimately dispose of the product. It is not intended as an in-depth assessment, but, rather, to get you started in the process of examining the entire life-cycle of products.

After you have examined the products that you actually produce, use, or sell, you should again use the Green Product Design Worksheet to evaluate any potential products that you may wish to create, use, or sell. A careful and considered evaluation of each stage in a product's life before it is even designed can help you formulate the best and most sustainable product design possible. The process of design analysis may, however, highlight materials issues or product traits that are not presently feasible for you to integrate into your manufacture, design, or use of the product. Although it is desirable to design the perfect green product, this is not always a viable business choice. The process of design analysis, however, can help point you in the direction toward sustainability.

A final set of six considerations for green design was developed by the EcoReDesign projects and Australian government. These considerations provide a quick checklist of the goals of any green design project:

*   Design for resource conservation by using minimal materials, renewable resources, and recycled or waste products.

*   Design for low impact by avoiding toxic or hazardous substances and avoiding the production of greenhouse gasses.

*   Design for cleaner manufacturing and pollution prevention by seeking the elimination of all waste—solid, liquid, and gaseous.

*   Design for efficient distribution by reducing the weight of the product and its packaging and insuring that any packaging is reusable or recyclable.

*   Design for energy and water efficiency in the production, distribution, use, and disposal of the product.

*   Design for durability, disassembly, remanufacture, reuse, recycling, degradability, and eventual safe disposal—a continual closed-loop system.

Sustainable Products and the Bottom of the Pyramid

Even if products are designed with the best techniques for incorporating all of these green attributes and with the greenest possible life-cycle, one question remains. The first question on the Green Product Design Worksheet—which penetrates to the very core of sustainable business practices—is, perhaps, the most difficult question of all to answer: *Is this product even necessary?* As the depth and breadth of a product's life-cycle begins to be understood, a deeper understanding of the product's environmental footprint becomes clearer. Of course, a consideration of the many other attributes of a product—besides its green design and production—are also necessary. Does the product fulfill a real need; solve a real problem; provide joy; serve an aesthetic purpose; foster education? These and many other factors also play into the decision to develop a particular product.

Green design finally, however, allows all of the various environmental factors of a product's existence to become a part of the equation.

Sustainability, however, calls for attention to three factors. Green design provides a way to examine two of them—the economic and environmental aspects of a product. But how do we measure the third factor—a product's impact on society?

As noted in Chapter 1, business is the only force on earth with the power, resources, personnel, and reach to confront and solve the problems that humanity faces. Paying attention to the environmental impacts of business provides a path for business to assist people in dramatically increasing the quality of their lives—without, in the process, destroying the environment. By minimizing—in every way possible—the impact of business on the natural world, global commerce can spread the economic progress enjoyed in the developed countries of the world to those who have not yet shared in that progress. By reducing or eliminating waste, decreasing and eventually ending our use of fossil fuels, conserving our fresh water, and using our limited natural resources in the most efficient ways possible, business can lead the world toward an era of greater health, safety, comfort, and security. But can businesses that are taking the road to sustainability do more to reach that era even faster?

One concept that can be used to help bring the benefits of progress to a wider cross section of humanity is referred to as *bottom of the pyramid*—an allusion to the lowest half of the pyramid of humanity. The top half of a pyramid, by height, may contain only 20 percent of its mass, while the lower half contains 80 percent. So too does the bottom part of humanity's pyramid contain the 4 billion people on earth who exist on a few dollars a day or less. This mass of people has enormous unmet needs that can be assisted by sustainable business practices. The concept of the bottom of the pyramid, as a business strategy, was first defined in 1998 by Professors C.K. Prahalad and Stuart L. Hart. It was later the subject of their books *The Fortune at the Bottom of the Pyramid*, by Prahalad, and *Capitalism at the Crossroads,* by Hart. Meeting the needs of the poorest in the world can provide an uplifting and inspiring new avenue for businesses to pursue.

The overwhelming success of the Grameen Bank, developed by Nobel Prize laureate Muhammad Yunus, and all of its many micro-credit offspring to aid the poor by extending credit, are an excellent example of a sustainable business model that achieves success by serving the bottom of the pyramid of humanity. Products such as a shampoo that works best in cold water or toothpaste sold in small, cheap, but environmentally sound packaging are but some of the ideas that have been introduced to meet the needs of this enormous market. Grameen Phone, an offshoot of Grameen Bank, began providing cell phones to women in Bangladesh in 1997. By providing phones to women in poor villages with no landline phone service and allowing the women to pay back the cost of the phones by selling phone usage to others in their villages, the Grameen Phone network has provided modern communication access to the rural poor. The nonprofit organization Light Up the World has developed rural off-the-grid lighting that combines very efficient LED lighting with energy supplied by low-cost solar panels. Innovative and low-cost products are being developed for this population in agriculture, construction, transportation, consumer goods, and services—in fact, in every area that has seen similar dramatic progress in developed countries. Any consideration of a new green product design should also include a consideration of its applicability to meeting the needs of the four billion people currently in the bottom half of humanity's pyramid.

Green Product Design Plan

① First, you will need to understand the life-cycles of both your current products and any potential future products. This assessment should include any products that you use in your business in the supplying of services. The best method for this is to perform a life-cycle analysis for each product. Chapter 4 and Chapter 11 also provide information on life-cycle assessments. In addition, a Limited Life-Cycle Assessment Worksheet is provided for you to develop your own very basic assessment of your product's life-cycle.

② You will then need to develop an approach to product design that will incorporate sustainability and environmental concerns into the design criteria. To assist in this process, a Green Product Design Worksheet is provided. This question-and-answer format worksheet begins with some basic questions regarding the product and then examines the product's attributes from raw materials to end of life. Your answers will allow you to assess how your product's characteristics can be altered at the design stage to lower its eventual environmental footprint.

③ In your analysis process, you need to actually identify the impacts of each product in your business. This analysis is designed to be part of the process of completing your Green Product Design Worksheet.

④ Finally, you will need to actually implement the design criteria that you have decided upon for each product. This will mean developing a set of specific design guidelines based on the details and explanations that you provided in your answers on your Green Product Design Worksheet. Your specific guidelines should be incorporated into your eventual Green Business Plan when you prepare it later, using the guidelines in Chapter 18.

Limited Life-Cycle Assessment Worksheet

Prepared by:	Business:
Date:	Address:

Description of Product Under Consideration:

Materials and Resources	Details
List the materials used in the creation of this product and its packaging.	
List the quantities of each that will be needed for the production of an individual unit of the product and packaging.	
Are these materials from renewable, nonrenewable, or recycled sources?	

Energy and Water Consumed	Details
How much and what type of energy will be consumed in the production of the product?	
During the distribution and sale of the product?	
During the ultimate use of the product?	
During the disposal of this product?	
How much water is necessary for the production of this product?	
During the ultimate use of this product?	

Waste and Emissions	Details
How much and what type of wastes are created during the creation of this product?	
During the ultimate use of the product?	
By the disposal of the product?	
Are any of the wastes toxic/hazardous?	
How many and what type of emissions are produced in the creation of the product?	
During the ultimate use of the product?	
By the disposal of the product?	

Green Product Design Worksheet

Prepared by:	Business:
Date:	Address:

Description of Product Under Consideration:

Initial Product Considerations	Yes/No	Details or Explanation
Is this product even necessary?		
What is the ultimate purpose of this product?		
What services will this provide to the customer?		
Can this product serve the needs of the "bottom of the pyramid"?		
Can the services that this product provides be leased or otherwise provided to customers without their actual purchase of the product?		
Can this product be redesigned to be provided as a service?		
Can you describe the details of the method or manner in which this product could be provided to customers as a service, including any closed-loop system that would be necessary?		
Materials Used in the Product	**Yes/No**	**Details or Explanation**
Can fewer overall types of materials be used in the creation of this product?		
Can more durable materials be used to create this product?		
Can the product be designed to be as durable, but with less overall use of material?		
Will any virgin raw materials be used in the creation of this product?		
Are any of the virgin raw materials that will be used nonrenewable?		

Can any plant-based or other natural materials be used in this product as a substitute for any virgin and nonrenewable raw materials?		
Can any material recycled from other processes in our own business be used in this product, instead of virgin raw materials?		
Can any by-products of other industrial processes or other types of recycled materials be used in this product as a substitute for any virgin raw materials?		
Can any of the materials planned for use in this product be made more recyclable, or can other more recyclable materials be substituted?		
Can any of the materials planned for use in this product be made fully compostable, or can other more compostable materials be substituted?		
Are all of the materials used in this product considered to have the least possible environmental impact of available materials?		
Are any of the materials in this product toxic or hazardous?		
Can any nontoxic or less hazardous materials be found to substitute for current materials?		
Are any of the materials to be used in this product hybrid or composite materials that are difficult or impossible to separate into their individual component parts or chemicals?		

Manufacture of the Product	Yes/No	Details or Explanation
Is the product designed to be used once and discarded?		
Can the product be designed to be reused many times over a longer life-cycle?		
Can the product design itself be made to be more durable than its initial or common design?		
Has the product been designed to avoid one-time use components such as cartridges, containers, or batteries?		
Can the product be designed to be easily disassembled and its component parts reused without change by our company?		
Are the methods used to fasten parts together designed to facilitate upgrade, repair, recycling, or disassembly of the product?		
If the product will use energy, has its use of energy been optimized as much as possible?		
If the product will use batteries, can they be rechargeable?		
If the product will use batteries, are the batteries easily identifiable and easily removable?		
Can the product be designed to be easily disassembled and the disassembled materials recycled for use in the creation of another product of equal or greater value by our company?		
Can the producut's disassembled parts or material be used or sold to another company for reuse?		

Have any barriers to recycling been eliminated from the product design (such as fillers, additives, painted plastics, embedded materials, etc.)?		
If the packaging absolutely must contain plastics, are they types that are easily recyclable and are they clearly marked as such?		
If it is not necessary for the product to be durable, can the product's components be designed to easily and quickly reenter the natural world, without causing any harm to the air, soil, water, or biodiversity of the earth?		
Does the proposed manufacturing process for this product produce any waste that can not be immediately reused or recycled?		
Does the manufacturing process or cleanup use any toxic or hazardous materials?		
Does the manufacturing process itself *produce* any toxic or hazardous materials?		
Can the proposed manufacturing process be designed to consume fewer materials?		
Is the manufacturing process designed with the least possible number and types of steps (to prevent errors and waste)?		
Can the proposed manufacturing process be designed to consume less energy and/or use lower processing temperatures?		
Is the manufacturing process designed to minimize water use?		

	Yes/No	Details or Explanation
Is the manufacturing process designed with the minimal amount of movement between manufacturing and assembly points?		
Can this product be designed to be easily repaired or upgraded by the consumer?		
Are parts readily available for any necessary repair of this product?		
Product Packaging Design	**Yes/No**	**Details or Explanation**
Does this product actually need any packaging at all?		
If it requires packaging, can the packaging be made entirely from recycled material?		
Has the packaging required been minimized to the extent possible?		
Has the number and type of different materials to be used in the packaging been minimized?		
Is the packaging designed to be totally recyclable without additional effort on the part of the user?		
Are any of the packaging materials hybrid or composite materials that are difficult or impossible to separate into their individual component parts or chemicals?		
If the packaging must contain plastics, are they easily recyclable and clearly marked as such?		
Can the packaging be designed to be easily compostable?		
Does the packaging contain any toxic or hazardous materials?		
Can the product be transported to its ultimate user in returnable packaging or shipping containers?		

End of Product Life Design	Yes/No	Details or Explanations
Are there components or materials used in this product or packaging that are considered "biological" nutrients that can be safely and easily composted or otherwise returned to the ecosystem near the location of their ultimate use?		
Are there systems in place that customers can use for the easy recycling or composting of this product and its packaging?		
Are there components or materials used in this product or its packaging that are considered "technical" nutrients that can be effectively and completely reused in some technological process?		
Are the materials that may be recycled or reused easy for the end user to separate and identify?		
Are there any systems in place to facilitate the return of the product, its components, or its packaging back to our company?		
Are there systems in place at this company for the disassembly and reuse of the components in this product?		
Are there systems in place for the disassembly and reuse of the actual individual materials in this product?		
If the components and materials are to be returned to the company for disposal, and there is no current use for the returned materials, has a potential purchaser of these returned materials been identified?		

Chapter 14

Green Business Eco-Labeling and Certification

For the world to utilize its resources on a sustainable basis will require changes in global consumption patterns to reduce the overall environmental impact of consumer choices. Unlike most environmental problems, consumption is not normally considered a problem. In fact, in most quarters, it is welcomed as a good, even essential, component of business. Consumption of materials and resources to provide all of the attributes of modern society, however, is not sustainable at today's levels and is one of the major causes of the continued deterioration of the global environment. The U.S. has a singular place in the consumption game—it is the largest single consumer of natural resources, including fossil fuels, and the greatest producer of wastes of all kinds. China, however, with its rapidly developing consumer society, is fast closing in on America's dubious titles and has passed the U.S. in the consumption of many raw materials.

Consumers understand that protecting the environment will require major changes. Consumer polls repeatedly indicate that around 75% of shoppers take environmental issues into consideration when making buying decisions. But it's not that easy to buy green. Even experts have a hard time making informed decisions with the bewildering array of product choices available. Deceptive and misleading advertising claims about the environmental safety of products makes the decisions even more difficult.

Two related new green business tools have emerged in recent years and are fast becoming a prominent feature in many industries. In response to growing consumer demand for a way to identify products and services that are environmentally friendly, *eco-labeling* has emerged as a vital new tool for consumer choice. *Environmental certification* systems provide the backbone of many of these labeling initiatives.

One of the greatest levers that can be applied to push business in the direction of a greener future is the trillions of dollars of annual consumer purchasing power. As the public becomes more willing to use its buying power to positively influence business, tools for consumers to use to differentiate among the overwhelming choices in the marketplace become necessary.

Eco-labeling and certification have emerged as a way to standardize environmental claims and to assure that businesses in a particular industry are playing by the same rules. Much like nutritional labels provide consumers with vital information about the dietary effects of food, eco-labeling can allow buyers to know the environmental impact of products and provide immediate, objective, and accurate evaluation of a product's environmental impact. They also provide an incentive for manufacturers and other businesses to meet such programs' standards by producing products that are found acceptable by unbiased, third-party certification. Any effective certification or labeling program must have open, verifiable, and peer-reviewed standards that are applied in a fair and unbiased manner. The cost of obtaining the certification or label should also not be prohibitively expensive so that small and medium-sized businesses can qualify.

Dozens of individual countries and numerous industries have developed labeling and certification programs to help consumers both understand a product's environmental impact and make more informed purchasing decisions. This chapter will review and provide information about the many eco-labeling and certification programs that have developed around the world. It is to your company's benefit to take advantage of these various programs to educate consumers about the greening of your business.

U.S. EPA Energy Star Program

The U.S. EPA's Energy Star program is one of the best-funded and most widespread of the eco-labeling programs. Begun in 1992, Energy Star was originally a voluntary labeling program designed to identify and promote energy-efficient products to reduce greenhouse gas emissions. Computers and monitors were the first labeled products. It was later expanded to label additional office equipment products and residential heating and cooling equipment. In 1996, EPA partnered with the U.S. Department of Energy for particular product categories. The Energy Star label is now on major appliances, office equipment, lighting, home electronics, and many more product categories. Energy Star provides a trustworthy label on over 50 product categories (and thousands of models) for the home and office. These products deliver the same or better performance as comparable models while using less energy and saving money. The EPA has also extended the label to cover new homes and commercial and industrial buildings, providing easy-to-use home and building assessment tools so that homeowners and building managers can start down the path to greater efficiency and cost savings.

Through its partnerships with more than 12,000 private and public sector organizations, Energy Star delivers the technical information and tools that organizations and consumers need to choose energy-efficient solutions and best management practices. Energy Star has successfully delivered energy and cost savings across the country, saving businesses, organizations, and consumers about $16 billion in 2007 alone. Over the past decade, Energy Star has been a driving force behind the more widespread use of such technological innovations as efficient fluorescent lighting, power management systems for office equipment, and low standby energy use. Over 1 billion Energy Star–certified products have been purchased since the program's inception.

There are many opportunities to save money by improving the efficiency of our industries using technologies and practices that already exist. However, many businesses do not take advantage of these opportunities because market barriers, such as lack of information and split incentives, limit their expenditures on what are, in fact, attractive financial investments when judged on the basis of complete information. The Energy Star program was designed to overcome many of the market barriers to the adoption of cost-effective energy efficiency products and services in a sustained manner and to help unleash the attendant savings. U.S. EPA Energy Star funding is used to provide businesses and consumers with information and tools that break down major market barriers and alter decision making for the long term. This approach, which helps direct private capital toward energy efficiency investments, provides a large environmental and economic payback for the government investment. Energy Star enhances the market for energy efficiency by reducing the transaction costs and lowering the investment risks to the point that many more projects become attractive.

The residential sector offers sizable opportunities for protecting the environment through energy efficiency. Consisting of more than 100 million households, this sector contributes about 17 percent of the nation's greenhouse gas emissions but could account for potential energy savings of up to 30 percent compared with current consumption. To capitalize on the possible savings, homeowners face numerous decisions. They receive information on energy efficiency options from many sources, including manufacturers, utilities, retailers, and contractors. Frequently this information comes in pieces, is inconsistent, and leaves homeowners with more questions than answers about the best options. Energy Star offers a straightforward, powerful, and reliable resource for answering many of these questions and showing the benefits of energy-efficient choices. The Energy Star® label is only awarded in product categories where the efficient products offer the features and performance consumers want and provide a reasonable payback if the initial purchase price is higher. The qualifying products offer a homeowner considerable savings: a home fully equipped with Energy Star products will operate on about 30 percent less energy than a house equipped with standard products, saving the typical homeowner about $400 each year.

For the Energy Star label to be attractive to businesses, consumers must not only recognize the label, but also understand that it represents cost savings and environmental protection. The EPA undertakes a variety of efforts to educate the public about how products and services carrying the Energy Star® label can protect the environment while saving them money, and about the hidden price tag of a product—the cost of energy to operate that product over its lifetime.

Beyond product labels, the EPA also offers the Energy Star partnership to organizations of all types and sizes. As part of this partnership, senior-level executives make a commitment to better energy management of their buildings or facilities. This top-level organizational commitment has proved to be the catalyst for energy efficiency investments in many of the most successful partner organizations. To engage top-level business managers, they must see the link between effective energy management and their core objectives. The EPA is working to demonstrate this connection and to provide organizations with new financial indices that help management understand how their energy costs affect their profitability relative to others in their sector.

The EPA has also collaborated with Innovest, a financial analysis firm, whose studies have determined that companies with effective energy management plans in place tend to be strong environmental performers and strong performers on Wall Street. Innovest research shows that leaders in corporate energy management outperform their competitors by 20 to 30 percent on Wall Street. This research has also demonstrated that:

- A commercial building owner can generate $2 to $3 of asset value for every $1 invested in energy performance improvements.

- A retail grocery can reap the equivalent of increasing sales by $85 when it reduces annual energy costs by $1, given this sector's low profit margins and relatively high energy expenses.

- A full service hotel can realize the equivalent of increasing its average daily rate by $1.35 (about 1.6 percent) from a 10 percent improvement in energy performance.

Through its work with thousands of partners, the EPA has identified the key elements of superior energy management.

- **_Top-level commitment to reduce energy waste._** Without this commitment, resources are often not allocated to energy projects, and efficiency programs are not sustained.

- **_Routine assessment of organization-wide performance._** Assessing energy use in all operations and all buildings results in resources being targeted to those facilities with the greatest potential for improvement. Organizations can rank their own properties, learn from the high performers, and upgrade the poor performers.

- **_Use of a systems-integrated approach to upgrade buildings._** Sizing heating and cooling equipment, integrating individual technical components, and controlling, operating, and maintaining equipment play a big role in the energy performance of a building.

Organizations using these guidelines have realized twice the energy savings for a given investment as alternative approaches. The case for these guidelines is clear given the findings from the past decade: The efficiency of building components such as windows, chillers, etc., has improved by more than 30 percent over the past 25 years, yet building energy use has not improved by nearly as much. An examination of U.S. buildings shows that the best performing buildings use 75 percent less energy than the worst performing buildings. It also shows that this difference cannot be accounted for by particular technologies, climate, building size, or building age. The EPA offers its proven energy management strategy to each of its 12,000 partners. EPA estimates that to date more than 47.5 billion kwh have been saved through these efforts.

Any type or size of business can begin a partnership with the Energy Star energy management program. The Energy Star program also maintains a list of energy engineers and consultants that have worked with the Energy Star energy management program within the past year. Please see the Energy Star website at **www.energystar.gov** and look under "Buildings and Plants" for more information.

If you need to purchase any products in the following categories, you should make your purchases based on Energy Star recommendations. In addition, if your business offers products in any of the following categories you should investigate working with the U.S. EPA's Energy Star product certification program to have your product Energy Star certified.

Energy Star Product Categories

Appliances

Battery chargers

Clothes washers

Dehumidifiers

Dishwashers

Refrigerators & freezers

Room air conditioners

Room air cleaners

Water heaters (in development)

Heating and Cooling

Air-source heat pumps

Boilers

Ceiling fans

Central air conditioning

Furnaces

Geothermal heat pumps

Home sealing & insulation

Light commercial products

Programmable thermostats

Ventilating fans

Home or Commercial Envelope Products

Roofing products

Windows, doors and skylights

Home Electronics

Battery charging systems

Cordless phones

Combination TV/VCR/DVD units

Digital to analog converters

DVD products

External power adapters

Home audio products

Televisions

VCRs

Office Equipment

Computers

Copiers and fax machines

Digital duplicators

Notebook & tablet PCs

Mailing machines

External power adapters

Monitors

Printers, scanners, all-in-ones

Lighting

Compact fluorescent bulbs

Residential light fixtures

Exit signs

Decorative light strings

Commercial Food Service

Commercial dishwashers

Commercial fryers

Commercial hot food cabinets

Commercial ice machines

Commercial refrigerators & freezers

Commercial steam cookers

Other Commercial Products

Vending machines

Solid state lighting (in development)

Water coolers

Enterprise servers (in development)

National Environmental Performance Track

A relatively new U.S. EPA certification program, begun in 2000, the National Environmental Performance Track, is designed to enhance facility-based environmental performance and to encourage facilities to achieve environmental excellence through continuous improvement. This program works with participating businesses to recognize facilities that have a sustained record of compliance and have implemented high-quality environmental management systems. Performance Track encourages facilities to continuously improve their environmental performance and to work closely with their community and employees. As an incentive for businesses, the U.S. EPA works with states to provide specific regulatory and administrative benefits, such as reduced self-reporting and low-priority status for routine federal inspections, that are designed to reduce a facility's costs without causing harm to the environment.

The EPA also encourages Performance Track facilities to take advantage of services such as the Green Suppliers Network (see **www.greensuppliers.gov**), which helps manufacturers and suppliers save money and improve environmental performance, or the Performance Track Mentoring Program, which matches Performance Track members or potential members with top-performing facilities currently in the program. Additionally, many leading financial advisory firms use Performance Track data in their research methods. This practice can benefit top-performing, publicly traded companies, making them more attractive to investors and increasing brand recognition.

The National Environmental Performance Track is open to facilities of all types, sizes, and complexity, public or private, manufacturing or service-oriented. It is an entirely free program for business participants. Once accepted, members remain in the program for three years, as long as they continue to meet the program criteria. After three years they may reapply. Facilities applying to Performance Track must meet the following criteria (note that separate criteria apply to small businesses):

- **Environmental Management System (EMS).** Applicants must have an EMS in place for at least one completed cycle (typically a one-year time frame). An EMS is a set of policies, processes, and practices that enable a facility to reduce its environmental impacts and increase its operating efficiency. A facility must have a comprehensive independent assessment of its EMS prior to acceptance to the program and every three years thereafter. We will take a look at the basics of EMS programs in Chapter 15.

- **Sustained Compliance.** Performance Track members must have a sustained record of compliance with environmental laws. They also commit to maintaining the level of compliance needed to qualify for the program. EPA has developed specific compliance screening criteria to determine eligibility for the Performance Track program.

- **Continuous Improvement.** Applicants must demonstrate past environmental achievements during the current and preceding year. Applicants also commit to four quantitative goals (small businesses commit to two goals) for improving their environmental performance. Goals range from upstream improvements (such as improving environmental performance of suppliers) to on-site improvements (such as reduce emissions or waste from a facility) to downstream improvements (such as reducing a product's packaging or its lifetime energy use). Performance Track members set and make good faith efforts to achieve their goals over the three-year term of participation. Performance Track encourages members to set ambitious "stretch" goals rather than setting goals they will be able to meet comfortably. Members commit to making progress toward their goals, and are normally expected to make progress in three of their four goals.

- **Public Outreach.** Applicants commit to remaining involved and active in their community, sharing their accomplishments with the public, and addressing any community concerns. They also complete an Annual Performance Report for each year of their membership, describing to EPA and the public their environmental accomplishments during the previous year.

The cost reductions and energy savings from participation in the Performance Track program are impressive. Hewlett-Packard Caribe operations in Puerto Rico developed a rigorous recycle and reuse plan which wound up diverting 85% of its solid waste from landfills, saving the company $1 million annually. Baxter Healthcare adopted new energy-efficient technologies that reduced its energy use by $8 million in 2005 alone. Baxter also saved another $6.9 million by reducing its generation of hazardous waste, and an additional $3.5 million by reducing product packaging—an annual savings of over $18 million. Since the program is available to large and small businesses alike, the knowledge gained since its inception can be readily scaled to virtually any business.

Applications for Performance Track membership can be completed online and submitted every year from April 1 through May 31 and September 1 through October 31. To apply for participation in the National Environmental Performance Track, please see **www.epa.gov/performancetrack/index.htm**.

Green Seal Program

In the United States, the Green Seal program has been certifying environmental products since 1991. It is an independent, nonprofit organization that works with manufacturers, businesses, purchasers, and governments at all levels to "green" the entire production and purchasing chain. The Green Seal program is somewhat unique in that it uses a detailed life-cycle evaluation of a product or service. This extensive assessment of the environmental impact of a product or service begins with the raw material extraction, continues on through the manufacturing and use of the product, and finally ends with recycling and disposal of the product. Products only become Green Seal–certified after very rigorous testing and standards-based evaluation, which includes on-site plant visits by Green Seal inspection teams.

The Green Seal program delivers clear, straightforward information to purchasers and individual consumers who want to make a positive impact on the environment with their purchases. One of its main benefits is in helping government agencies and other institutions fulfill green procurement policies by providing a certifiable rating system of various green products. It also aids businesses by enabling manufacturers to create more sustainable products, save money, and increase the overall efficiency of its product development.

The Green Seal program also has developed two related partnership programs that can assist businesses by providing "best practices" assistance. The Green Seal Purchasing Partnership and the Green Seal Facilities Partnership programs provide both recognition and technical assistance to businesses that are working to develop internal practices that enhance environmental performance. These two programs are not standards-based programs, like the traditional Green Seal program, but rather are efforts to assist businesses of all sizes in greening either their purchasing process or their facilities management. Any organization wishing to participate in these two pilot partnership programs should see **www.greenseal.org/programs/partnership.cfm**.

The main Green Seal program is based on sets of standards for environmentally preferable products. Certification of a product earns the right to display the Green Seal label and the recognition as a certified environmentally sound product. The label and certification is valuable to both consumers and, importantly, to institutional purchasing agents who are always seeking to fulfill state and federal mandates to purchase green products. If your company produces one of the products for which Green Seal has set standards, meeting those standards can earn you the right to use the Green Seal label. Its website is **www.greenseal.org**. The various categories of Green Seal Product Standards are outlined on the following page.

Green Seal Environmental Standards

Alternative Energy Vehicles	Anti-Corrosive Paints
Cleaning and Degreasing Agents	Cleaning Services
Coated Printing Paper	Commercial Adhesives
Electric Chillers	Energy Efficient Lighting (CFLs)
Fleet Vehicle Maintenance	Food Service Packaging
General Purpose Household Cleaners	Industrial Hand Cleaners and Soaps
Industrial Floor Care Products	Lodging Properties
Newsprint	Occupancy Sensors
Paints	Food Service Paper Products
Paper Towels and Napkins	Powdered Laundry Bleach
Printing and Writing Paper	Recycled Content Latex Paint
Re-refined Engine Oil	Reusable Utility Bags
Tissue Paper	Windows and Window Films

In addition to the various environmental standards that the Green Seal program has developed, it has also prepared Green Reports for a number of product categories. These reports are peer-reviewed overviews of a particular product that provides information regarding the environmental and financial savings possible by using the greenest products available and various purchasing criteria based on a life-cycle analysis of the products. The reports offer recommendations of specific brands and models that meet the Green Seal criteria. If your company sells or manufactures any of the following products, it would be beneficial to seek Green Seal certification and listings in the appropriate Green Report for your product.

Green Seal Green Reports Available

Carpet	Compact Fluorescent Lighting
CFL Downlighting	Floor Care Products
High Intensity Discharge Lighting	Lawn Care Equipment
Linear Fluorescent Lighting	Occupancy Sensors
Office Furniture	Office Supplies
Paper, Alternative Fiber	Paper, Paper Towels and Tissue
Paper, Printing and Writing	Particleboard and Fiberboard
Quick Serve Food Packaging, Rigid	Room Air Conditioning
Tires, Low Rolling Resistance	Wood Finishes and Stains

Scientific Certification Systems

This nonprofit program has also developed a system to certify environmental claims of various products and services. It has been around since 1984 and was the first certifying organization to verify seafood product claims for the Marine Stewardship Council and is a leading certifier of forestry practices for the Forest Stewardship Council (both of which will be discussed later in this chapter). They maintain a website that provides for online applications for various certification programs as well as an online database of certified products. Please see **www.scscertified.com** for additional details of their certification programs and services.

SCS Certifications Available

Nutri-Clean® (Pesticide-residue free) for fruits and/or vegatables

Certi-Clean® Facilities for certified food safety programs

Veri-Flora® for sustainably grown flowers and potted plants

Certified Organic for USDA National Organic products program

Certifed Fair Labor Practices (in development)

Certified Sustainable Agriculture (in development)

Forest Stewardship Council certification for sustainably-managed forests and forest product chain of custody

Marine Stewardship Council for sustainable fisheries certifcation

Eco-products certification for the following products and services:

Flooring Adhesives and Sealants	Composite Wood Products
Decking and Fencing	Doors and Windows
Building Hardware	Insulation
Interior Molding and Trim	Masonry
Roofing, Siding, and Exterior Trim	Salvagable Wood
Wallboard	Wood Flooring
Carpet	Laminate Flooring
Resilient Flooring	Flooring Tiles
Flooring Underlayment	Furniture
Home Cleaning Products	Fireplaces
Paints, Stains and Primers	Plastic Bags and Liners
Plastic Pellets	Reclaimed Carpet
Waste Quarry Rock	Upholstery
Wall Coverings	Fabric Treatments

Global Eco-Labeling Network

For eco-label programs outside the United States, the Global Eco-Labeling Network maintains a website for all member certifcation programs at **www.gen.gr.jp**. If your company does business in any of the following countries, check their website for certification and eco-labeling program details.

Country/Region	Member
Australia	Good Environmental Choice Australia Ltd.
Brazil	Associacao Brasileira de Normas Tecnicas (ABNT)
Croatia	Ministry of Environmental Protection and Physical Planning
Czech Republic	Ministry of the Environment
EU	European Commission—DG ENVIRONMENT (G2)
Germany	Federal Environmental Agency (FEA) Blue Angel
Hong Kong (GC)	Green Council
Hong Kong (HKFEP)	Hong Kong Federation of Environmental Protection (HKFEP) Limited
India	Central Pollution Control Board (CPCB)
Indonesia	Ministry of Environment
Japan	Japan Environment Association (JEA)
Korea	Korea Eco-Products Institute (KOECO)
New Zealand	Environmental Choice New Zealand
Nordic 5 Countries	Nordic Ecolabelling Board
North America (Canada)	Terra Choice Environmental Service Inc, Environment Canada
North America (U.S.A.)	Green Seal
Philippines	Clean & Green Foundation, Inc.
Russia	Saint-Petersburg Ecological Union
Taiwan,China	Environment and Development Foundation (EDF)
Singapore	Singapore Environment Council
Sweden (SSNC)	Swedish Society for Nature Conservation (SSNC)
Sweden (TCO)	TCO Development
Thailand	Thailand Environment Institute (TEI)
Ukraine	Living Planet
United Kingdom	Department for Environment, Food and Rural Affairs (DEFRA)

European Eco-Labeling Programs

The European Union maintains its own eco-lableing program that provides an EU-wide eco-label: The Flower logo eco-label. The Scandinavian countries of Norway, Sweden, Finland, Iceland, and Denmark also maintain their own Swan logo eoclabel. These two labels are provided for any manufacturer, retailer, or service provider who meets the criteria for a product group. The qualifying company can then market their eco-labeled product throughout the entire European Union or Nordic region. The EU maintains a searchable database of certified products at the following website: **www.eco-label.com.** The main websites for these two programs are as follows: European Union: **http://ec.europa.eu/environment/ecolabel** Nordic Nations: **www.ecolabel.nu**.

The following table indicates the general range of products and services that may be certified and receive the respective eco-label from each program.

The EU Flower Logo Eco-Label	The Nordic Swan Logo Eco-Label
Bed Mattresses	Floor Coverings
Paint And Varnishes	Personal Computers
Light Bulbs	Adhesives
Graphic Paper	Hotels
Textiles	Coffee Filters
Detergents	Paper Envelopes
Dishwashing Detergents	Grease-Proof Paper
Refrigerators	Batteries
Washing Machines	Automatic Dishwashing Detergents
All-Purpose Cleaners	AV Equipment
Hand Dishwashing Detergent	All-Purpose Cleaners
PCs and Portable Computers	Detergents
Vacuum Cleaners	Industrial Cleaning & Degreasing Agents
Furniture	Furniture
Tourism Accommodations	Garden Machinery
Furniture	Photographic Development Services
Printed Matter	Kitchen Appliances
	Cleaning Services
	Supermarkets/Grocery Stores

Forest Stewardship Council

Formed in 1993, this nonprofit organization has become the leader in the certification of sustainably managed forests and forest products. Many retailers now stock FSC-certified products, including Home Depot, Lowe's, and Kinko's. Home Depot and Lowe's came into the FSC fold following an intense lobbying and consumer pressure campaign orchsetrated, in part, by the Rain Forest Action Network. In recent years, the FSC has had some growing pains as it reduced its originally strict criteria to allow for mixed-source forest products and certification of wood from forests in which only 50% of the lumber is sustainably harvested. This has forced the FSC to downgrade their labels which formerly applied to lumber from "sustainably-managed" forests to the current standard of "well-managed" forests, a rather vague and somewhat ambiguous standard. (Of course, *sustainable* is also a rather elusive and nebulous term itself.) The program is in the process of redesigning its criteria and auditing process with stronger standards. For more information, please see **www.fscus.org**.

Marine Stewardship Council

In the seafood industry, the Marine Stewardship Council is the main cerfication organization, with offices in the UK, USA, Australia, Japan, and the Netherlands. Though it has operated independently since 1999, the MSC was founded two years earlier in a unique joint effort by the World Wildlife Fund and Unilever, the world's largest purchaser of seafood. This program has brought the world's focus on sustainable fishing practices and is instrumental in assuring consumers that the seafood with the MSC label is fished in a sustainable manner. The MSC label is now affixed more than 7 percent of the world's wild-caught seafood. It maintains both a consumer-oriented and an industry-oriented website at **www.msc.org**.

Chlorine-Free Products Association

This non-profit organization provides certification for paper, paper products, and pulp manufacturers that their products are either totally chlorine free or processed chlorine free. A number of large paper companies have been certified to use the eco-label from the CFPA, including Cascade Paper, National Envelope, Neenah Paper, Dolphin Blue Paper, and Greenline Paper Products. Their website is **www .chlorinefreeproducts.org**.

Greener Choices EcoLabels Center

The respected U.S. nonprofit *Consumer Reports* maintains an extensive database of eco-labels for many products and services. Over 140 various eco-labels are indexed by product category, eco-label logo, and certifying organization. The eco-labels range from "100% Vegan" to "Dolphin Safe" to "Fair Trade" and cover an amazing range of products and services. No matter what product or service you use, manufacture, or provide, you should check out the profusion of eco-label programs that are tracked on this website at **www.greenerchoices.org/eco-labels**.

EcoLabeling.org

Another good source of information on various available eco-labels, this website provides a very easy-to-use searchable database of over 200 eco-labels and eco-label organizations. See **www.eco-labeling.org** for more information.

Whether you decide to have the products that your company produces certified to use a particular eco-label, or if you simply wish to assure that the products that your company uses are ecologically safe, the use of eco-labels and certification programs is an important way for you to assure your customers that your company is doing all that it can to protect the environment and act as a good citizen.

Chapter 15

Environmental Management Systems

An environmental management system is a formal set of policies and procedures that define how a company will evaluate, manage, and track its overall environmental impacts. In recent years, there has been a concerted effort to standardize the way that business, at least big business, handles its environmental management. Led by the International Organization for Standardization and its ISO 14001 standards, the development of environment management systems has been a major success in integrating environmental decision making into the mainstream of the business world. Such a system serves as an excellent tool for achieving cost-effective environmental improvements through methods spurred by a company's own initiative rather than government regulation.

This structured approach to environmental management has allowed many different types of businesses to adopt a similar set of management policies aimed at improving environmental performance. The complex ISO 14001 process itself is designed to lead to the eventual certification of a business as being in compliance with the environmental standards that are the core of the program. Increasingly, as environmental issues receive more prominence in the greater business world, this type of environmental management system certification is being required of more companies within the supply chains of larger corporate businesses.

In the United States, thousands of organizations—large corporations, small businesses, local governments, state and federal agencies, schools, and nonprofits—all use environmental management systems to systematically manage their environmental matters. Implementing a systematic environmental management system can produce a variety of benefits, including:

- **Improved environmental performance.** An environmental management system can help monitor energy and water conservation, resource efficiencies, and pollution prevention. By tracking the reductions in greenhouse gas emissions that result from these activities, an environmental management system helps demonstrate a company's commitment to reducing the risk of climate change. Improvements that lead to resource conservation and pollution prevention can also translate into reduced purchasing and disposal costs.

- **Better regulatory compliance.** An environmental management system can increase a company's regulatory compliance, which is especially important for companies that have spent time and resources dealing with regulatory violations. By providing a way to systematically identify and track environmental, health, and safety problem areas, an environmental management system enables employers to improve workplace safety and correct problems before they draw enforcement actions. This improvement can also help companies obtain needed permits and authorizations and reduce the cost of insurance.

- **Certification and recognition.** Environmental management system implementation can also enhance a company's image and improve public and community relations. As consumers place an increasing value on environmental performance, they will favor companies that show a commitment to measurable environmental management. An effective environmental management system can improve access to capital by satisfying investor and lender criteria for environmental progress. It can also increase sales by helping a company meet vendors' certification criteria. By reducing the risk of injury to workers through environmental improvements and additional training, employers can also enhance recruitment and employee morale.

Several organizations offer environmental management system certification programs, including the American Chemistry Council, the American Forest and Paper Association, the International Chamber of Commerce, and the Coalition for Environmentally Responsible Economies (CERES). The International Organization for Standardization (ISO) developed the most widely recognized environmental management system standard, ISO 14001, in 1996. ISO 14001 establishes a rigorous management framework by which a company's impacts on the environment can be systematically identified and reduced. It does not set technical or performance standards. A company can achieve ISO 14001 certification by hiring an accredited, third-party auditor to evaluate its environmental management system. To maintain this certification, the company must show continual improvement and invite a third-party auditor back to review the environmental management system every three years. Obtaining ISO 14001 certification can be expensive and time-consuming, although the cost and complexity depends on a company's size, activities, and existing environmental policies. To date, nearly 37,000 organizations around the world have achieved ISO 14001 certification. However, for many businesses, full ISO 14001 certification may be beyond their means or budget and not wholly appropriate. Small and medium-sized businesses can face unique challenges in developing an environmental management system. In particular, they often find it difficult to dedicate the necessary personnel and resources to the effort. Additionally, the level of documentation required for a certified environmental management system can be daunting.

Note also that in 2007, ISO Standard 14064, regarding greenhouse gases, has been recently added to the environmental standardization process. This standard and its related details can be used to set up a system for the reporting of greenhouse gas emissions and their removal from a business's waste stream.

Basic Environmental Management System

Even if your business decides not to pursue full environmental management system certification, developing your own company's environmental management program can help you streamline your operations and decision-making processes. This chapter will provide a basic overview of the steps that are generally required to develop an internal environmental management system. Although much of the framework for developing such a system is similar to the procedures necessary for ISO 14001 certification, the following process is *not* designed to meet ISO standards. Although the ISO 14001 standards provide more detail and are somewhat more complex, this book provides many of the elements that comprise a typical environmental management system. (FYI: The 15 basic requirements of a full ISO 14001 system are outlined at the end of this chapter. In addition, numerous ISO 14001 resources are detailed in Appendix B if you wish to pursue this issue further). The main elements of a basic environmental management system are as follows.

Commitment and Policy

Under most environmental management systems, a company commits to continual environmental improvement and establishes a company environmental policy statement that is specific to its own environmental concerns. The statement should be adopted by the company's management and should include a commitment to compliance with all legal and other industry requirements, to pollution prevention, and to continual improvement. The policy should be reviewed periodically (typically annually) and should be communicated to all employees. This aspect of an environmental management system is covered in Chapter 18 of this book.

Planning

The core of an environmental management system provides that a company conduct a full review of its operations, identifying legal requirements and environmental concerns, establishing objectives, evaluating alternatives, setting targets, and devising a plan for meeting those targets. Whenever possible, the goals selected should also be measurable and take into account both the technological feasibility of the various options and the costs involved. These elements of an environmental management system are also a key component of this book. These items are covered by the assessments, process maps, and economic analyses in the various topic-specific chapters in Part Two of this book, including energy use, water use, waste management, travel and transportation, supply chain and purchasing, materials use, product design, and building design, as well as Chapter 18 on Green Business Plans.

Implementation and Operation

The company follows through with the plan by clearly identifying those individuals who are responsible for developing, managing, and implementing the different components of the system. This aspect of the company system should also include training, communication, and documentation to ensure that environmental targets are met. For any environmental management plan to be effective, each employee must be trained in his or her role in addressing the significant aspects identified by the plan, and procedures must exist for orienting new employees into the system. These aspects of a company environmental management system are covered in Chapters 18 on personnel responsibility and green business plan implementation.

Monitoring, Evaluation, and Review

The company then monitors its operations to evaluate whether the targets are being met, and, if not, takes corrective action to optimize the effectiveness of the plan. This evaluation and review stage creates a loop of continuous improvement for the company that allows it to periodically check its environmental goals against specific criteria to ensure that the company plan is operating as intended. The success of this phase depends on the company's ability to accurately monitor and measure key activities and to track progress by maintaining a usable recordkeeping system. Tracking environmental progress allows a company to quantify the successful components of its environmental program and identify areas that need improvement. These aspects are also covered in Chapter 18 on green business plan implementation.

These four key elements of any basic environmental management system can be outlined and compiled in the Green Business Plan that you will prepare for your business in Chapter 18 of this book. Using that plan as your outline will enable you to plan, implement, and monitor all of the various action steps that you decide to include in your company's plan. If your company wishes to eventually go further and seek full certification under ISO standards, by following the outline in this book you will already have set up many of the required elements.

ISO 14001 Environmental Management Systems

For full ISO certification of a company environmental management system, it is necessary to implement all 15 phases of the ISO standards. There are many resources relating to ISO Environmental Management Systems noted in Appendix B of this book. In addition, two useful manuals developed by the U.S. EPA are included on the CD that accompanies this book: *Practical Guide to Environmental Management for Small Businesses* and *Integrated Environmental Management Systems Implementation Guide*. This second guide is intended for small and medium sized companies and associations, as well as large companies. It offers a step-by-step approach to help organizations develop and implement an environmental management system; its simple, thorough directions are clear even to those unfamiliar with environmental management planning. The environmental management system approach described in this document follows the guidelines of ISO 14001, but enhances this standard by emphasizing chemical risk management, use of cleaner technologies, and pollution prevention. This guide is most effective when used in tandem with the various other tools, such as the sample Company Manual Template for Small Businesses, and various Integrated Environmental Management Systems Worksheets, all of which are included on the CD. Following is an overview of the full 15 requirements of an ISO environmental management system. As you will see, implementation of such a comprehensive system, particularly for smaller businesses, can be an overwhelming task. Note, however, that many, but not all, of the basic requirements of these standards can be met with the basic Green Business Plan that you will prepare using this guidebook.

Environmental Policy

A company is required to develop an environmental policy statement that is defined by the top management and is specific to the nature, scale, and environmental impacts of its activities, products, and services. The statement must be signed by the organization's senior management representative and must include a commitment to compliance with all legal and other requirements to which the company subscribes, to pollution prevention, and to continual improvement of the environmental management system. It must also provide a framework for setting and reviewing environmental objectives and targets. The policy must be reviewed periodically (typically annually) and must be communicated to all employees and made available to the public.

Significant Environmental Aspects

A company is required to identify the environmental interactions (i.e., aspects) of its activities, products, and services (i.e., processes or tasks) and to determine the actual and/or potential impacts of those aspects on the environment. When considering the actual or potential severity of the impacts, as well as the legal and other requirements that govern the aspects, companies will identify certain aspects as being significant environmental aspects and set objectives to achieve a certain level of performance associated with them.

Legal and Other Requirements

A company must have in place a procedure to identify and have access to any legal or other requirements that must be complied with pertaining to any and all of their environmental interactions. The company must also have procedures in place to make certain that the requirements are being met, to periodically review compliance with the laws, and to keep accurate and complete records of the company's efforts in this regard.

Objectives and Targets

A company is required to establish objectives and targets to achieve a specific level of environmental performance for its significant environmental aspects. These objectives and targets must be consistent with the organization's environmental policy and the legal and other requirements to which it adheres. They should also be measurable, whenever possible, and take into account the technological feasibility of the various options, the costs involved, the organization's operational requirements, and the views of interested persons and companies.

Environmental Management Programs

Companies are also required to develop internal environmental management programs to provide the structure and accountability needed to achieve the objectives and targets. They must also provide both the means and the appropriate time to allow for the accomplishment of the environmental objectives. The program must be designed to apply to new developments and activities, as well as new products or services that the company offers.

Structure and Responsibility

An organization is required to clearly identify those individuals who are responsible for developing, managing, and implementing the different components of the system. Resources must be provided to fully implement the company's environmental management system. Specific people must be appointed to fulfill the company's requirements as well as report on the company's environmental performance to top management.

Training, Awareness, and Competence

A company should ensure that all individuals who work for or on behalf of it are aware of the requirements of the environmental management system and the importance of adhering to the company's environmental policy. These individuals should also be made aware of the company's significant environmental aspects and resulting impacts, and how their work activities relate to them. Finally, they should be made aware of the benefits of improved environmental performance and the consequences of deviating from the environmental management system requirements. Any personnel who are performing tasks that could cause significant environmental impacts must be trained and competent.

Communication

The company must establish procedures for internal communications among varying company levels or functions. This communication is designed to assure that the goals and objectives of the environmental management system are understood by everyone in the company and that a feedback system is in place. It must also develop a procedure for handling inquiries from external parties, and these procedures should include documentation of any such inquiries.

Document Control

A company must manage documents associated with the environmental management system in a manner that ensures they are easily identifiable and regularly reviewed or revised as necessary. The company documentation system must provide current versions of relevant documents at all locations where they are needed and promptly remove any obsolete documents from service. Similarly, records relevant to the environmental management system must be controlled in a manner that ensures they are properly collected, identified, indexed, filed, stored, and maintained. Records must also be retained in accordance with applicable laws, regulations, and/or other requirements to which the company subscribes.

Emergency Preparedness and Response

A company must generally develop written procedures to provide instructions preventing, mitigating, and identifying potential accidents or emergency situations. The procedures should also outline responses to such accidents and emergencies and ensure that such response plans are clear to everyone involved and followed in a consistent, repeatable manner. Such procedures should be tested periodically and reviewed and revised when necessary. The company should work with relevant government agencies to coordinate such emergency response planning with current government emergency preparedness plans.

Monitoring and Measurement

A company must periodically evaluate its compliance with the legal and other requirements applicable to its environmental aspects to ensure the commitment to compliance articulated in its environmental policy statement. This should include recording information to track performance, operations controls, and conformance with company environmental objectives. Any monitoring equipment must be calibrated and maintained and any documentation of the monitoring and measurement activities should be retained by the company.

Nonconformance and Corrective and Preventive Actions

A company must have a systematic process for identifying and correcting compliance and environmental management system-conformance deficiencies. In addition, a company must have a similar process for identifying potential deficiencies and correcting them before they become a problem. Most deficiencies are discovered during the audit process and corrected using the corrective and preventive action process. Any changes in procedures stemming from this process should be documented.

Records

A company must establish a clear system to identify and maintain environmental records, including any training and audit results. The records should provide a method to identify and trace the records to a particular activity, product or service and they should be easily retrieved and protected from loss or destruction. Times for retention or disposal of such records should be established and recorded.

Environmental Management System Audit

A systematic program and procedures must be established for periodic audits of the company's environmental performance. Such audits must also ensure that the system is structured and functioning in accordance with the ISO 14001 standards. The audit program should outline the scope, frequency, procedures, and personnel responsibilities for both conducting and reporting the results of the audits.

Management Review

Finally, a company's senior management must periodically review the environmental management system to evaluate its ongoing suitability, adequacy, and effectiveness towards achieving the desired level of environmental performance. Such review should consider any need for changes to the system resulting from audit results, changing conditions, and the company's commitment to continual improvement.

As you can see, a complete and comprehensive environmental management system that conforms with ISO standards is a major undertaking. This type of standardization, however, has provided many larger companies with a detailed and verifiable system with which to track its own environmental performance against that of its competitors. As more large corporations begin to place more environmental pressure on participant's in supply chains, the use of detailed environmental management systems will become more widespread, even to smaller companies.

Additional useful resources for developing a basic environmental management system are provided on the CD that accompanies this book—the U.S. EPA's guide *Documenting your Environmental Management Plan—A Workbook for Small Businesses,* and *Integrated Environmental Management Systems: A Company Manual Template for Small Businesses.* In addition, the basic steps in this book for developing your business green plan can also provide an introduction into the use of a systematic approach for bringing environmental issues into any businesses' decision-making process.

Chapter 16

Green Business Sustainability Reporting

Financial information reporting has long been a feature of modern business. From annual financial reports to detailed Securities and Exchange reports, corporate and public business financial records have been the subject of intense scrutiny and regulation. But what about the other impacts of business? How is the public able to judge the environmental, social, and even ethical effects of business operations?

Beginning in the early 1970s in the U.S., citizens concerned about these impacts began asking large businesses for information regarding their social and environmental impacts. These efforts were spurred, in part, by the 1969 passage of the federal National Environmental Protection Act that required, for the first time, government agencies to produce Environmental Impact Statements outlining the effects of government activities on the natural world. Most of the early efforts to obtain such reporting were sporadic and met with refusals or hostilities on the part of big business. The second phase of social and environmental reporting began, in 1989, with the extraordinary move by Ben and Jerry's Ice Cream to hire a "social auditor" to examine the company's impact on society and the environment. This led to the first-ever public report of the impacts of a company on its "stakeholders," everyone involved or impacted by the business. Though there were, as yet, no verifiable standards by which to measure the effectiveness or authenticity of the report or the steps that Ben and Jerry's took to improve its performance in these areas, this path-breaking step moved the concept of business social and environmental reporting into the limelight of public attention. Other socially responsible companies, notably the late Anita Roddick's BodyShop, soon followed suit. Corporate social responsibility reporting, as it came to be called, was on its way to transforming the relationship between business and the public by making it more transparent and open to examination.

The current stage has introduced third-party certification of social responsibility and the development of verifiable standards of conduct. The nonprofit group SustainAbility, led by John Elkington (originator of the term *triple bottom line*) and Julia Hailes, began the process of examining corporate reporting standards with a survey conducted for the U.N. Environmental Program in 1994. The United Nations began to develop a set of "sustainability reporting guidelines" shortly thereafter. The first such actual third-party certification of this kind in the United States took place in 1998, when Avon opened its New York operations to inspection by the newly-formed nonprofit Social Accountability International. In the years since, social responsibility and more recently its offspring, sustainability, have grown to become an important part of how business is monitored by the public. Such reporting communicates a wide range of subject matter about the environmental, social, and economic impacts of a company's activities, products, and services.

Today, corporate sustainability reporting has become both an integral component of how the public tracks business performance and a vital tool for business to begin to understand its own impacts on society and the environment. Sustainability reporting, like the institution of a clear environmental management system, can help businesses identify and address their current and potential risks and their often misunderstood or unappreciated impacts on the greater world. All of the reasons and benefits for greening a business apply equally to reporting the impacts of a business in a systematic way to the public. Reporting improves your relationship with the public, investors, and employees as they begin to see the concrete efforts that you are taking to better your operations. Cost savings are achieved through the improved performance by looking more closely at how your business uses energy, water, and other resources. Such reporting can be both an early-warning signal of potential problems and a self-diagnostic tool for finding, and solving, those problems.

If you have begun to use the foregoing chapters to develop green business actions for your company, you have already taken many of the steps that sustainability encompasses. Your company may not yet have been asked to report any of its environmental initiatives publicly or even privately to other companies in its supply chain. However, as the public seeks more knowledge and accountability from the business world, sustainability reporting is quickly spreading down the supply chains of big business to encompass more and more smaller businesses every day, and the public and the companies themselves will continue to seek to verify the impacts of their operation on society and the natural world. To assist in these efforts, a number of organizations have developed standards and certification programs to standardize and verify the reports that companies make public. Taking a look at a few of the more prominent sustainability reporting programs will help you understand this increasingly important aspect of greening your business.

The Global Reporting Initiative and Ceres Principles

Launched in 1999, this program was a joint effort between the United Nations Environmental Program and the U.S. nonprofit organization, CERES (now Ceres), the Coalition for Environmentally Responsible Economics. Ceres itself had been formed in 1989, partly in response to the Exxon Valdez tragedy in Alaska. Ceres's first action was to develop a clear set of principles, first known as the Valdez Principles, for corporate environmental conduct which was intended to be publicly endorsed by companies as an environmental mission statement or ethic. Now known as the Ceres Principles, this code of environmental ethics included a call for public reporting of company environmental management and efforts. The Ceres Principles are still a clear and concise statement of core environmental standards that all businesses should abide by. Two decades after their development, they remain a hallmark of business responsibility. In Chapter 18, as you seek to develop an environmental mission statement for your company, the Ceres Principles can provide an excellent example. The principles are:

Protection of the Biosphere
We will reduce and make continual progress toward eliminating the release of any substance that may cause environmental damage to the air, water, or the earth or its inhabitants. We will safeguard all habitats affected by our operations and will protect open spaces and wilderness, while preserving biodiversity.

Sustainable Use of Natural Resources
We will make sustainable use of renewable natural resources, such as water, soils and forests. We will conserve non-renewable natural resources through efficient use and careful planning.

Reduction and Disposal of Wastes
We will reduce and where possible eliminate waste through source reduction and recycling. All waste will be handled and disposed of through safe and responsible methods.

Energy Conservation
We will conserve energy and improve the energy efficiency of our internal operations and of the goods and services we sell. We will make every effort to use environmentally safe and sustainable energy sources.

Risk Reduction
We will strive to minimize the environmental, health and safety risks to our employees and the communities in which we operate through safe technologies, facilities and operating procedures, and by being prepared for emergencies.

Safe Products and Services

We will reduce and where possible eliminate the use, manufacture or sale of products and services that cause environmental damage or health or safety hazards. We will inform our customers of the environmental impacts of our products or services and try to correct unsafe use.

Environmental Restoration

We will promptly and responsibly correct conditions we have caused that endanger health, safety or the environment. To the extent feasible, we will redress injuries we have caused to persons or damage we have caused to the environment and will restore the environment.

Informing the Public

We will inform in a timely manner everyone who may be affected by conditions caused by our company that might endanger health, safety or the environment. We will regularly seek advice and counsel through dialogue with persons in communities near our facilities. We will not take any action against employees for reporting dangerous incidents or conditions to management or to appropriate authorities.

Management Commitment

We will implement these Principles and sustain a process that ensures that the Board of Directors and Chief Executive Officer are fully informed about pertinent environmental issues and are fully responsible for environmental policy. In selecting our Board of Directors, we will consider demonstrated environmental commitment as a factor.

Audits and Reports

We will conduct an annual self-evaluation of our progress in implementing these Principles. We will support the timely creation of generally accepted environmental audit procedures. We will annually complete the Ceres Report, which will be made available to the public.

The last of these principles became the spark for the development of the Global Reporting Initiative Guidelines that have become the hallmark of sustainability reporting worldwide. The Guidelines provide an overview of what such reports should generally contain and how they should be developed and monitored. There is no enforced standard, other than public scrutiny, for these reports. Their purpose is to inform both the public and the company how it is performing.

General Sustainability Report Guidelines

A sustainability report should generally contain the following elements:

- A statement of the company's vision and strategy regarding its contribution to sustainability, including a statement from the CEO or owners.

- A profile of the company, describing its major products or services, type of company, and the markets it serves. Details regarding its stakeholders (who the company and its products impact) are also useful.

- A description of the environmental management system that the company has developed to provide direction and strategies for its approach to these issues.

- A set of "performance indicators" that provide a measurable method for the company to monitor and report on its progress in achieving its sustainability goals. These indicators are the core of sustainability reporting. These indicators generally fall into three categories:

  - *Economic indicators* that generally show the net sales and geographic breakdown of its product or services sales to customers; the costs of all goods, materials, and services purchased from suppliers; the total payroll and benefits paid to employees; and finally payments to investors and taxing bodies.

  - *Environmental indicators* that generally report the company's overall impact on the environment, including: the total amount of materials, energy, and water used; any land or management practices that impact biodiversity; a measurement of its greenhouse gas emissions, other pollution, and wastes; any significant impact of its products or services on the environment,; and any fines or penalties for non-compliance with environmental regulations.

  - *Social indicators* that report on the size, diversity, and makeup of the company's workforce; representation of employees by trade unions; any occupational or health accidents or diseases; any training of employees; evidence of adherence to basic human rights standards regarding non-discrimination, collective bargaining, child and forced labor, indigenous rights, corruption, fair competition, and disciplinary standards; and finally any issues relating to customer health, safety, and privacy, such as proper labeling, customer service, and complaints.

Other Sustainability Reporting Standards

EMAS

This is the voluntary European Union Environmental Management and Audit Scheme which provides similar method for EU companies to report their improvements in environmental performance on a continuous basis. EMAS-registered companies certify that they are in compliance with all environmental laws, that they use an environmental management system, and that they report on their environmental performance through the publication of an independently verified environmental statement. They may then use the EMAS logo, which guarantees the reliability of the information provided. For more infomation, see **http://ec.europa.eu/environment/emas**.

ISO 14031 Environmental Performance Evaluation

As part of the overall ISO 14000 environmental standards (of which we looked at the ISO environmental management system in the last chapter), this standard provides a formal process for measuring, analyzing, reporting, and communicating an organization's environmental performance against criteria set by its management. The information may then be communicated to the public under the ISO 14063 standards for communication. Also the ISO 1404 standard provides for the measurement and reporting of a company's greenhouse gas emissions. For more information, see **www.iso-14001.org.uk/index.htm**.

SA 8000

This set of standards has been developed by Social Accountability International and deals primarily with working conditions, similar to the workplace portion of the social indicators of the Global Reporting Initiative. Certification of adherence to the standards is provided for a company's places of employment. Many workplaces, primarily in Brazil, India, and China, have been certified. See **www.sa8000.org**.

Greenhouse Gas Protocol Initiative

Developed jointly by the World Resources Institute and the World Business Council for Sustainable Development, these standards provide for the measurement and reporting of a company's overall greenhouse emissions. Several of their Excel spreadsheets for carbon emission measurements are provided on the accompanying CD. See also: **www.ghgprotocol.org** for more information.

Climate Counts

This very simple online method for reporting carbon emissions has been developed in recent years using a fillable online guide. See **www.climatecounts.org**.

Chapter 17

U.S. Environmental Regulations

Environmental regulations in the United States remain the model for governmental regulation in many countries. Since their main beginnings in the late 1960s, they have been modified and updated to deal with many of the most serious environmental issues that have confronted America. Covering clean air, clean water, pesticides, community right to know, toxic waste cleanups, chemical accidents, oil spills—these powerful laws have been behind many of the major environmental headlines that have shaped the environmental movement. Although the U.S. Congress has failed to confront the most serious environmental issue of our time—climate change and its attendant greenhouse gas emissions— the framework of environmental regulations remains the backbone of protection of the country's environment. Although the current predominantly compliance-based regulatory system has produced many benefits, it has often not provided the flexibility necessary to try alternative and more cost-effective methods. The current system focuses attention on cleanup and control, rather than on product or process redesign that could prevent pollution in the first place. This orients decision makers to "end-of-the-pipe" solutions and removes the focus from whole-systems approaches to environmental issues. In addition, the current system has created an administrative burden for both government and industry. Improvements in this regulatory system to a more performance-based system would allow more innovative approaches to a wide range of environmental issues.

Nevertheless, it is an important step in greening your business to be certain that you make sure that you are obeying all applicable federal, state, and local environmental laws and regulations. All American businesses, no matter how small, must comply with these often stringent rules and regulations. Many businesses are subject to these wide-reaching laws without their knowledge or understanding. The scope and range of the regulations is daunting—filling literally thousands of pages of law and code books. In the U.S., most environmental regulations are under the authority of the Environmental Protection Agency, although other agencies may also share authority in some cases. It is often difficult to find out what laws apply, who they apply to, how the apply, and when they may take effect in a particular situation. In some cases, compliance may mean obtaining permits and filing required paperwork. But complying with these regulations is serious business.

Should you discover that your business may have been violating a federal environmental regulation, the U.S. EPA provides several major incentives for businesses to voluntarily come into compliance with federal environmental laws and regulations. To take advantage of these incentives, essentially you must voluntarily discover, promptly disclose to EPA, quickly correct, and work to prevent recurrence of future environmental violations. If you meet the following conditions, you will be eligible for complete protection from any penalties resulting from the violation. Even if you fail to meet the first condition—systematic discovery—you can still be eligible for 75 percent penalty reduction, and a recommendation for no criminal prosecution based on the violations. Total penalty mitigation requires:

- Systematic discovery of the violation through an environmental audit or the implementation of a regulatory compliance management system.
- Voluntary discovery of the violation was not detected as a result of a legally required monitoring, sampling, or auditing procedure.
- Prompt disclosure in writing to EPA within 21 days of discovery or such shorter time as may be required by law. Discovery occurs when any officer, director, employee, or agent of the facility has an objectively reasonable basis for believing that a violation has or may have occurred.
- Independent discovery and disclosure before EPA or another regulator would likely have identified the violation through its own investigation or information provided by a third party.
- Correction and remediation of the violation within 60 calendar days, in most cases, from the date of discovery.
- Prevention of recurrence of the violation.
- Cooperation by the business is required.

The following table provides only a general overview of the twelve main categories of U.S. regulatory requirements. It is not all-inclusive and does not describe state or local requirements. Its purpose is to give you an overall understanding of the range of U.S. environmental regulations so you will be better prepared to seek assistance from the U.S. or your Environmental Protection Agency and begin looking in more detail at specific regulations that may apply to your business. An Environmental Regulation Compliance Worksheet is also provided at the end of this chapter.

Major Categories of U.S. Environmental Regulations

Type of Impact	Details of Regulation	Applicable Law
Waste disposal liability **Example:** The company that took your waste 10 years ago went bankrupt, leaving a contaminated landfill. Now you may be required to share in the cost for the site's cleanup.	**Overview:** Maintains "Superfund" to pay for cleanup of hazardous waste sites up front. Later, the Environmental Protection Agency (EPA) can recover costs from each "Responsible Party." Those who once owned the site, presently own the site, or sent waste to the site can be an RP. **Thresholds:** Anyone who owned or contributed waste to a site can be a "responsible party." **Requires Permit?** No. **Regulatory Reports?** No, but lots of other paperwork. **Important Considerations: If you ever receive a letter that suggests your business may be an RP, get a good environmental attorney before you reply.**	Comprehensive Environmental Response, Compensation, and Liability Act (CERCLA)

Type of Impact	Details of Regulation	Applicable Law
Wastes containing chemicals even in tiny amounts **Examples:** Parts washing fluids, paint thinners, acids, caustics, toxic chemicals like pesticides or chlorinated solvents, and wastes that have toxic metals in them like lead, cadmium, or chromium.	**Overview:** Tells you what a hazardous waste is and sets requirements for taking care of it on-site, moving it from one place to another, and where and how it may be treated or disposed. Regulation includes special provisions to make recycling easier for universal wastes: mercury-containing lamps, batteries, mercury switches, and recalled pesticides. **Thresholds:** Applies to any amount of hazardous waste. **Requires Permit?** Yes, for certain hazardous waste activities. **Regulatory Reports?** Yes, annually, for some, but not all, generators, and any business that must have a permit. May also require notification of the regulatory agency of hazardous waste activities depending on the amount of waste generated. **Important Considerations: The law requires your business to determine whether any of its wastes are legally classified as hazardous. Make sure this is done properly to avoid severe financial and liability risk if wastes are illegally disposed of (even by accident).**	Resource Conservation and Recovery Act (RCRA) of 1976 and subsequent amendments

Type of Impact	Details of Regulation	Applicable Law
Air pollutants released from business operations **Examples:** Boilers and furnaces, paint and dye application, parts cleaning, sand blasting or other dusty operations.	**Overview:** Sets up a system of controls to be sure that pollutants coming from a business's operations or heating plant do not hurt the overall air quality in the region. It regulates numerous pollutants. Of particular concern to small businesses are volatile organic compounds (VOCs), nitrous oxides (NOx), and hazardous air pollutants (HAPs), though additional ones may apply. **Thresholds:** Numerous thresholds for specific air contaminants, usually given in tons or pounds per year. These thresholds are based on your business's potential to emit (PTE), assuming 24 hour production at peak rates, as well as its actual emissions, so your business could be covered even if its actual emissions are low. **Requires Permit?** Yes, depending on what contaminants are emitted and the amount of actual and potential emissions. **Regulatory Reports?** Yes, annually, if your business is subject to a permit. Daily monitoring and quarterly reporting may also be required depending on the type of operation. **Important Considerations: A business may require a permit based on its potential to emit, even if its actual emissions do not exceed thresholds. Also, you may have to obtain a permit before you can begin construction of operations that will increase air emissions.**	Clean Air Act (CAA) and its amendments

Type of Impact	Details of Regulation	Applicable Law
Contaminated water from business operations or property **Examples:** Process water going off your property through a drain. Storm water that runs off your property through a storm drain or another waterway.	**Overview:** Sets up a system of controls to be sure that contaminated water coming from cities, businesses, and farms does not hurt waterways such as wetlands, ponds, streams, and lakes, or harm groundwater quality. Industrial wastewater cannot be discharged into a septic system. If you put anything but sanitary waste down the drain, you must abide by the local sanitary sewer ordinance. **Thresholds:** Varies for each type of contaminant, based on where it is going and what authority has control. It can be very small, such as a couple of parts per million. **Requires Permit?** Yes, if your business dumps contaminated water into a waterway, onto the ground, or into the street, a storm drain, or a ditch, you may have to obtain a permit, even if you treat the wastewater first. Some local authorities also require a permit for discharges to the sanitary sewer. Under storm water regulations, even if you are not required to have a storm water permit, you still may have to file a "no exposure certification." **Regulatory Reports?** Yes, if your business is covered by the permit requirements. Monitoring may also be required. Businesses required to have a storm water permit will also have to submit a storm water pollution prevention plan.	Clean Water Act (CWA) and its amendments

Type of Impact	Details of Regulation	Applicable Law
Chemical spills to air, water, or land **Examples:** A chemical leaks into a storm drain and contaminates a stream. A valve on your refrigeration unit fails, releasing ammonia gas to the air.	**Overview:** Makes possible a national emergency response program for certain spills and accidental releases. If your business releases certain chemicals, called "hazardous substances," you must notify the National Response Center. **Thresholds:** Amount of a substance released is more than or equal to its listed "Reportable Quantity," or "RQ." These amounts vary by substance and can be as small as one pound. The RQ requirements are found at **www.epa.gov/superfund/programs/er/triggers/haztrigs/rqover.htm** **Requires Permit?** No. **Regulatory Reports?** Yes, in follow-up to reported releases.	Comprehensive Environmental Response, Compensation, and Liability Act (CERCLA)
	Overview: Requires you to notify state and local emergency planning commissions immediately if your business has an unplanned release of certain chemicals. In addition to the CERCLA hazardous substances mentioned just above, it covers "extremely hazardous substances" that are listed in regulations put in place to carry out the Emergency Planning and Community Right-to-Know Act. **Thresholds**: Amount of a substance released is more than or equal to its "Reportable Quantity" (RQ). **Requires Permit?** No. **Regulatory Reports?** Yes, in follow-up to reported releases.	*Emergency Release Notification* under the Emergency Planning and Community Right-to-Know Act (EPCRA)

Type of Impact	Details of Regulation	Applicable Law
Emergency planning for chemicals stored and used at your business site **Example:** Your business has hazardous chemicals on-site that could pose a danger to the local community if they spilled, were released, or involved in a fire.	**Overview:** Puts in place coordination and planning so that state and local government agencies can prepare for and respond to hazardous chemical spills. If your business is covered by these requirements, you must notify state and local planning commissions and assist these agencies with maintaining the local emergency plan, including providing pertinent information. **Thresholds:** If the amount of a listed substance kept on-site at your business is more than or equal to the listed Threshold Planning Quantity (TPQ), then you must participate in local emergency planning as described above. TPQs vary by substance and can be as little as one pound. **Requires Permit?** No. **Regulatory Reports?** Notification of any changes at your facility that affect emergency planning.	*Emergency Planning* under the Emergency Planning and Community Right-to-Know Act (EPCRA)

Type of Impact	Details of Regulation	Applicable Law
Telling the community and local responders about chemicals stored and used at your business site **Example:** Your business has hazardous chemicals on-site that could pose a danger to the local community if they spilled, were released, or involved in a fire.	**Overview:** Provides a way for the public to access information about hazardous chemicals that community businesses use, store, or release to the environment. Requires you to submit copies of Material Safety Data Sheets for certain hazardous chemicals you keep and use at your business, and to report how much of each you have. **Thresholds:** For listed substances, the Threshold Planning Quantity (TPQ) or 500 pounds, whichever is less; for all other OSHA hazardous chemicals, 10,000 pounds. **Requires Permit?** No. **Regulatory Reports?** Yes, an annual chemical inventory report, called a "Tier 1" or "Tier 2" report, is required. Which report your business will have to file depends on local and state requirements.	*Hazardous Chemical Reporting: Community Right-to-Know* under the Emergency Planning and Community Right-to-Know Act (EPCRA)

Type of Impact	Details of Regulation	Applicable Law
Telling the community and regulators about chemicals released into the environment as part of your normal business operations **Example:** Your business has hazardous chemicals on-site that could pose a danger to the local community if they spilled, were released, or involved in a fire.	**Overview:** For certain hazardous chemicals used by certain industries (as determined by SIC code), requires you to measure or estimate the amount that came on your site during the year and what happened to it, such as, how much went into your waste stream. You are exempt if your business does not have 10 or more full-time employees. This information is made available to the public, such as on EPA's EnviroFacts web site. See **www.epa.gov/enviro**. **Thresholds:** You manufacture or process 25,000 pounds or otherwise use 10,000 pounds of a listed hazardous substance at your site in a year. (Certain chemicals of special concern have lower thresholds, like mercury at 10 pounds, lead at 100 pounds, and polycyclic aromatic compounds at 100 pounds.) **Requires Permit?** No. **Regulatory Reports?** Yes, an annual Toxic Release Inventory (TRI) that identifies the amounts of toxic chemicals, covered by the requirement, that your business releases to the environment.	*Toxic Chemical Release Reporting: Community Right-to-Know* under the Emergency Planning and Community Right-to-Know Act (EPCRA)

Type of Impact	Details of Regulation	Applicable Law
Managing Chemical Risks **Example:** You have a process within your business operations that could release a dangerous amount of toxic chemicals to the air if it malfunctioned.	**Overview:** Requires you to evaluate certain processes of your business operations to determine whether they could pose a danger to your neighbors through an accidental chemical release. If so, you must undertake planning to prevent malfunctions from occurring and to reduce the harm from a chemical release if it does occur. **Thresholds:** The amount of a chemical in a process is equal to or more than its listed threshold. **Requires Permit?** No. **Regulatory Report?** Yes, requires initial submission of Risk Management Plan and registration form that documents that your business has completed the hazard assessment, analysis, and planning necessary to prevent and respond to accidental chemical releases from any process covered by the regulation. Also, requires updates according to a schedule given in the regulation.	*Chemical Accident Prevention* under the Clean Air Act

Type of Impact	Details of Regulation	Applicable Law
Pesticide Use **Examples:** Your staff applies weed killers on outdoor property, or uses pesticides to control rodents or insects, or you hire a pesticide applicator to do this.	**Overview:** Governs the use and disposal of all pesticides to prevent harm to people and the environment. Requires that you be sure that people using certain pesticides at your business are certified, and, if you are an agricultural business, that you put in place an extensive Worker Protection program for employees who work with pesticides. (There are many additional requirements if your business manufactures pesticides or creates plants that are genetically pest resistant.) **Thresholds:** Applies to any amount of restricted-use pesticide, and certain other pesticides. **Requires Permit?** Requires certification of persons who apply certain pesticides. **Regulatory Report?** No.	Federal Insecticide, Fungicide and Rodenticide Act (FIFRA)

Type of Impact	Details of Regulation	Applicable Law
Polychlorinated Biphenyls (PCBs) **Examples:** You have equipment that uses a PCB-containing transformer as a component; you have to replace PCB-containing electrical ballasts in your lighting fixtures.	**Overview:** Requires identification and extensive recordkeeping for PCB-containing items. Sets requirements for taking care of these items on-site, moving them from one place to another, and where and how they may be treated or disposed. **Thresholds:** Applies to certain PCB-containing material (depends on whether PCB concentration of the source of contamination was 50 ppm or greater). **Requires Permit?** Yes, if your business treats or disposes of any PCB-containing wastes. **Regulatory Report?** Yes, requires submission of annual report if you use or store greater than 45 kg at one time. Reporting requirements are identified in 40 CFR 761.180.	*Polychlorinated Biphenyls (PCBs)* under the Toxic Substances Control Act (TSCA)

Type of Impact	Details of Regulation	Applicable Law
Storage, management, and disposal of petroleum products **Examples:** Your business has one or more storage tanks for petroleum products such as gasoline, diesel fuel, or heating oil. Your business drains used oil from motor vehicles. Your business has potential to spill petroleum products into a waterway.	**Overview:** Applies to petroleum products stored and used, such as vehicle fuel, heating oil, and motor oil. Underground petroleum storage tanks must meet performance standards, the purpose of which is to prevent leaks into soil or groundwater. (Underground storage tanks containing other hazardous chemicals may also be regulated.) Requires additional controls and management practices to detect, prevent, and respond to petroleum leaks or spills. If your property becomes contaminated by a petroleum spill, there are specific cleanup requirements that apply. **Thresholds:** Your business is required to develop a Spill Prevention Control and Countermeasure Plan if your business has a total on-site storage capacity of more than 1,320 gallons of petroleum products in aboveground tanks and containers (containers less than 55 gallons in capacity are exempt) or has underground petroleum storage capacity of greater than 42,000 gallons (completely buried tanks regulated under 40 CFR Parts 280 and 281 are exempt), and can reasonably be expected to discharge oil in harmful quantities into waters of the United States. **Requires Permit?** No. **Regulatory Report?** Yes, in follow-up to reportable releases.	*Underground storage tank and used oil regulations* of the Resource Conservation and Recovery Act (RCRA) of 1976 and subsequent amendments. EPA's *Oil Pollution Prevention Regulation, part* of the Clean Water Act (CWA).

Additional U.S. Environmental Regulations

In addition to the foregoing 12 major regulatory categories, there are numerous other regulations that might apply to your particular type of business. The following listing provides a generalized survey of the various types of categories of federal environmental regulations and initiatives. If your business impacts any of the following areas, please check for details at **www.epa.gov/lawsregs/envtopics/index.html.** (By the way, don't be fooled by the listing of "climate change," it does not yet provide any regulations, merely a link to the various U.S. policy responses to climate change, such as they are.)

Acid Rain
Agriculture
Air
Asbestos
Automotive Industry
Beaches
Brownfields
Cars, Trucks, Motorized Equipment
Chemicals
Children
China
Cleanup
Climate Change
Computers/ Electronics
Construction
Cooperative Conservation
Coral Reef Protection
Drinking Water
Dry Cleaning
Energy
Enforcement
Environmental Justice
Extraction
Federal Facilities
Fishing
Food Quality
Forest
Furniture
Garment/ Textiles

Healthcare/ Hospitals
International Affairs
Leather
Low-Income Populations
Lumber
Mercury
Metals
Minerals/ Mines
Ocean
Oil Spills
Paper
Particulate Matter
Pesticides
Petroleum
Pharmaceuticals
Plastics
Pulp
Radiation
Rubber
Shipbuilding
Solid Waste
Superfund
Tires
Toxic Substances
Transportation
Tribes
Underground Storage Tanks
Universal Waste
Wetlands

Environmental Regulation Compliance Worksheet

Prepared by:	Date:	Business:	
Address:			Phone:
Business Operation Involved	Type and or Name of Regulation	Local, State, or Federal?	Compliance Requirements

Chapter 18

Preparing Your Green Business Plan

Once you have completed all of the initial steps for greening your business that have been outlined thus far in this book, you'll be ready to prepare your company's Green Business Plan. Why does your company even need a formal green plan? It helps you to keep track of all of your environmental activities so you can better streamline and organize them, helping to keep the time and effort that you and your employees will have to devote to them at a reasonable level. Done well, your green business plan will make implementing your environmental plans easier and more natural for everyone in your business. Employees will appreciate that your green plan spells out exactly what's expected of them. Your green business plan will provide a framework that allows you to more easily see opportunities for improvement and additional cost savings that may be available. Finally, if you have been thinking about developing an environmental management system that would be certified or recognized by an organization outside of your business, developing your green plan will put you in a good position to do that.

Develop a Green Mission and Policy Statement

The first task in actually preparing your green plan is to write a company environmental policy or green mission statement. Your company's environmental policy is the shared starting point for people to understand the basic environmental beliefs, commitments, and goals that you would like to become a central element of how your company does business. It can state how environmental concerns are considered in the company's decision making and how these concerns fit into its day-to-day activities. It should be relatively short, to the point, and communicated throughout your company so that employees understand and remember the policy. All the other steps for improving the environmental performance of your company will be geared towards meeting the environmental goals stated in the policy. An environmental mission statement usually begins with a declaration of your business's commitment to the environment. It often includes a commitment to continuously improve your company's environmental performance. Many businesses also commit to keeping employees and community members safe as part of their environmental policy. In addition to a declaration, the environmental policy states how the business will live up to its declaration. The environmental policy does not have to be lengthy or wordy. The more to the point, the more effective it will be in communicating your intent. When putting the policy together, consider what your company is trying to achieve with your environmental activities and how you will accomplish your goals. It should only include strategies and actions that you are willing to commit your business's resources to. Also think about how the policy will be regarded by employees within your business. Later, once you get it fine-tuned, you will find that your environmental policy can be helpful to communicate your business's approach to environmental issues to local officials, customers, the media, and others outside your company.

Look back at the Ceres Principles that were outlined in Chapter 16. These can provide a good starting point for concepts that you may wish to include in your company green mission statement. Think about what your company wants to achieve through your environmental policy. You may wish to brainstorm with your management or employees and develop a list of action words or very short phrases that reflects your company's environmental commitment. Drawing on the list of words, phrases, and concepts that you have brainstormed, put them together into a few-sentence statement. The next step should be to list the ways that your company plans to use to achieve the commitments or goals expressed in the initial statement. Finally, combine your initial mission or goal statement with your stated outline of how you will fulfill your new green mission.

Determine Each Person's Responsibilities

For your efforts in greening your business to be as successful as possible, you will need to determine who in your company will be responsible for the various aspects of your green business plan. For the one-person business, this part is easy—you, the owner, are responsible. For any business with employees (and even sole proprietorships can have employees), ultimate success for your green plan may well rest on involving everyone in your business in both the planning and implementation stages. You will need support for all aspects of your green plan for it to become a core value in your business. Everyone who will be impacted by your green business efforts should understand the benefits and scope of the plan as well as any additional responsibilities or work required. Having roles and responsibilities clearly written out helps employees understand what part of the company's greening activities they are responsible for and how their role relates to the roles of others. By establishing who is responsible for what, your green business plan will also help to increase accountability within the company and help motivate employees to take more personal responsibility because their tasks are well defined and not overwhelming. By making sure all tasks are assigned, it is less likely that they will fall between the cracks or be neglected if a key employee leaves. Each small business is unique and has to work out environmental roles and responsibilities in a way that fits into its particular business culture. It will also be beneficial to find a balance of responsibilities among all employees so that environmental management will not take up too much of anyone's time and will truly be a team effort. Some of the added work that employees or management may have to take on are:

- Collecting information for various environmental assessments of the business, such as for energy use, water use, waste disposal, etc.

- Preparation of the various worksheets and process maps regarding your business green plan.

- Participating in training or education efforts to understand any new policies, methods, or procedures your company green plan may require.

- Implementation of any of the changes that your company environmental plan requires, such as changes in production, equipment, storage, or processes.

- Communicating your new environmental commitment to customers and the public.

This chapter provides a simple chart-based method of identifying and assigning responsibility for various aspects of your business environmental plan. You will need to give careful thought to who should handle each of the various tasks that are necessary for your green plan to succeed. Different people may need to handle the assessment than will handle the actual implementation of the plans. Likewise, your bookkeeper or accountant may need to be involved in the various economic analyses that may be required. The following table (which is also included on the enclosed CD as a fillable PDF form) should help you identify who will have the responsibility for making your environmental plan a success. Refer to this chart regularly to see if it needs updating and to check on who needs to be consulted regarding progress toward your company's green goals. When you have completed this chart, be sure to include it in your overall green business plan.

Green Plan Responsibility Worksheet

Green Plan Function	Person	Regular Job
Company Policy: Development of company green mission statement and policy		
Company Policy: Overall responsibility for preparation of company green plan		
Energy use: Preparation of company carbon footprint, process map, and action worksheet		
Energy use: Preparation of company energy use survey and economic analysis of company energy use		
Energy use: Implementation and monitoring of new company energy use plans		
Water Use: Preparation of company water use assessment, water consumption worksheet, process map, and action worksheet		
Water Use: Preparation of water consumption worksheet and economic analysis of company water use		
Water Use: Implementation and monitoring of new company water use plans		
Waste Management: Preparation of company waste assessment, process map, and action worksheet		
Waste Management: Preparation of economic analysis of company waste reduction plans		
Waste Management: Review of hazardous waste regulations and study of company compliance		
Waste Management: Implementation and monitoring of new company waste management plans		
Transportation: Preparation of company travel and transportation assessment, transportation carbon footprint, process map, and action worksheet		
Transportation: Preparation of economic analysis of company travel and transportation plans		
Transportation: Implementation and monitoring of new company travel and transportation plans		

Office Equipment and Computing: Preparation of equipment and computer survey and equipment and computer action worksheet		
Office Equipment and Computing: Implementation and monitoring of new company green equipment and computing plans		
Purchasing: Preparation of company green purchasing assessment, process map, supply chain worksheet, action worksheet, and distribution of supply chain and purchasing questionnaire		
Purchasing: Preparation of purchasing life-cycle assessments and economic analysis of company green purchasing plans		
Purchasing: Implementation and monitoring of new company green purchasing plans		
Building: Development of company green building or remodeling plans and preparation of company building plan action worksheet		
Building: Preparation of economic analysis of company green building or remodeling plans		
Building: Implementation and monitoring of new company green building or remodeling plans		
Product Design: Evaluation of company products and future product designs using product design worksheet		
Product Design: Preparation of limited life-cycle assessment (or more detailed life-cycle assessments) of company product design plans		
Product Design: Implementation and monitoring of new company materials and design plans		
Eco-Labeling/Certification/Reporting: Preparation of any applications for eco-labeling, environmental certification, or sustainability reporting paperwork		
Environmental Management System: Development and implementation of any company environmental management system		
Environmental Regulations: Study of environmental regulation requirements and preparation of environmental regulation compliance worksheet		

Prepare Your Green Business Plan and Manual

After you have developed your company green mission statement and policy and you have assigned the responsibilities for each aspect of your overall green business plan, you will then need to compile and create the formal plan and put it in a company green manual. Compiling all of the paperwork and information may be a rather time-consuming task, but it will more than repay itself in time saved in the future because your green business plan will allow you to find information when you need it, even if the responsible person is not around. This will help ensure that all of the necessary tasks are done consistently throughout the business.

This phase of the green business plan process is simply a matter of assembling into one place all the various paperwork that you will be using for your overall assessments, surveys, and action plans—including your newly prepared policy statement and green plan responsibility worksheet. You will need to provide a simple cover sheet and table of contents (both of which are shown in this chapter and provided on the accompanying CD as either a fillable PDF form or a text form that you may alter as necessary). Then, you'll need to assemble the underlying information you have gathered into a simple manual that will help your business follow its green plan.

Your initial green business plan can consist of uncompleted paperwork—essentially all of the various forms and worksheets that are included in this book. The basic idea is to compile all of the needed paperwork material into one place so that they'll be accessible and easily located. The blank forms can be used to complete the various assessment or action tasks, or you can use the fillable PDF forms on the CD to complete the forms on your computer. Once you (or the person assigned to the task) have completed each worksheet, survey, or assessment, the completed form should be placed in your green business plan manual. If desired, you can cut and paste the actions that you have selected (from each text version of the action worksheets) to implement for each issue into an overall text file plan of action, or you may simply use the completed PDF forms for that purpose. If you have used any of the additional software, online resources, or the Excel spreadsheets that are included on the CD to prepare additional reports (such as more detailed carbon footprint analyses), you will also need to include that paperwork in your final green business plan manual. Once you have compiled all of your initial paperwork, simply put it all together in a hard-copy version so that it can be referred to frequently and all of the necessary materials can be found in one place. A simple three-ring binder is all you'll need. Following is a standard-format cover sheet and basic table of contents of all of the paperwork that you may wish to include in your green business plan and the chapter numbers for reference.

Green Business Plan

Name of Company	
Address of Company	
Phone Number	
Fax Number	
Main Email Address	
Website Address	
Blog Address	
General description of business	

Basic Contents of Green Business Plan Manual

Cover sheet (Chapter 18)

Table of Contents (Chapter 18)

Company Green Mission Statement and Policy (Chapter 18)

Green Plan Responsibility Worksheet (Chapter 18)

Energy Use Worksheet (Chapter 6)

Energy Survey Worksheet (Chapter 6)

Basic Carbon Footprint Worksheet (Chapter 6)

Energy Use Process Map (Chapter 6)

Energy Efficiency Action Worksheet (Chapter 6)

Energy Efficiency Economic Analysis Worksheet (Chapter 6)

Water Consumption Worksheet (Chapter 7)

Water Survey Worksheet (Chapter 7)

Water Use Process Map (Chapter 7)

Water Conservation Action Worksheet (Chapter 7)

Water Conservation Economic Analysis Worksheet (Chapter 7)

Waste Expense Worksheet (Chapter 8)

Waste Survey Worksheet (Chapter 8)

Waste and Recycling Process Map (Chapter 8)

Waste and Recycling Action Worksheet (Chapter 8)

Waste Reduction Action Worksheet (Chapter 8)

Waste Reduction Economic Analysis Worksheet (Chapter 8)

Business Transportation Carbon Footprint Worksheet (Chapter 9)

Travel and Transportation Action Worksheet (Chapter 9)

Travel and Transportation Economic Analysis Worksheet (Chapter 9)

Equipment and Computer Survey (Chapter 10)

Equipment and Computer Action Worksheet (Chapter 10)

Supply Chain Process Map (Chapter 11)

Supply Chain Worksheet (Chapter 11)

Supply Chain Action Worksheet (Chapter 11)

Supply Chain and Purchasing Questionnaire (Chapter 11)

Green Building Action Worksheet (Chapter 12)

Building Upgrade Economic Analysis (Chapter 12)

Limited Life-Cycle Assessment Worksheet (Chapter 13)

Green Product Design Worksheet (Chapter 13)

Environmental Regulation Compliance Worksheet (Chapter 17)

Performance Monitoring Worksheet (Chapter 18)

Performance Monitoring Worksheet

Date of Review:	Company:	
Name of Reviewer:	Title:	
Goal and Unit of Measure	Annual Target	Target Met
Energy Use in kWh per month	10% less	
Natural Gas Use in therms per month	15% less	
Purchased Energy Carbon Footprint lbs/mo	10% less	
Water Use in gallons per month	20% less	
Waste Reduction in pounds per month	25% less	
Recycling Rate in pounds per month	20% more	
Transportation Use in miles per month	10% less	
Transportation Carbon Footprint in lbs/mo	10% less	

Implement and Monitor Your Green Business Plan

Your green business plan manual outlines and details how environmental management activities will be organized within your business. You should already have involved your management and employees in the entire process of developing your green business plan from the start—from brainstorming a company green mission statement to assigning responsibilities and deciding which actions are most viable for your company.

If your business has employees, after you have defined their various responsibilities and determined which action steps will need to be implemented, you need a way to implement the plan and communicate it to each employee. This is best done formally by giving each employee a copy detailing his or her specific responsibilities, such as any worksheets they will need to complete or action plans that they will be expected to carry out. You will probably wish to hold a company-wide meeting to discuss the specifics of your new company policies and the various overall approaches that you hope to take with its implementation. As owner or manager, it will be your responsibility to make sure that the overall tasks are being implemented in a timely fashion.

Setting Targets and Performance Monitoring

This task verifies whether or not goals stated in the your mission statement and the actions that you have implemented are being achieved. On a regular basis you need to review the goals of your green plan, consider the system of action and accountability it has established throughout your company, and look at the results of monitoring to see how well the plan is working towards its stated goals. For this activity to be effective, you will need to set some targets for your actions. It is a good idea to set aside some time at least once a quarter to see if the goals and targets are being met. It may also make sense to seek out the opinions of your employees and management and see how they are perceiving the overall success of the green plan. However you decide to approach it, you can use the Performance Monitoring Worksheet in this chapter as a guide.

To effectively monitor your company's environmental improvement, you will need some way to measure progress towards your goals. Measures are usually expressed in numbers—tons of waste generated, pounds of carbon emitted, or actual dollars saved on energy bills. For example, if your *goal* is to reduce hazardous waste, then your *measure* might be the pounds of waste generated over a year's time. You may also wish to set specific targets for your goals. A *target* tells you by how much you want to achieve with your goal, as expressed by your chosen measure. For example, if your goal is to reduce waste, and your measure is the amount of waste generated over one year, then a target might be to reduce that amount by 10 percent within one year. Specific goals and targets are useful to everyone in your company who has to help achieve your company's environmental goals, by allowing them to know exactly what they should be shooting for. The Performance Monitoring Worksheet shown previously will guide you in identifying meaningful targets and in monitoring the progress towards those targets. As your green business plan matures, both your goals and targets will need to be revisited. You may choose to keep the same goal but change the target to reflect a higher performance expectation. Or, you may choose to retire certain goals and adapt new ones to reflect new environmental challenges your business is facing. The idea is that the goals and targets work together to spark ongoing improvement in your business's green performance. A few generalized goals and targets are provided on the worksheet in this book to give you an idea on how to complete this worksheet. Both the PDF and text versions of this worksheet, provided on the CD, are blank to allow you to set specific goals and targets that are tailored to the needs of your company's green plan.

Beyond Greening Your Business

As you work to implement all of the various changes that the development of a company green plan entails, you may begin to find other exciting avenues for your business to pursue. You may decide to develop your own renewable energy system and work with others in your community who are doing the same. Your recycling efforts may lead you in the direction of using more recycled products or even developing ways to use more recycled material in your own business, perhaps in the manufacture of better, more efficient products. Your green business actions may lead you to take more initiative in greening your home energy, water, and waste decisions. Choices that you make in considering your company's transportation and travel needs may lead you toward working in your community to develop better and more public transportation for your region. The investigation of the life-cycles of your products may lead you to decide to develop radically more efficient products for your own company or for sale to others. You may decide, in fact, to change the entire direction of your company and fully pursue the goal of making it a truly sustainable business.

Whatever direction the greening of your business helps you to take, you will be taking the journey with millions of others who are also seeking to lessen their—and their businesses'—impact on the earth. The steps that you take, regardless of how small or halting they may be, will be in the right direction—toward a future in which our collective system of commerce begins to heal the earth and begins to restore our sense of harmony with our environment. You'll be taking those steps, with millions of other people around the earth, toward the ultimate goal of sustainability—toward assuring that somehow life—in all its myriad forms—continues forever.

Bibliography

Books

Anderson, Ray. *Mid-Course Correction: Toward a Sustainable Enterprise: The Interface Model*. Atlanta: Peregrinzilla Press, 1999.

Ausubel, Kenny, and J. P. Harpignies. *Nature's Operating Instructions: the True Biotechnologies*. San Francisco: Sierra Club Books, 2004.

Benyus, Janine M. *Biomimicry: Innovation Inspired by Nature*. New York: William Morrow, 2002.

Bornstein, David. *How to Change the World: Social Entrepreneurs and the Power of New Ideas*. New York: Oxford UP, 2007.

Bradford, Travis. *Solar Revolution: the Economic Transformation of the Global Energy Industry*. Cambridge MA: The MIT Press, 2006.

Brown, Lester R. *Eco-Economy: Building an Economy for the Earth*. New York: W. W. Norton & Company, 2001.

Cairncross, Frances. *Green, Inc.: A Guide To Business And The Environment*. Washington D.C.: Island Press, 1995.

Cohen, Ben, and Mal Warwick. *Values-Driven Business: How to Change the World, Make Money, and Have Fun*. San Francisco: Berrett-Koehler Publishers, 2006.

Conley, Chip, and Eric Friedenwald-Fishman. *Marketing That Matters: 10 Practices to Profit Your Business and Change the World*. San Francisco: Berrett-Koehler Publishers, 2006.

Edwards, Adres R. *The Sustainability Revolution: Portrait of a Paradigm Shift*. Gabriola Island BC Canada: New Society, 2005.

Epstein, Marc J. *Making Sustainability Work: Best Practices in Managing and Measuring Corporate Social, Environmental and Economic Impacts*. San Francisco: Berrett-Kohler Publishers, 2008.

Esty, Daniel C., and Andrew S. Winston. *Green to Gold: How Smart Companies Use Environmental Strategy to Innovate, Create Value, and Build Competitive Advantage*. New Haven CT: Yale University Press, 2006.

Forbes, Peter. *The Gecko's Foot: Bio-Inspiration: Engineering New Materials From Nature*. New York: W. W. Norton & Company, 2005.

Frankel, Carl. *In Earth's Company: Business, Environment and the Challenge of Sustainability*. Stony Creek CT: New Society Publishers, 1998.

Gardner, Gary, and Thomas Prugh. *State of the World 2008: Toward a Sustainable Global Economy*. New York: W. W. Norton & Company, 2008.

Geiser, Kenneth. *Materials Matter: Toward a Sustainable Materials Policy*. Cambridge MA: The MIT Press, 2001.

Gordon, Pamela J. *Lean and Green: Profit for Your Workplace and the Environment*. San Francisco: Berrett-Koehler Publishers, 2001.

Grant, John. *The Green Marketing Manifesto*. West Sussex England: John Wiley & Sons Ltd., 2007.

Hart, Stuart L. *Capitalism At the Crossroads: Aligning Business, Earth, and Humanity*. Upper Saddle River NJ: Wharton School Publishing, 2007.

Hawken, Paul, Amory Lovins, and L. Hunter Lovins. *Natural Capitalism: Creating the Next Industrial Revolution*. Boston: Little, Brown and Company, 2002.

Hawken, Paul. *Blessed Unrest: How the Largest Movement in the World Came Into Being and Why No One Saw It Coming*. New York: Viking, 2007.

Hawken, Paul. *The Ecology of Commerce*. New York: HarperCollins, 1993.

Hirshberg, Gary. *Stirring It Up: How to Make Money and Save the World*. New York: Hyperion, 2008.

Hitchcock, Darcy, and Marsha Willard. T*he Business Guide to Sustainability: Practical Strategies and Tools for Organizations*. Sterling VA: EarthScan, 2006.

Hoffman, Andrew J., and John G. Woody. *Climate Change: What's Your Business Strategy?* Boston: Harvard Business Press, 2008.

Hoffman, Andrew J. *Carbon Strategies: How Leading Companies are Reducing Their Climate Change Footprint*. Ann Arbor MI: The University of Michigan Press, 2007.

Johnston, David, and Kim Master. *Green Remodeling : Changing the World One Room At a Time*. Gabriola Island BC Canada: New Society Publishers, 2007.

Laszlo, Chris. *The Sustainable Company: How to Create Lasting Value through Social and Environmental Performance.* Washington D.C.: Island Press: 2005

Laszlo, Chris. *Sustainable Value: How the World's Leading Companies Are Doing Well by Doing Good.* Stanford CA: Stanford Business Books: 2008

Lerner, Steve. *Eco-Pioneers: Practical Visionaries Solving Today's Environmental Problems.* Cambridge MA: The MIT Press, 1998.

Lockwood, Charles, Kimberly O'Neill Packard, Forest L. Reinhardt, Amory B. Lovins, L. H. Lovins, Paul Hawken, Stuart L. Hart, Jonathan Lash, Fred Wellington, Bill Sells, and Alissa J. Stern. *Harvard Business Review on Green Business Strategy.* Boston: Harvard Business School Press, 2007.

Lovins, Amory B., Jonathan G. Koomey, and Nathan J. Glasgow. *Winning the Oil Endgame: Innovation for Profits, Jobs and Security.* Snowmass CO: Rocky Mountain Institute, 2005.

Makower, Joel. *The E Factor - the Bottom-Line Approach to Environmentally Responsible Business.* New York: Penguin Group, 1994.

McDonough, William, and Michael Braungart. *Cradle to Cradle: Remaking the Way We Make Things.* New York: North Point Press, 2002.

McKay, Kim, Jenny Bonnin, and Tim Wallace. *True Green At Work: 100 Ways You Can Make the Environment Your Business.* Washington DC: National Geographic Press, 2008.

Molella, Arthur, and Joyce Bedi. *Inventing for the Environment.* Cambridge MA, The MIT Press, 2003.

Myers, Norman, and Jennifer Kent. *Perverse Subsidies: How Misused Tax Dollars Harm the Environment and the Economy.* Washington DC: Island Press, 2001.

Nattrass, Brian and Mary Altomare. *Dancing with the Tiger: Learning Sustainability Step by Natural Step.* Gabriola Island BC Canada: New Society Publishers, 2002.

Nattrass, Brian and Mary Altomare. *The Natural Step for Business: Wealth, Ecology & the Evolutionary Corporation.* Gabriola Island BC Canada: New Society Publishers, 1999.

Orr, David. *The Nature of Design: Ecology, Culture, and Human Intention.* New York: Oxford University Press, 2004.

Pernick, Ron, and Clint Wilder. *The Clean Tech Revolution: the Next Big Growth and Investment Opportunity.* New York: HarperCollins, 2007.

Popoff, Frank and Livio D. DeSimone. *Eco-Efficiency: The Business Link to Sustainable Development.* Cambridge MA: The MIT Press, 2000.

Robert, Karl-Henrik. *The Natural Step Story: Seeding a Quiet Revolution.* Gabriola Island BC Canada: New Society Publishers, 2002.

Ruhl, J. B., Steven E. Kraft, and Christopher L. Lant. *The Law and Policy of Ecosystem Services.* Washington DC: Island Press, 2007.

Savitz, Andrew. *The Triple Bottom Line: How Today's Best-Run Companies Are Achieving Economic, Social and Environmental Success - and How You Can Too.* Somerset NJ: Josey-Bass, 2006.

Schmidheiny, Stephan and the World Business Council for Sustainable Developmen. *Changing Course: A Global Business Perspective on Development and the Environment.* Cambridge MA, The MIT Press, 1992.

Sitarz, Daniel. *Agenda 21: The Earth Summit Strategy to Save Our Planet.* Boulder CO: EarthPress, 1994.

Sitarz, Daniel. *Sustainable America: America's Environment, Economy, and Society in the 21st Century.* Carbondale IL: EarthPress, 1998.

Smil, Vaclav. *Transforming the Twentieth Century: Technical Innovations and Their Consequences.* New York: Oxford University Press, 2006.

Townsend, Amy K. *Green Business: A Five-part Model for Creating an Environmentally Responsible Company.* Atglen PA, Schiffer Publishing, 2006

Van der Ryn, Sim and Stuart Cowan. *Ecological Design.* Washington D.C.: Island Press, 1995

Von Weizsacker, Ernst, Amory B. Lovins, and L. Hunter Lovins. *Factor Four: Doubling Wealth, Halving Resource Use.* London: Earthscan, 2001.

Wackernagel, Mathis, and William Rees. *Our Ecological Footprint: Reducing Human Impact on the Earth.* Gabriola Island BC Canada: New Society Publishers, 1996.

Watts, Philip and Chad Holliday and Stephan Schmidheiny. *Walking the Talk: The Business Case for Sustainable Development.* San Fransisco: Berrett-Kohler Publishers, 2002

Willard, Bob. *The Sustainability Advantage: Seven Business Case Benefits of a Triple Bottom Line.* Gabriola Island BC Canada: New Society, 2002.

Reports

(Note: All information contained on the CD accompanying this book was also consulted in the preparation of this work. Please see the listings for Publications and Spreadsheets in Appendix A.)

A New Vision: An Organizational Guide to Pollution Prevention. U.S. Environmental Protection Agency. 124 pp., 2001.

Audit and Reduction Manual for Industrial Emissions and Wastes. United Nations Industrial Development Program. 124 pp., 1991.

Better By Design: An Innovation Guide Using Natural Design Solutions. Minnesota Office of Environmental Assistance. 36 pp., 2006.

Building the UN Global Compact Principles into Business: A Practical Integration Guide. Business for Social Responsibility. 33 pp., 2005.

Build It Right: Cleaner Energy for Cleaner Buildings. Renewable Energy Policy Project, American Council for an Energy-Efficient Economy. 24 pp., 2000.

Business and Economic Development: The Impact of Corporate Responsibility Standards and Practices. AccountAbility, 76 pp., 2003.

Business and the Environment: Solutions for a Changing World. Business Guide to Waste Reduction and Recycling (Guide and Workbook). Xerox Corporation. Guide: 53 pp., Workbook: 81 pp., 1998.

Business Guide to a Sustainable Supply Chain: A Practical Guide. New Zealand Business Council for Sustainable Development. 52 pp., 2003.

Buy Recycled Guidebook. Buy Recycled Business Alliance, National Recycling Coalition, 27 pp., Undated.

Cleaner Production Manual for Small and Medium Enterprise. Curtin University of Technology. 100 pp., 2001.

Clean, Green, and Read All Over: Ten Rules for Effective Corporate Environmental and Sustainability Reporting. J. Emil Morhardt, ASQ Quality Press. 26 pp., 2002.

Concise Self-Assessment Guide to Environmentally Sustainable Commerce. West Michigan Sustainable Business Forum. 13 pp., 1997.

Deloitte Sustainability Reporting Scorecard. Deloitte & Touche Global Environmental & Sustainability Services. 42 pp., 2002.

Design for Environment Guide. National Research Council of Canada. 200 pp., 2001.

Design for Environment Toolkit. Minnesota Office of Environmental Assistance, Minnesota Technical Assistance Program. 70, pp. Undated.

Designing Products and Services with Sustainable Attributes. West Michigan Sustainable Business Forum. 16 pp., 1999.

Driving Success: Marketing And Sustainable Development. World Business Council for Sustainable Business. 20 pp., 2005.

Eco-Efficiency Learning Module. World Business Council for Sustainable Development. 225 pp., 2005.

Eco-Mapping. International Network for Environmental Management. 17 pp., 1998.

Energy Accounting: A Key Tool in Managing Energy Costs. California Energy Commission. 30 pp., 2000.

Environmental Management Systems: An Implementation Guide for Small and Medium-Sized Organizations. National Science Foundation International. 201 pp., 2001.

Facility Manager's Guide to Water Management. Arizona Municipal Water Users Association. 83 pp., 1999.

Field Guide for Sustainable Construction. Partnership for Achieving Construction Excellence, The Pennsylvania State University and the Pentagon Renovation and Construction Program Office. 311 pp., 2004.

G3 Draft Sustainability Reporting Guidelines. Global Reporting Initiative. 56 pp., 2005.

Good Housekeeping Guide for Small & Medium-Sized Enterprises. German Agency for Technical

Cooperation. 32 pp., 1998.

Green at Work Guide: Making Your Workplace Activities More Environmentally Friendly. Commonwealth of Pennsylvania, Governor's Green Government Council. 52 pp., 2002.

Greening Your Products. U.S. Environmental Protection Agency. 52 pp., 2002.

Green Office Guide: A Guide to Greening Your Bottom Line Through a Resource-Efficient Office Environment. City of Portland, Office of Sustainable Development. 43 pp., 2001.

High 5! Communicating your Business Success through Sustainability Reporting: A Guide for Small and Not-So-Small Businesses. Global Reporting Initiative. 56 pp., 2005.

Improving Environmental Performance and Compliance: 10 Elements of Effective Environmental Management Systems. Commission for Environmental Cooperation, North American Free Trade Agreement. 9 pp., 2000.

International Declaration on Cleaner Production: Implementation Guidelines for Companies. United Nations Environmental Programme, Division of Technology, Industry, and Economics, Production and Consumption Branch, 21 pp, 2001.

Introduction to EcoReDesign: Improving the Environmental Performance of Manufactured Products. Commonwealth of Australia. 16 pp., 2001.

ISO 14001 Implementation Manual. National Center for Environmental Decision-Making Research. 97 pp., 1998.

Learning Eco Efficiency. World Business Council for Sustainable Development. 240 pp., 2005.

Measuring Eco-efficiency: A Guide to Reporting Company Performance. World Business Council for Sustainable Development. 39 pp., 2000.

Model Green Building Guidelines. National Association of Home Builders. 170 pp., 2006.

Pollution Prevention Planning Handbook. Environment Canada. 153 pp., 2001.

Product Innovation: The Green Advantage. Commonwealth of Australia. 19 pp., 2001.

Pursuing Perfection: Case Studies Examining Lean Manufacturing Strategies, Pollution Prevention, and Environmental Regulatory Management Implications. U.S. EPA .68 pp., 2005.

Small Business Waste Reduction Guide. University of Wisconsin-Extension. 250 pp., 1997.

Standardizing Excellence: Working with Smaller Businesses to Implement Environmental Management Systems. Green Business Network, The National Environmental Education and Training Foundation. 53 pp., 2001.

Strategic Challenges for Business in the Use of Corporate Responsibility Codes, Standards, and Frameworks. World Business Council for Sustainable Development. 48 pp., 2004.

State of Green Business 2008. Joel Makower and the editors of Greenbiz.com. 64 pp., 2008.

Sustainability Reporting Guidelines on Economic, Environmental, and Social Performance. Global Reporting Initiative. 104 pp., 2002.

The Greenhouse Gas Protocol for Project Accounting. World Resources Institute, 148 pp., 2006.

The Nothing to Waste Program: Incorporating Pollution Prevention into Small Businesses. New Mexico Environmental Alliance. 70 pp., 2001.

Three Steps to Eco Efficiency. Environment Canada. 15 pp., 2000.

Waste Minimization: An Environmental Good Practice Guide for Industry. United Kingdom Environment Agency. 89 pp., 2001.

Waste Minimization: Getting Staff Involved. United Kingdom Environment Agency. 36 pp., 2001.

Appendix A

Installation Instructions and Contents of CD

Installation Instructions for PCs

1. Insert the enclosed CD in your computer.
2. The installation program will start automatically. Follow the onscreen dialogue and make your appropriate choices.
3. If the CD installation does not start automatically, click on START, then RUN, then BROWSE, and select your CD drive, and then select the file "Install.exe." Finally, click OK to run the installation program.
4. During the installation program, you will be prompted as to whether you wish to install the Adobe Acrobat Reader® program. This software is necessary to view and fill in the PDF forms that are included on the Forms-on-CD. If you do not already have this program, you will need to select the full installation that will install the program on your computer.

Installation Instructions for MACs®

1. Insert the enclosed CD in your computer.
2. Copy the folder "Forms for Macs" to your hard drive. All of the PDF and text-only forms are included in this folder.
3. If you do not already have the Adobe Acrobat Reader® program installed on your hard drive, you will need to download the version of this software that is appropriate for your particular MAC operating system from **www.adobe.com**. Note: The latest versions of the MAC operating system (OS-X) has PDF capabilities built into it.

Instructions for Using CD

All of the forms that are included in this book have been provided on the CD for your use. A number of Excel Spreadsheets have also been included on the CD for your use. In addition, numerous publications have also been provided on the CD as PDF files. If you have completed the CD installation program, all of the forms, spreadsheets, and publications will have been copied to your computer's hard drive. By default, these files are installed in the C:\Green Business folder which is created by the installation program. (Note for MAC users: see instructions on prior page). Within this folder, there is one document (BOOK WEB ADDRESSES-a PDF form that provides interactive web-addresses for all of the websites noted in this book) and 3 sub-folders: Publications, Spreadsheets, and Forms.

For access to the forms, click on the Forms folder. Opening this folder will provide you with access to folders for each of the topics corresponding to chapters in the book. Within each chapter, the forms are provided in two separate formats:

TEXT forms may be opened, prepared, and printed from within your own word processing program (such as Microsoft Word®, or WordPerfect®). The text forms all have the file extension: .txt. These forms are located in the folders supplied for each chapter's forms. You will use the forms in this format if you will be making changes to any of the text on the forms or if you wish to cut and paste any of the information into your green business plan.

PDF forms may be filled in on your computer screen and printed out on any printer. This particular format provides the most widely-used format for accessing computer files. Files in this format may be opened as images on your computer and printed out on any printer. The files in PDF format all have the file extension: .pdf. Although this format provides the easiest method for completing the forms, the forms in this format can not be altered (other than to fill in the information required on the blanks provided). If you wish to alter the language in any of the forms, you will need to access the forms in their text-only versions.

Please note that on the five Economic Analysis PDF documents that are contained on the CD, you will often receive a message that notes that "The value entered does not match the format ...". This message is caused by a quirk in the Adobe Acrobat formatting program. Whenever you see this message, please click OK. You may need to click OK several times to move on to the next data entry point.

Forms from Book Included on CD

(All forms are provided as fillable PDF documents. Some are also provided as text forms.)

Green Business Energy Use (Chapter 6)
Energy Use Worksheet
Energy Survey Worksheet
Business Carbon Footprint Worksheet
Energy Efficiency Action Worksheet
Energy Efficiency Economic Analysis Worksheet

Green Business Water Use (Chapter 7)
Water Consumption Worksheet
Water Survey Worksheet
Water Conservation Action Worksheet
Water Conservation Economic Analysis Worksheet

Green Business Waste and Recycling (Chapter 8)
Waste Expense Worksheet
Waste Survey Worksheet
Waste and Recycling Action Worksheet
Waste Reduction Economic Analysis Worksheet

Green Business Transportation and Travel (Chapter 9)
Business Transportation Carbon Footprint Worksheet
Travel and Transportation Action Worksheet
Travel and Transportation Economic Analysis Worksheet

Green Business Office Equipment and Computing (Chapter 10)
Equipment and Computer Survey
Equipment and Computer Action Worksheet

Green Business Supply Chain and Purchasing (Chapter 11)
Supply Chain Worksheet
Supply Chain and Purchasing Action Worksheet
Supply Chain and Purchasing Questionnaire

Green Business Building (Chapter 12)
Green Building Action Worksheet
Building Upgrade Economic Analysis

Green Product and Service Design (Chapter 13)
Limited Life-Cycle Assessment Worksheet
Green Product Design Worksheet

U.S. Environmental Regulations (Chapter 17)
Environmental Regulation Compliance Worksheet

Preparing Your Green Business Plan (Chapter 18)
Green Business Plan Cover Sheet
Table of Contents
Green Plan Responsibility Worksheet
Performance Monitoring Worksheet

Publications Included on CD

(All publications are provided as PDF documents. File title on CD shown in parenthesis.)

Documenting Your Environmental Management Plan (Documenting Your EMP.pdf), U.S. Environmental Protection Agency, Small Business Division, 80 pp., 2003.

EPA Hazardous Waste Listings. (EPA Hazardous Waste Listings.pdf) U.S. Environmental Protection Agency, 118 pp., March 2008.

Greenhouse Gas Protocol, A Corporate Accounting and Reporting Standard, (Greenhouse Gas Protocol.pdf), World Resources Institute, 116 pp., 2004.

Hands-on-Solutions to Improve Profits and Productivity: Energy Saving Tips for Small Businesses. (DOE Energy Guide.pdf) U.S. Department of Energy, 32 pp., 1996.

Hot Climate, Cool Commerce: A Service Sector Guide to Greenhouse Gas Management, (Hot Climate Cool Commerce.pdf), World Resources Institute, 80 pp., 2006.

Integrated Environmental Management Systems: A Company Manual Template For Small Business, (IEMS Company Manual Template.pdf), U.S. Environmental Protection Agency, 65 pp., 2000.

Integrated Environmental Management Systems Implementation Guide, (IEMS Implementation Guide.pdf), U.S. Environmental Protection Agency, 268 pp., 2005.

Integrating Green Purchasing Into Your Environmental Management System (EPA Integrating Green Purchasing.pdf) U.S. Environmental Protection Agency, 70 pp., 2005.

Introduction to Environmental Accounting as a Business Management Tool. (EPA Environmental Accounting.pdf), U.S. Environmental Protection Agency, 26 pp., 1995.

Lean and Energy Toolkit. (EPA Lean Energy Toolkit.pdf), U.S. Environmental Protection Agency, 56 pp., 2007.

Lean and Environment Toolkit. (EPA Lean Enviro Toolkit.pdf) U.S. Environmental Protection Agency, 96 pp., 2007.

Lean Manufacturing and the Environment: Research on Advanced Manufacturing Systems and the Environment and Recommendations for Leveraging Better Environmental Performance. (EPA Lean Manufacturing.pdf), U.S. Environmental Protection Agency, 68 pp., 2003.

Los Alamos National Laboratory Sustainable Design Guide, (Sustainable Design Guide.pdf), Los Alamos National Laboratory, 264 pp., 2002.

Practical Guide to Environmental Management for Small Businesses, (Practical Guide to EM.pdf), U.S. Environmental Protection Agency, 50 pp., 2002.

Principles of Pollution Prevention and Cleaner Production: An International Training Course Manual, (EPA Pollution Prevention Manual.pdf), U.S. Environmental Protection Agency, 119 pp., 1998.

Promoting Green Purchasing: Tools and Resources to Quantify the Benefits of Environmentally Preferable Purchasing, (EPA Promoting Green Purchasing.pdf), U.S. Environmental Protection Agency, 15 pp., 2006

Putting Energy Into Profits: Energy Star Guide for Small Businesses. (Energy Star Business Guide.pdf), U.S. Environmental Protection Agency, 39 pp., 2007.

Solid Waste Management And Greenhouse Gases: A Life-Cycle Assessment of Emissions and Sinks (EPA Solid Waste and GHG.pdf), U.S. Environmental Protection Agency, 170 pp., 2006.

Switching To Green: A Renewable Energy Guide For Office And Retail Companies, (Switching to Green Renewables.pdf), World Resources Institute, 26 pp., 2006.

Working 9 to 5 on Climate Change: An Office Guide (Working 9 to 5 on Climate Change.pdf), World Resources Institute, 70 pp., 2002.

Spreadsheets Included on CD

(Spreadsheets are all Excel-formatted. You may need to enable macros on your computer.)
The following spreadsheets (with two exceptions) were prepared for and are copyrighted by the World Resources Institute, in cooperation with the World Business Council for Sustainable Development and the Greenhouse Gas Protocol Initiative, and are provided with their permission. Their use acknowledges these copyrights. The Computer Power Savings Calculator and the Waste Reduction Emissions Calculator were provided by the U.S. Environmental Protection Agency.

Business Travel Emissions Calculator.xls (Version date: August 2005)
> This tool will enable you to calculate your company's CO_2 emissions from business travel, including air, rail, bus, and car travel. Two approaches are provided, calculating emissions based on fuel use, and calculating emissions based on distance traveled. This tool is intended to be used in conjunction with *Hot Climate, Cool Commerce: A Service Sector Guide to GHG Management*, a WRI report also available on the CD.

Carbon Value Analysis Tool.xls (Version date: March 2008)
> This is a screening tool that allows you to integrate the value of carbon dioxide emissions reductions into energy-related project financing decisions. You are able to conduct cash-flow, return on investment, and risk analysis using this spreadsheet.

Combined Heat and Power Plant.xls (Version date: September 2006)
> This tool intends to facilitate the allocation of GHG emissions attributable to the purchase or sale of energy from a combined heat and power (CHP) plant. Can be used by all companies whose operations involve the purchase or sale of energy from a CHP plant.

Computer Power Savings Calculator.xls (Version date: September 2007)
> Use this simple calculator to estimate typical savings from Energy Star qualified computers and/or power management features.

Employee Commuting Emissions Calculator.xls (Version date: June 2006)
> This tool will enable you to calculate your company's employee's emissions from commuting to work. This tool is intended to be used in conjunction with *Hot Climate, Cool Commerce: A Service Sector Guide to GHG Management*, a WRI report also available on the CD.

Facility Fuel Use Emissions Calculator.xls (Version date: March 2008)
> This tool provides for the allocation of GHG emissions attributable to combustion of fossil fuels on site at a facility, such as with a boiler, furnace, etc.

Purchased Electricity Emissions Calculator.xls (Version date: December 2007)
> This spreadsheet allows the calculation of greenhouse gas emissions attributable to the use of purchased electricity. This tool is intended to be used in conjunction with *Hot Climate, Cool Commerce: A Service Sector Guide to GHG Management*, a WRI report also available on the CD.

Stationary Combustion Emissions Calculator.xls (Version date: December 2007)
> This tool is applicable to the calculation of direct CO_2 emissions from the combustion of fuels at stationary facilities. It also provides basic methods for the calculation of CH_4 and N_2O emissions. This spreadsheet tool is to be used in conjunction with two additional documents: 1) *GHG Protocol Guidance: Direct Emissions from Stationary Combustion* 2) *The GHG Protocol: A Corporate Accounting and Reporting Standard, Revised Edition (Available on the CD)*

Transportation Emissions Calculator.xls (Version date: January 2005)
> This tools allows the calculation of emissions from road vehicles, trains, ships, and aircrafts used in a business. Two approaches are provided, calculating emissions based on fuel use, and calculating emissions based on distance traveled.

WARM.xls (Waste Reduction Emissions Calculator) (Version date: April 2008)
> This tool calculates greenhouse gas emissions from various waste management practices, such as recycling, source reduction, composting, combustion, and landfilling. The spreadsheet can use various scenarios to assess potential projects.

Appendix B

Resources for a Greener Business

This Appendix is arranged by the substantive chapter topics to provide additional resources for the various topics covered. In addition, the first section provides general green business resources.

General Green Business Resources

Business for Social Responsibility (BSR) is a global organization that helps member companies achieve success in ways that respect ethical values, people, communities and the environment. **www.bsr.org**

CERES - Coalition for Environmentally Responsible Economies. CERES encourages corporate environmental responsibility in a number of ways, from encouraging companies to endorse the CERES Principles, working with endorsing companies both on meeting their commitment and on environmental reporting through the Global Reporting Initiative, and mobilizing the network in activist projects like the Sustainable Governance Project and the Green Hotel Initiative. They also convene forums for discussion among diverse groups, from the annual CERES conference to industry-specific dialogues. **www.ceres.org**

Cool Companies. A resource featuring best practices for strategies and technologies that save energy, cut costs and reduce pollution. **www.cool-companies.org**

Corporate Social Responsibility (CSR) Europe. CSR Europe is a business-driven membership network. Their mission is to help companies achieve profitable, sustainable growth and human progress by placing corporate social responsibility in the mainstream of business practice. **www.csreurope.org**

GreenBiz.com harnesses the power of technology to bring environmental information, resources, and tools to the mainstream business community. Its mission is to provide accurate and balanced information and resources to help companies of all sizes and sectors combine ecological sustainability with profitable business practices. **www.greenbiz.com**

Global Reporting Initiative. GRI is an international effort to create a common framework for sustainability reporting on economic, environmental and social performance. The mission of the GRI is to elevate the comparability and credibility of sustainability reporting practices worldwide. **www.globalreporting.org**

SustainableBusiness.com serves as the Internet community for businesses that integrate economic, and social and environmental concerns into their core strategy. They exist to help green business grow. **www.sustainablebusiness.com**

World Business Council on Sustainable Development. Formed in the wake of the 1992 Rio Earth Summit, the World Business Council for Sustainable Development (WBCSD) is a coalition of 165 international companies united by a shared commitment to sustainable development via the three pillars of economic growth, ecological balance and social progress. **www.wbcsd.org**

WorldCSR.com is a gateway to the websites of the leading business-led organizations on corporate social responsibility, worldwide. **www.worldcsr.com**

Energy Efficiency and Renewable Energy Resources (Chapter 6)

The resources under this heading are cited in this chapter and are also found on the interactive PDF document BOOK WEB ADDRESSES that is contained on the CD, which will allow you to access these sites without the need to retype the web addresses.

The Greenhouse Gas Protocol Initiative:
    www.ghgprotocol.org/calculation-tools
The Building Energy Software Tools Directory:
    www.eere.energy.gov/buildings/tools_directory
Department of Energy Best Practices website:
    www1.eere.energy.gov/industry/bestpractices/software.html
Energy Plus Software:
    www.eere.energy.gov/buildings/energyplus
Quick Plant Energy Profiler:
    www1.eere.energy.gov/industry/quickpep
Save Energy Now Initiative:
    www1.eere.energy.gov/industry/saveenergynow
Federal Energy Management Program Energy Cost Calculators:
    www1.eere.energy.gov/femp/procurement/eep_eccalculators.html
Building Life-Cycle Cost Software:
    www1.eere.energy.gov/femp/information/download_blcc.html
Utility Company Energy Efficiency Programs:
    http://eetd.lbl.gov/EnergyCrossroads/2ueeprogram.html
Online Business Energy Analysis:
    www.energyguide.com
Solar America Cities:
    www1.eere.energy.gov/solar/solar_america
Wind and Hydropower Technologies website:
    www1.eere.energy.gov/windandhydro
Geothermal Technologies Program:
    www1.eere.energy.gov/geothermal
Green Power Options Available for Your State:
    www.eere.energy.gov/greenpower/buying/buying_power.shtml
Certified Sources of Renewable Energy Credits:
    www.green-e.org
Native Energy CoolWatts Program:
    www.NativeEnergy.com
Green-e Climate Certification Programs:
    www.green-e.org/getcert_ghg_products.shtml
Database for State Incentives for Renewables and Efficiency:
    www.dsireusa.org
Small Producer Biodiesel and Ethanol Credit:
    www.irs.gov
Manufactured Home Tax Credit:
    www.irs.gov
Energy Cost Calculator for Compact Fluorescent Lamps:
    www1.eere.energy.gov/femp/procurement/eep_fluorescent_lamps_calc.html
U.S. EPA's Climate Leaders Program:
    www.epa.gov/stateply
Belkin Conserve Surge Protector:
    www.belkin.com
Smart Strip Power Strip:
    http://bitsltd.net/ConsumerProducts/

The Isole Plug Load Controller:
   www.wattstopper.com
U.S. EPA's Energy Star Label Program:
   www.energystar.gov

Additional Energy Resources

The U.S. Department of Energy, Industrial Technology Best Practices program has a varied and expanding software collection. **http://www1.eere.energy.gov/industry/bestpractices/software.html**. A few packages must be ordered from the EERE Information Center via E-mail at **www1.eere.energy.gov/informationcenter** or by calling 1-877-EERE-INF (877-337-3463).

The Decision Tools for Industry CD contains the following software tools the MotorMaster+ (MM+), Pump System Assessment Tool, Steam System Tool Suite, 3E Plus and the new AirMaster+ software packages. Please order the CD via E-mail from the EERE Information Center at **www1.eere.energy.gov/informationcenter** or call the EERE Information Center at 1-877-EERE-INF (877-337-3463).

Energy Analysis Software

EnergyPlus from the US Department of Energy. EnergyPlus is a free building energy simulation software program for modeling building heating, cooling, lighting, ventilating, and other energy flows. **http://www.eere.energy.gov/buildings/energyplus/**

DOE 2/ DOE 2.1 E/ DOE 2.2 from the Energy Science and Technology Software Center; DOE2.com; others - all adaptions of the original software developed by Lawrence Berkeley National Laboratory. Hourly energy usage and energy costs software for commercial or residential; $300, costs differ for commercial adaptions. **http://www.doe2.com**

Building Loads Analysis and System Thermodynamics (BLAST) from the U.S. Army Engineer Research and Development Center (ERDC). Software estimates of building energy needs by simulation of air handling systems and central plant equipment; $450-1500. **http://www.eere.energy.gov/buildings/energyplus**

Simulation Problem Analysis and Research Kernel (SPARK); VisualSPARK from Lawrence Berkeley National Laboratory (NBNL). Free software that is equation-based, object-oriented simulation environment for construction and running models of complex systems. **http://simulationresearch.lbl.gov**

THERM from Lawrence Berkeley National Laboratory. Free software to model two-dimensional heat-transfer effects in building components. **http://windows.lbl.gov/software/therm/therm.html**

ENERGY-10 from the Sustainable Buildings Industry Council (SBIC) (in coordination with NREL, LBNL, Berkeley Solar Group). Simulation software that analyzes energy and cost savings for different design strategies; $325. **www.sbicouncil.org/storelistitem.cfm?itemnumber=1**

Building Design Advisor from Lawrence Berkeley National Laboratory. Free software design tool using database of prototype buildings types/materials to guide decision makers through project from design to specification - links to other software tools. **http://gaia.lbl.gov/BDA/**

SUNREL from National Renewable Energy Laboratory. Energy simulation software, small buildings; $50. **http://www.nrel.gov/buildings/sunrel/**

Energy Scheming from the Energy Studies in Buildings Lab at the University of Oregon. Energy analysis software program based on graphical interface (architectural renderings); $250. **www.uoregon.edu/~esbl/esbl_web/index2.htm**

eQuest from the U.S. Department of Energy. Free energy analysis software program based on graphical interface (architectural renderings). **http://doe2.com/equest/**

Energy Star Green Building Design from the U.S. EPA. Website with guidance for new buildings to improve energy efficiency. **http://www.energystar.gov/index.cfm?c=new_bldg_design.new_bldg_design**

Clean Power Estimator from the California Energy Commission. Free economic evaluation software to estimate benefits in investing in a PV solar or small wind electric generating system. **http://www.consumerenergycenter.org/renewables/estimator/index.html**

PV Design-Pro from Maui Solar, based on Sandia National Labs Algorithms. Software model to predict the electrical output of photovoltaic panels included with several other solar design tools, $250. **http://www.mauisolarsoftware.com**

PV Watts from the National Renewable Energy Laboratory. Free software to calculate electrical energy produced by grid-connected PV system. **http://rredc.nrel.gov/solar/codes_algs/PVWATTS/**

REM Design from Architectural Energy Corporation. Home energy analysis software; $297. **http://www.archenergy.com/products/rem**

EnergyPro from Energy Soft. Energy analysis software based on California Title 24; $200-$1200. **http://www.energysoft.com/**

Building Energy Software Tools Directory from the US Department of Energy, Energy Efficiency and Renewable Energy Program. Free database of detailed information on software tools, including strengths and weakness. **http://www.eere.energy.gov/buildings/tools_directory/**

National Center for Photovoltaics from the National Renewable Energy Laboratory. **http://www.nrel.gov/ncpv**

Green Building Studio. Web-based energy engineering analysis software solution that integrates with today"s 3D-CAD/BIM applications; first runs on a project free (demonstration phase). **http://www.greenbuildingstudio.com**

Home Energy Efficient Design (HEED), from the University of California, Los Angeles. Free, fast, easy to use, and highly graphic energy analysis software. **http://www2.aud.ucla.edu/energy-design-tools/**

Energy Gauge USA from the University of Central Florida. Code compliance and energy rating software; $100-$150. **http://energygauge.com/usares/default.htm**

Energy Assessment Service Providers

U.S. Department of Energy Industrial Assessment Centers (IACs). IACs, which are located at 26 universities across the United States provide no-cost energy and waste assessments to eligible small and medium-sized manufacturers. Teams of engineering faculty and students from IACs conduct energy audits or industrial assessments of manufacturing facilities and recommend actions to improve productivity, reduce waste, and save energy. **www1.eere.energy.gov/industry/bestpractices/iacs.html**

U.S. DOE Best Practices Plant-Wide Energy Assessments. Mid-size and large manufacturers can apply for a cost-shared Plant-Wide Energy Assessment offered by U.S. DOE. The assessments are comprehensive and systematic examinations of energy use reduction opportunities at industrial facilities. All major aspects of energy consumption are addressed, including process operations and plant utility systems. **http://www1.eere.energy.gov/industry/bestpractices/plant_assessments.html**

U.S. DOE Save Energy Now Energy Savings Assessments. Through the Save Energy Now program, the U.S. DOE offers Energy Savings Assessments to the nation's most energy-intensive manufacturing facilities. The focus of these assessments is on immediate opportunities to save energy and money, primarily by focusing on energy-intensive systems such as process heating, steam, pumps, fans, and compressed air. **www1.eere.energy.gov/industry/saveenergynow/**

ENERGY STAR Directory of Energy Service and Product Providers. The U.S. EPA and U.S. DOE ENERGY STAR Program offers a searchable on-line directory of private energy service and product providers, that includes energy management service companies, energy improvement contractors, and energy service companies, as well as other types of service providers and equipment manufacturers. **http://www.energystar.gov/index.cfm?fuseaction=find_a_product.**

Energy Assessment Resources and Tools

Energy Efficiency Toolkit for Manufacturers: Eight Proven Ways to Reduce Your Costs. The National Association of Manufacturers has developed this toolkit outlining energy conservation strategies, case studies, and resources for manufacturers seeking to reduce energy use and costs. The toolkit is based on the results of an energy-efficiency survey of over 400 manufacturing companies. **www.fypower.org/pdf/manufacturer_toolkit.pdf**

ENERGY STAR Guidelines for Energy Management. The ENERGY STAR website describes a seven-step process for effective energy management. The guidelines are based on the successful practices of ENERGY STAR partners for improving the energy, financial, and environmental performance of businesses. In addition to practical guidelines, the ENERGY STAR website offers several energy assessment tools and resources.
www.energystar.gov/index.cfm?c=guidelines.guidelines_index

IAC Self-Assessment Workbook for Small Manufacturers. This workbook presents a step-by-step methodology for small manufacturers to identify opportunities to reduce energy use, improve operations, and reduce costs at their facilities. The workbook includes practical tips, checklists, and examples of common energy cost savings opportunities.
iac.rutgers.edu/redirect.php?rf=selfassessment

Industrial Audit Guidebook Developed by the Bonneville Power Administration. The Bonneville Power Administration's Industrial Audit Guidebook provides practical instructions, tips, and guidance for performing walk-through energy audits of industrial facilities to identify opportunities to reduce electrical energy consumption. Organized as a checklist of questions, the guidebook is intended for technical and non-technical audiences to assist with the first step in an energy audit: touring a facility and quickly identifying energy savings opportunities.
www.bpa.gov/Energy/N/projects/industrial/audit/index.cfm

Green Suppliers Network Lean and Clean Assessments. The Green Suppliers Network (GSN) is a collaborative partnership between EPA and the National Institute of Standards and Technology Manufacturing Extension Partnership (NIST MEP) that works with large companies to provide low-cost "Lean and Clean " facility assessments to small and medium-sized businesses in several sectors. These assessments include detailed consideration of energy reduction opportunities.
www.greensuppliers.gov

Resource Efficiency Management Resources from Washington State University has developed several workbooks, checklists, and other guidance for conducting energy audits. Other resources available on the website include fact sheets describing energy-efficiency opportunities for commercial and industrial users. **www.energy.wsu.edu/pubs/default.cfm**

Water Conservation Resources (Chapter 7)

The resources under this heading are cited in this chapter and are also found on the interactive PDF document BOOK WEB ADDRESSES that is contained on the CD, which will allow you to access these sites without the need to retype the web addresses.

WaterSense® Program:
    www.epa.gov/watersense
American Water Works Association:
    ww.awwa.org/waterwiser
Low-flow Water products:
    www.zeroflush.com

Waste Reduction and Recycling Resources (Chapter 8)

The resources under this heading are cited in this chapter and are also found on the interactive PDF document BOOK WEB ADDRESSES that is contained on the CD, which will allow you to access these sites without the need to retype the web addresses.

Waste Reduction Model (WARM):
www.epa.gov/climatechange/wycd/waste/calculators/Warm_home.html
Reduce your advertising mail:
www.dmachoice.org
Reduce the number of catalogs you receive:
www.CatalogChoice.org
Advertise surplus and reusable waste items:
www.govlink.org/hazwaste/business/imex
Reselling cardboard boxes:
www.UsedCardboardBoxes.com
Selling equipment or other items aren't recyclable:
www.freecycle.org
Selling used business items:
www.craigslist.com
State environmental protection agencies:
www.epa.gov/osw
Notification of Hazardous Waste Activity:
www.epa.gov/epaoswer/hazwaste/data/form8700/forms.htm
To drop off packing peanuts:
www.loosefillpackaging.com
Universal Waste List:
www.epa.gov/epaoswer/hazwaste/id/univwast/index.htm

Travel and Transportation Resources (Chapter 9)

The resources under this heading are cited in this chapter and are also found on the interactive PDF document BOOK WEB ADDRESSES that is contained on the CD, which will allow you to access these sites without the need to retype the web addresses.

Carbon footprint calculator:
www.carbontrust.co.uk/solutions/CarbonFootprinting/FootprintCalculators or
www.carbonfootprint.com/businessregister.aspx
General travel carbon footprint calculator:
www.nativeenergy.com/pages/travel_calculator/30.php
Excel® spreadsheets for calculating transportation emissions:
www.ghgprotocol.org/calculation-tools
To promote carpooling:
www.carpoolworld.com or www.erideshare.com
Hybrid company-owned cars:
www.hybridcenter.org
EPA SmartWay Transport Partnership:
www.epa.gov/smartway
'Green' hotels:
www.greenhotels.com
Hybrid car rentals:
www.evrental.com
Carbon offsetting for required travel:
www.nativeenergy.com

Office Equipment and Computing Resources (Chapter 10)

The resources under this heading are cited in this chapter and are also found on the interactive PDF document BOOK WEB ADDRESSES that is contained on the CD, which will allow you to access these sites without the need to retype the web addresses.

EPEAT (Electronic Product Environmental Assessment Tool):
www.epeat.net
U.S. Department of Energy's Federal Energy Management Program:
www1.eere.energy.gov/femp/procurement/eep_computer.html
Energy Efficiency and Renewable Energy, Industrial Technology Program:
www1.eere.energy.gov/industry/bestpractices/software.html
Dell computer free recycling program:
www.dell.com/recycling or
www.dell.com/assetrecovery
IBM computer and equipment purchasing program:
www-03.ibm.com/financing/us/recovery/small/buyback.html
Apple Computer free take-back and recycling program:
www.apple.com/environment/recycling
Hewlett-Packard recycling program:
www.hp.com
Electronic Industries Alliance recycling program:
www.eiae.org
E-waste overseas electronics recycling to developing countries:
www.ban.org
Good Deed Foundation:
www.gooddeedfoundation.org/recycle
Evaluating dollar savings by using power management techniques:
www.energystar.gov/index.cfm?c=power_mgt.pr_power_mgt_users
For purchasing used or refurbished equipment:
www.dell.com/outlet or
www.refurbdepot.com .
Energy Star® products:
www.energystar.gov
EPEAT products:
www.epeat.net
Leasing of computers and equipment:
www.ibm.com
EZ Wizard:
www.energystar.gov/index.cfm?c=power_mgt.pr_power_mgt_ez_wiz
Oxford University climate modeling software:
www.climateprediction.net

Supply Chain and Purchasing Resources (Chapter 11)

The resources under this heading are cited in this chapter and are also found on the interactive PDF document BOOK WEB ADDRESSES that is contained on the CD, which will allow you to access these sites without the need to retype the web addresses.

U.S. EPA Database of Environmental Products Information:
http://yosemite1.epa.gov/oppt/eppstand2.nsf
Analytica Software:
www.lumina.com/ana/player.htm
Life-Cycle Assessment Tool:
www.earthster.org
The Recycled Content (ReCon) Tool:
http://epa.gov/climatechange/wycd/waste/calculators/ReCon_home.html
Product assessment for your environmental purchasing goals:
www.earthster.org or www.openLca.org

Green Building Resources (Chapter 12)

The resources under this heading are cited in this chapter and are also found on the interactive PDF document BOOK WEB ADDRESSES that is contained on the CD, which will allow you to access these sites without the need to retype the web addresses.

New York State Energy Research and Development Authority:
    www.nyserda.org
New York State tax credit program for sustainable design:
    www.dec.state.ny.us
New Jersey SmartStart Building Program:
    www.njcleanenergy.com/commercial-industrial/programs/nj-smartstart-buildings
New Jersey Clean Energy Program:
    www.njcleanenergy.com
Pennsylvania Governor's Green Government Council:
    www.gggc.state.pa.us
Connecticut Clean Energy Fund:
    www.ctcleanenergy.com
Oregon's Business Energy Tax Credit:
    www.oregon.gov/energy/cons/bus/betc.shtml
Database for State Incentives for Renewables and Efficiency:
    www.dsireusa.org
Green Building Initiative and Green Globes rating system:
    www.thegbi.org/commercial
LEED certification program:
    www.usgbc.org
Greenguard Environmental Institute:
    www.greenguard.org
Green Building Certification Institute:
    www.gbci.org
The Energy Building Investment Decision Support (eBIDS) database:
    http://cbpd.arc.cmu.edu/ebids
eVALUator:
    www.energydesignresources.com/resource/131
U.S. EPA's Sustainable Redevelopment of Brownfields Program:
    www.epa.gov/brownfields/sustain.htm
Green roofs:
    www.greenroofs.com
Certified 'green' power suppliers:
    www.green-e.org

Green Building Life-Cycle Cost Tools

Building Investment Decision Support (BIDS) from the Carnegie-Mellon University Center for Building Performance and Diagnostics. Case-based decision-making software that calculates the economic value added of investing in high performance building systems based on the findings of building owners and researchers around the world; subscription required. **http://cbpd.arc.cmu.edu/bids/**

Energy Building Investment Decision Support (eBIDS) from the Carnegie-Mellon University Center for Building Performance and Diagnostics. Detailed case study information with ROI data; Free database. **http://cbpd.arc.cmu.edu/ebids/**

Building Life-Cycle Cost (BLCC) Program from the National Institute of Standards and Technology (NIST). Analysis of capital investments in buildings; Free software. **http://www1.eere.energy.gov/femp/information/download_blcc.html**

Life Cycle Costing Manual for the Federal Energy Management Program from the National Institute of Standards and Technology (NIST). Free publication available on line; contains specific LEED guidance; referenced in LEED. **http://www.bfrl.nist.gov/oae/publications/handbooks/135.pdf**

Envest from Building Research Establishment Limited (BRE). Software for LCC and LCA - intended for use with BREEAM rating tool; $150 and up. **http://envestv2.bre.co.uk**

Clean Power Estimator from the California Energy Commission. Free economic evaluation software to estimate benefits in investing in a PV solar or small wind electric generating system. **http://www.consumerenergycenter.org/renewables/estimator/index.html**

Energy Price Indices and Discount Factors for Life-Cycle Cost Analysis Annual Supplement to Handbook 135 (ASHB 135). **http://www1.eere.energy.gov/femp/pdfs/ashb08.pdf**

eVALUator from Energy Design Resources. Calculates the life-cycle benefits of investments that improve building design. It analyzes the financial benefits from buildings that reduce energy cost, raise employee productivity, and enhance tenant satisfaction; Free with registration; software. **http://www.energydesignresources.com/resource/131/**

LIFE from Elite Software. Software for LCC, user definable cost items; about $400. **http://www.elitesoft.com/web/hvacr/elite_life_info.html**

Additional Green Building Organizations

EEBA-Energy & Environmental Building Association:
www.eeba.org

SBIC-Sustainable Buildings Industry Council:
www.SBICouncil.org

AAMA-American Architectural Manufacturers Association:
www.aamanet.org

CRRC-Cool Roof Rating Council: www.coolroofs.org

ASHRAE-American Society of Heating, Refrigerating and Air Conditioning Engineers:
www.ashrae.org

The Energy Efficient Mortgages Program:
www.hud.gov/offices/hsg/sfh/eem/energy-r.cfm

NRC-National Recycling Coalition, Inc.:
www.nrc-recycle.org

IAQA-Indoor Air Quality Association, Inc.:
www.iaqa.org

ASES-The American Solar Energy Society:
www.ases.org

SEPA-The Solar Electric Power Association:
www.solarelectricpower.org

DSIRE-Database of State Incentives for Renewable Energy:
www.dsireusa.org

GHPC-Geothermal Heat Pump Consortium-State Incentives:
www.geoexchange.com/incentives/incentives.htm

CEE-Consortium for Energy Efficiency, Inc.:
www.cee1.org

SCAQMD-South Coast Air Quality Management District:
www.aqmd.gov

NFRC-National Fenestration Rating Council:
www.nfrc.org

EWC-Efficient Windows Collaborative:
www.efficientwindows.org

NSF-National Sanitation Foundation:
    www.nsf.org
RESNET-Residential Energy Services Network:
    www.natresnet.org
CRI-Carpet & Rug Institute-IAQ Green Label Program:
    www.carpet-rug.com
Green Guard Environmental Institute:
    www.greenguard.org
Green Seal, Inc.:
    www.greenseal.org
SCS-Scientific Certification Systems:
    www.scscertified.com
GreenSpec® (Materials Directory):
    www.buildinggreen.com
ACEEE-American Council for Energy Efficient Economy:
    www.aceee.org
Iris Communications, Inc.:
    www.oikos.com/green_products/index.php
Athena™ Environmental Impact Estimator-Sustainable Materials Institute:
    www.athenaSMI.ca
SFI-Sustainable Forest Initiative®:
    www.aboutsfi.org
Green Prints-Southface Energy Institute:
    www.greenprints.org
NAHBRC-NAHB Research Center:
    www.nahbrc.com
EEBA-Energy & Environmental Building Association: Regional Workshops:
    www.eeba.org
SBIC-Sustainable Buildings Industry Council: Regional Workshops:
    www.sbicouncil.org
ASES-American Solar Energy Society:
    www.ases.org
EPAs Energy Star Label Program:
        www.energystar.gov

Green Building Material & Product Specification Tools

Architecture Record Green Product Guide from McGraw Hill Construction. Free online directory of green products with active links to identify quantifiable, easily verifiable standards, where these can be defined. **http://archrecord.construction.com/products/green/default.asp**

Federal Green Construction Guide for Specifiers from the U.S. EPA Whole Building Design Guide. Free on-line database; specification language by type of construction product. **http://www.wbdg.org/design/greenspec.php**

Forest Stewardship Council Certified Product Locator. Free online locator for products with Forest Stewardship Council Certification. **http://www.fscus.org/faqs/fsc_products.php**

EPA Environmentally Preferable Purchasing from the U.S. EPA. Compilation of tools and resources to estimate the environmental and economic benefits of both past and projected Environmentally Preferable Purchasing choices. **http://www.epa.gov/epp/tools/epp_metrics.pdf**

Cool Roofing Materials Database from Lawrence Berkeley National Laboratory. Free database of roofing materials, other research and reference materials on heat island effects. **http://eetd.lbl.gov/CoolRoofs/**

GreenSpec Directory. Product information service, screened by staff, no advertising money for inclusion; printed copy $89, online subscription $200 per year. **http://www.buildinggreen.com**

Professional's Guide to Energy Efficient Building Products from eBuild. Free product listings, commercial advertising. **http://www.ebuild.com/products.hwx**

The Sustainable Design Resource Guide from the American Institute of Architects, Colorado. Free online guide is organized according to divisions of the Construction Specifications Institute. Outlines specific concerns related to the products and systems; gives product listings and information designed to help specify sustainable building products; provides list of organizations, publications and computer software. **http://www.aiasdrg.org/**

Oikos Green Product Information. Searchable online database, commercial sponsors - but focus on green products. **http://oikos.com/green_products/index.php**

General Services Administration Environmental Products and Services Guide. Free online publication with GSA recommended products and services. **http://www.fedcenter.gov/Documents/index.cfm?id=517&pge_prg_id=0&pge_id=0**

U.S. EPA Database of Environmental Information for Products and Services. Online searchable database of environmental information for products and services, get product information or additional resources. **http://yosemite1.epa.gov/oppt/eppstand2.nsf**

Energy Star from the U.S. EPA. Online listing of Energy Star certified products. **http://www.energystar.gov**

Green-e Certification Program from the Center for Resource Solutions. Independent certification and verification program for renewable energy. **http://www.green-e.org/about_cert.shtml**

Recycled Content Product Directory from the California Integrated Waste Management Board. Free online product listings and links to manufacturers by type. **http://www.ciwmb.ca.gov/rcp/**

Green Seal Certified Products. Online product listings. **http://www.greenseal.org/findaproduct/index.cfm**

Construction Criteria Base from the Whole Building Design Guide. Free online library of construction guide specifications, manuals, standards and many other essential criteria documents. **http://www.wbdg.org/ccb/**

Green Format from the Construction Specification Institute. Online product data guide for green properties. **http://www.csinet.org/s_csi/sec.asp?CID=1958&DID=13641**

Green Sage. Listing of sustainable building materials and furnishings (commercial sponsorship). **http://www.greensage.com/**

Green Guard Product Certification from Green Guard Environmental Institute. Certification program and product listings regarding indoor air quality. **http://www.greenguard.org/**

Product Database, Green Building Pages. Online database with ability to search for products by LEED point or CSI (Construction Specification Institute) categories. **http://www.greenbuildingpages.com/main_md.html**

Green Product database. Online product listings by CSI categories. **http://www.greenerbuilding.org/**

Green Products Network. Online information on bio-based products, research, links to suppliers. **http://www.greenproducts.net/**

Green Design Resources (Chapter 13)
Life Cycle Assessment Tools

ATHENA Environmental Impact Estimator (EIE) from the Athena Sustainable Materials Institute. Easy-to-use design tool (software) for selection of materials; life cycle assessments of various designs based on extensive database of materials and products; $540-1200. **http://www.athenasmi.ca/tools/software/index.html**

BEES 4.0. Free software for analyzing life cycle implications of building products, can be used for balancing the environmental and economic performance of building products. BEES 3.0 can be downloaded free of charge from the NIST website: **www.bfrl.nist.gov/oae/software/bees.html**

Boustead Model 5.0. Extensive database in which data such as fuels and energy use, raw materials requirements, and solid, liquid, and gaseous emissions are stored. It also includes software which enables the user to manipulate data in the database and to select a suitable data presentation method from a host of options. **http://www.boustead-consulting.co.uk/products.htm**

eiolca.net. This web site allows users to estimate the overall environmental impacts from producing a certain dollar amount of a commodity or service in the United States. Carnegie-Mellon University **http://www.eiolca.net**

Environmental Impact Indicator. Prepared for architects, engineers, and researchers to get LCA answers about conceptual designs of new buildings or renovations to existing buildings: **www.athenaSMI.ca**

GaBi 4 Software System and Database. Different versions are available from educational to professional use of Life Cycle Analysis to evaluate life cycle environmental, cost, and social profiles of products, processes and technologies. GaBi offers databases with worldwide coverage as well as Ecoinvent data. A demo version is available for download. **www.gabi-software.com**

GEMIS (Global Emission Model for Integrated Systems). A life cycle analysis program and database for energy, material, and transport systems. The GEMIS database offers information on fossil fuels, renewables, processes for electricity and heat, raw materials, and transports. Free from the website. **www.oeko.de/service/gemis/en/index.htm**

GREET. The U.S. Department of Energy's Office of Transportation Technologies fuel-cycle model called GREET (Greenhouse gases, Regulated Emissions, and Energy use in Transportation) allows researchers to evaluate various engine and fuel combinations on a consistent fuel-cycle basis: **www.transportation.anl.gov/software/GREET**

TEAM 4.0. Offered by Pricewaterhouse Coopers Ecobilan Group (also known as Ecobalance), a professional tool for evaluating the life cycle environmental and cost profiles of products and technologies. It contains comprehensive database of over 600 modules with worldwide coverage. An online demo is available from the website. **www.ecobalance.com/uk_lcatool.php**

US LCI Data. In May 2001, NREL and its partners created the U.S. Life-Cycle Inventory (LCI) Database to provide support to public, private, and non-profit sector efforts in developing product life cycle assessments and environmentally-oriented decision support systems and tools. The objective of the U.S. LCI Database Project is to provide LCI data for commonly used materials, products and processes following a single data development protocol consistent with international standards. Since the goal is to make the creation of LCIs easier, rather than to carry out full product LCIs, database modules provide data on many of the processes needed by others for conducting LCIs. However, the modules do not contain data characterizing the full life cycles of specific products. The data protocol is based on ISO 14048 and is compatible with the EcoSpold format. The LCI data are available in several formats: a streamlined spreadsheet, an EcoSpold format spreadsheet, an EcoSpold XML file, and a detailed spreadsheet with all the calculation details. **www.nrel.gov/lci/**

Additional Green Design Resources

Green Design Institute. An academic-industry-government consortium based at Carnegie-Mellon University to develop research and education programs to improve environmental quality. **http://www.ce.cmu.edu/GreenDesign/**

Biomimicry Institute.
www.biomimicryinstitute.org

Natural Capitalism.
www.natcap.org (Paul Hawken)
www.natcapinc.org (L. Hunter Lovins)
www.rmi.org (Amory Lovins)

The Natural Step.
www.naturalstep.org

William McDonough and Partners.
  http://www.mcdonoughpartners.com/
The Bottom of the Pyramid.
  http://www.12manage.com/methods_prahalad_bottom_of_the_pyramid.html

Eco-Labeling and Certification Resources (Chapter 14)

The resources under this heading are cited in this chapter and are also found on the interactive PDF document BOOK WEB ADDRESSES that is contained on the CD, which will allow you to access these sites without the need to retype the web addresses.

Green Suppliers Network:
  www.greensuppliers.gov
National Environmental Performance Track:
  www.epa.gov/performancetrack/index.htm
Green Seal Facilities Partnership programs:
  www.greenseal.org/programs/partnership.cfm
Green Seal program:
  www.greenseal.org
Scientific Certification Systems:
  www.scscertified.com
European Union eco-lableing program:
  www.eco-label.com
European Union:
   http://ec.europa.eu/environment/ecolabel
Nordic Nations:
  www.ecolabel.nu
FSC-certified products:
  www.fscus.org
Marine Stewardship Council:
  www.msc.org
Chlorine-Free Products Association:
  www.chlorinefreeproducts.org
Greener Choices EcoLabels Center:
  www.greenerchoices.org/eco-labels
Eco Labeling:
  www.ecolabeling.org

Environmental Management System Resources (Chapter 15)

The resources under this heading are cited in this chapter and are also found on the interactive PDF document BOOK WEB ADDRESSES that is contained on the CD, which will allow you to access these sites without the need to retype the web addresses.

EPA Environmental Management Systems Resource Center. This center provides EMS information and resources, including research reports, best-practice manuals, and EMS templates. **www.epa.gov/ems**

EPA's Environmental Management System. View the outline of EPA's EMS, which focus-es on compliance, pollution prevention, purchasing, and public outreach. **www.epa.gov/ems**

EPA's National Environmental Performance Track Program. Performance Track is a voluntary program designed to recognize facilities that consis-tently meet their legal requirements and have implemented high-quality EMSs. **www.epa.gov/performancetrack**

International Organization for Standardization (ISO). The ISO Web site provides a range of information about the organization and its standards, including press releases, news bulletins, guidance documents, training materials, a calendar of ISO-related events, and contact information. **http://www.iso.org/iso/home.htm**

Industrial Pollution Prevention Gateway. Provides various tools for environmental management, self-assessments, and publications. **http://www.eeaa.gov.eg/IPPG/cp_tools.htm**

The PEER Center. The Public Entity Environmental Management System Resource (PEER) Center provides EMS guidance, tools, and training. This Web site connects you with real-life mentors, technical assistance, and problem-solving strategies. **www.peercenter.net**

The ISO 14001 Guidance Manual. The National Center for Environmental Decision-Making Research (NCEDMR) developed this manual to assist organizations interested in developing an EMS consistent with the ISO 14001 standard. **http://www.usistf.org/download/ISMS_Downloads/ISO14001.pdf**

Sustainability Reporting Resources (Chapter 16)

The resources under this heading are cited in this chapter and are also found on the interactive PDF document BOOK WEB ADDRESSES that is contained on the CD, which will allow you to access these sites without the need to retype the web addresses.

E*uropean Union Environmental Management and Audi Scheme:*
> http://ec.europa.eu/environment/emas

ISO 14031 Environmental Performance Evaluation:
> www.iso-14001.org.uk

Social Accountability International: SA 8000:
> www.sa8000.org

Greenhouse Gas Protocol Initiative:
> www.ghgprotocol.org

Climate Counts:
> www.climatecounts.org

U.S. Environmental Regulations Resources (Chapter 17)

The resources under this heading are cited in this chapter and are also found on the interactive PDF document BOOK WEB ADDRESSES that is contained on the CD, which will allow you to access these sites without the need to retype the web addresses.

Reportable Quantity (RQ):
> www.epa.gov/superfund/programs/er/triggers/haztrigs/rqover.htm

EPA's EnviroFacts:
> www.epa.gov/enviro

Additional U.S. Environmental Regulations:
> www.epa.gov/lawsregs/envtopics/index.html

Index

Agriculture, 19
Allenby, Braden, 216
Alternative fuel tax credits, 75
American Chemistry Council, 249
American Forest and Paper Association, 249
American Water Works Association, 99
Analytica software, 177
Anderson, Ray, 10, 37
Apple Computer recycling program, 165
Australia, and EcoReDesign, 223
Automobiles
    mileage standards, 17–18
    and outmoded technology, 19
Avon, 258

Ben and Jerry's Ice Cream, 257
Benyus, Janine, 37, 212, 218
Best Practices software, 65–66
Biodiesel tax credit, 75
Biomimicry, 29, 31, 36–37
    and green design, 213–214, 218–219
Biomimicry: Innovation Inspired by Nature, 37, 212
Blessed Unrest, 13
BodyShop, 257
Bottom of the pyramid, 224–225
Braungart, Michael, 37, 214–215
Brown, Lester, 21
Bruntland Commission, 13
Building Energy Software Tools Directory (online), 65
Building Life-Cycle Cost software, 43, 67–68, 199
        Building Upgrade Economic Analysis, 209
Buildings
    carbon emissions, 187
    commercial, and water use, 98–99, 106–108, 198,
        204
    energy use, 186, 187, 198, 205
    upgrades, 59
    See also Green buildings
Business
    advantages of greening, 13
    cutting energy and raw material inputs, 15
    decisions as root cause of all environmental
        problems, 16–18
    and elimination of toxic materials, 15
    as force to correct environmental problems, 9, 12,
        14–15, 20–22
    impact on natural world, 12
    reasons for engaging in, 13
    reimagining, 21–22
    and resilience to change and risk, 15
    role in global economy, 12, 20
    and sustainability, 9
Business Carbon Footprint Worksheet, 83, 88, 200
Business Transportation Carbon Footprint Worksheet,
    151, 153

California, and green building incentives, 189
Cap-and-trade system, 55–56
Capitalism at the Crossroads, 224
Carbon Disclosure Project, 149–150
Carbon emissions
    and business challenges, 54, 56
    corporate reduction efforts, 57
    corporate reporting of, 56–57
    direct, 63, 150
    energy use as main source of, 54, 56
    indirect from purchased energy, 63, 150
    other indirect, 63, 150
    price of, 55–57
    reduction required, 54
Carbon footprints, 63–64
    assessment tools and services, 64–69
    calculators, 152
    and taxes and credits, 64
    See also Business Carbon Footprint Worksheet;
        Business Transportation Carbon Footprint
        Worksheet
Carbon offsets, 74
Carbon taxes, 28–29, 55
Carbon trading, 28–29, 55–56
Carnegie-Mellon University Center for Building
        Performance and Diagnostics, 199
Cascade Paper, 246
Cell phones, recycling, 165
CERCLA. See Comprehensive Environmental
        Response, Compensation, and Liability Act
CERES/Ceres. See Coalition for Environmentally
        Responsible Economies
Ceres Principles, 259–260
Changing Course: A Global Business Perspective on
        Development and the Environment, 33
Chemical sustainability, 34
Chicago
    green building incentives, 189
    and solar energy, 70
Chicago Climate Exchange, 56
China, and sustainable progress, 14
Chlorine-Free Products Association, 246
Clean Air Act, 19, 267, 273
Clean Water Act, 19, 268, 276
Cleaner production, 32
    and democratic oversight, 32
    life-cycle approach, 33
    precautionary principle, 32
    preventive approach, 32
Climate change, 263
    UN panel on, 16
    and water availability, 98
    See also Carbon emissions; Carbon footprints;
        Carbon offsets; Carbon taxes; Carbon
        trading; Chicago Climate Exchange; Kyoto
        Protocol on Climate Change
Climate Counts, 262
Closed-loop systems, 34
Coalition for Environmentally Responsible Economies
        48, 249, 259
        Principles, 259–260

Company environmental policy statement, 51
Company Manual Template for Small Businesses, 252
Comprehensive Environmental Response, Compensation, and Liability Act (CERCLA), 265, 269
Computers. See Office equipment and computers
Connecticut Clean Energy, 190
Consumer Reports, 247
CoolWatts program, 74
Corporations, 10
Cost payback analysis, 43, 44
    green buildings, 208
    lighting, 95
    travel and transportation, 152, 158–159
    waste, 119–120, 145–146
    water use, 101, 110
Cradle-to-cradle design, 29, 31, 37–38, 214–215
Customer loyalty, 27

Database for State Incentives for Renewables and Efficiency, 75
DC Pro (data center energy efficiency assessment tool), 164
Dell Computer, 149
    computer recycling program, 164
Design for the environment (DfE), 29, 34
Documenting Your Environmental Management Plan, 256
Dolphin Blue Paper, 246
Drought, 98

Earth Policy Institute, 21
Earth Summit (1992), 13
Earthster.org, 65, 177, 178
Eco-effectiveness, 38
Eco-efficiency, 33–34, 38
Eco-labeling and certification, 48, 233–234
    Chlorine-Free Products Association, 246
    EcoLabeling.org, 247
    Flower logo ecolabel (European Union), 245
    Forest Stewardship Council, 243, 246
    Global Eco-Labeling Network, 244
    Green Seal, 241–242
    Greener Choices EcoLabels Center, 247
    Marine Stewardship Council, 243, 246
    National Environmental Performance Track, 239–240
    Scientific Certification Systems, 243
    Swan logo ecolabel (Scandinavia), 245
    See also Energy Star program
Eco-mapping, 41–42
EcoLabeling.org, 247
The Ecology of Commerce, 20, 21–22, 31
EcoReDesign, 223
Einstein, Albert, 21
Electric Power Research Institute, 57
Electricity, 19
Electronic Industries Alliance, 165
Electronics Survey Worksheet, 166
Elkington, John, 258

EMAS (European Union Environmental Management and Audit Scheme and logo), 262
Emergency Planning and Community Right-to-Know Act (EPCRA), 269, 270, 271, 272
Employee motivation, 26
Employee responsibilities, 51–52
Energy Building Investment Decision Support (eBIDS) database, 199
Energy Cost Calculator for Compact Fluorescent Lamps, 82
Energy cost calculators, 67, 82
Energy Design Resources, 199
Energy efficiency, 57–58, 62
    assessment tools and services, 64–69
    and building upgrades, 59
    commercial building tax deduction, 76
    and computers, 165–166, 170, 171
    conservation subsidies, 76
    food service businesses, 62
    government incentives, 75–77
    and green building design, 195, 205
    and heating and cooling, 58–59
    home builders' tax credits, 76
    keys to managing, 237
    lighting as major energy use, 58, 59
    and lodging businesses, 61–62
    and office equipment and computers, 59
    and office-based businesses, 60–61
    online analysis tool, 68
    plan, 83–85
    reducing or eliminating purchased energy, 58, 62
    and refrigeration equipment, 62
    replacing purchased with renewable energy, 58, 62
    and retail businesses, 59–60
    and travel and transportation, 59
    USDA improvements program, 77
    utility company programs, 68
    and water heating, 61
    See also Energy Star program
Energy Efficiency Action Worksheet, 85, 90–94
Energy Efficiency Economic Analysis, 97
Energy Star program, 48, 68, 234–235
    and business energy savings programs, 236–237
    computer specifications, 163
    and homes and commercial buildings, 234–236
    and Innovest, 236
    and organizations, 236
    product categories, 238
    Target Finder (and building energy benchmarks), 191, 197
Energy use, and process maps, 41
Energy Use Process Map, 84, 89
Energy Use Survey, 84
Energy Use Worksheet, 83, 86, 87
EnergyPlus software, 43, 66
Engel, Heinz-Werner, 41
Environmental accounting, 47, 211
Environmental certification and reporting programs. See Eco-labeling and certification

Environmental management systems (EMS), 39–40, 239, 248–250
  basic approach, 250–252
  benefits of, 248–249
  commitment and policy, 250
  implementation and operation, 251
  monitoring, evaluation, and review, 251
  planning, 251
  steps in, 40
  See also ISO 14001 Standard for Environmental Management
Environmental problems, 9
  as result of business decisons, 16–18
Environmental Regulation Compliance Worksheet, 264, 278
Environmental regulations, 27–28, 263–264
  on air pollutants, 267
  on chemical risk management, 273
  on chemical spills,269
  on emergency planning, 270
  on hazardous chemical release, 272
  on hazardous chemical storage, 271
  on hazardous wastes, 136, 266
  list of general categories, 277
  on pesticides, 274
  on polychlorinated biphenyls (PCBs), 275
  on storage, management, and disposal of petroleum products, 276
  on waste disposal liability, 265
  on water contamination, 278
EPA. See U.S. Environmental Protection Agency
EPCRA. See Emergency Planning and Community Right-to-Know Act
EPEAT (Electronic Product Environmental Assessment Tool), 163
Equipment and Computer Action Worksheet, 166, 168–172
Equipment and Computer Survey, 167
European Union
  carbon trading system, 56
  EMAS (Environmental Management and Audit Scheme and logo), 262
  Flower logo ecolabel, 245
  Waste Electrical and Electronic Equipment legislation, 164
  and wind energy, 70–71
eVALUator, 199
Extended product responsibility, 35
Extractive industries, 18, 19
Exxon Valdez, 259

Factor Four, 31, 36
Federal Insecticide, Fungicide and Rodenticide Act (FIFRA), 274
Fishing industry, 19
Flower logo eco-label (European Union), 245
  products and services certified, 245
Fluorescent lighting, 18–19
Food service businesses, 62
Forest Stewardship Council, 243, 246

The Fortune at the Bottom of the Pyramid, 224
Fossil fuels, 17–18
Fowler, Susan, 13–14

GaBi software, 46
General Electric, 56
Geothermal energy, 71–72
Gifford, Kathy Lee, 174–175
Global Eco-Labeling Network, 244
Global Fusion, 174–175
Global Reporting Initiative, 48
  Guidelines, 260
Global warming, and human activities, 16–17
Goldman Sachs, 149
Governments, and role in sustainability, 18
Grameen Bank and Phone, 224–225
Green assessment, 50–51
Green Building Action Worksheet, 200, 202–207
Green Building Certification Institute, 195
Green Building Initiative Green Globes Program, 190, 191, 193, 197, 200
Green buildings, 186–187
  and access to public transportation, 198–199
  and building systems, 194–195, 207
  cost analysis tools, 199, 201
  cost payback analysis, 208
  and energy consumption, 198
  and energy efficiency, 195, 205
  and green design, 188
  greening leased properties, 196–199
  incentive programs, 189–190
  and indoor air quality, 197, 207
  and life-cycle assessment, 191, 201
  and materials in older buildings, 198
  materials use, 194, 205–207
  new construction, 193–195
  plan for, 200–201
  plan implementation, 201
  preliminary considerations, 202
  rating programs, 190–192
  reasonable cost of, 188
  and recycling, 198
  remodeling, 195–196
  renovations, 186, 188–189
  return on investment analysis, 208
  site selection and development, 194, 202–204
  and up-to-date design and construction professionals, 195
  and water use, 198, 204
  whole-system design, 193
  and workforce productivity, 187–188
Green business plan, 51, 279
  company environmental policy statement, 51, 279–280
  compiling, 52, 284
  cover sheet, 285
  employee responsibilities, 51–52, 280–281
  and going beyond, 288
  implementing, 52, 287
  manual, 284

manual contents, 286
mission statement, 279–280
performance monitoring, 287–288, 289
targets, 287
See also Ceres Principles; Green Plan
   Responsibility Worksheet
Green chemistry, 34, 215–216
Green design, 29–30, 210–211
   and adaptability to innovations, 216
   and all energy to produce material transformation,
      217
   and all process elements as products, 216
   assessing necessity of product, 223, 227
   and avoidance of toxics, 217
   and biomimicry, 213–214, 218–219
   and bottom of the pyramid, 224–225
   and buildings, 188
   checklist of considerations, 223
   and cradle-to-cradle design, 214–215
   designing for reuse or recycling, 217, 223
   and distribution stage, 220–221
   and efficient distribution, 223
   and end of product's life, 221–223, 232
   and energy efficiency, 223
   and green chemistry, 215–216
   implementation of plan, 225
   and improving local habitat and species diversity,
      217
   key concepts, 212–216
   and life-cycle assessment, 210, 219, 225
   and low impact, 223
   and manufacturing stage, 220, 229–231
   and minimum of materials and energy, 217
   and natural capitalism, 213–214
   and The Natural Step, 212–213
   and natural systems, 212
   and packaging, 217, 231
   plan, 225
   and producing no waste, 216
   and product's impact on society, 224
   and raw materials stage, 219, 227–228
   recycled rather than raw materials, 217
   and resource conservation, 223
   and restorative investment in natural capital, 214
   rules of, 216–217
   and services rather than products, 214, 221
   and user stage, 221
   and waste elimination, 223
   and water efficiency, 223
Green energy certificates, 72–73
Green Plan Responsibility Worksheet, 282–283
Green Product Design Worksheet, 222, 223, 225,
      227–232
Green Seal, 46, 48, 241
   Environmental (Product) Standards, 241, 242
   Facilities Partnership, 241
   Green Reports, 242
   Purchasing Partnership, 241
Green Suppliers Network, 239
Green-e

Climate (carbon offset program), 74
   renewable energy certification program, 73
Greener Choices EcoLabels Center, 247
Greenguard Environmental Institute, 190
   building products certification program, 194
Greenhouse Gas Protocol Initiative, 64–65, 262
Greenhouse gases, 16–17
Greening
   and competitive advantage, 27–29
   and cost savings, 24–25
   and customer loyalty, 27
   defined, 10
   and employee motivation, 26
   myth that it is more expensive, 23–24
   overview, 50
   and product and service design. See Green
      design
   and waste reduction, 24–25
Greenline Paper Products, 246

Hailes, Julia, 258
Hands-on Solutions to Improve Profits and Productivity:
      Energy Saving Tips for Small Businesses,
      69
Hart, Stuart, 21, 224
Hawken, Paul, 13, 20, 21–22, 31, 213
Hazardous chemicals, 19
Hazardous waste, 114, 115, 136
   avoiding mixing, 136
   batteries, 140
   characteristic, 137–138
   compliance categories, 138
   Conditionally Exempt Small Quantity Generators
      (CESQGs), 138, 141
   federal and state regulations, 136
   lamps containing mercury or lead, 140–141
   Large Quantity Generators (LQGs), 138, 142, 143
   listed, 137
   measuring amounts generated, 139–140
   pesticides, 140
   recycling and reusing, 136
   regulations, 136, 266
   replacing with less wasteful materials or
      processes, 136
   safe storage, 136
   Small Quantity Generators (SQGs), 138, 142
   thermostats, 140
   typically generated by small businesses, 144
   Universal Waste Rule, 140–141
Heating and cooling, 58–59
Herbicides, 19
Hewlett-Packard, 149, 240
   computer recycling program, 165
Hollender, Jeffrey, 30
Home Depot, 57, 246
HVAC systems, 197

IBM, 163
   computer recycling program, 164
India, and sustainable progress, 14

Innovest, 236
Integrated Environmental Management Systems, 256
Integrated Environmental Management Systems Implementation Guide, 252
Integrated Environmental Management Systems Worksheets, 252
Integrating Green Purchasing Into Your Environmental Management System (EMS), 176
Interface Inc., 10, 37, 221
International Chamber of Commerce, 249
International Network for Environmental Management, 41
International Organization for Standardization, 40, 48. See also ISO 1404; ISO 9000 Quality Management Program; ISO 14001 Standard for Environmental Management; ISO 14031 Environmental Performance Evaluation; ISO 14064
International Society for Industrial Ecology, 216
Introduction to Environmental Accounting as a Business Management Tool, 47
ISO 1404, 262
ISO 9000 Quality Management Program, 40
ISO 14001 Standard for Environmental Management, 40, 46, 48, 248, 249–250, 252, 256
    on communication, 254
    on document control, 254
    on emergency preparedness and response, 254–255
    on environmental management programs, 253
    on environmental management system audits, 255
    on legal and other requirements, 253
    on management review, 255–256
    on monitoring and measurement, 255
    on nonconformance and corrective and preventive actions, 255
    on objectives and targets, 253
    on policy statements, 252
    on records, 255
    on significant environmental aspects of business, 253
    on structure and responsibility, 253–254
    on training, awareness, and competence, 254
    See also Environmental management systems
ISO 14031 Environmental Performance Evaluation, 262
ISO 14064, 250

Johnson, Fisk, 21

Kinko's, 246
Kyoto Protocol on Climate Change, 74

Land development, 19
Lawrence Berkeley Laboratory, Environmental Technologies Division, 68
Leadership in Energy and Environmental Design (LEED) Program, 190, 192, 197
    and certification of building professionals, 195
    green building checklists, 193, 200

rating system for Commercial Interiors and Renovations., 197
    standards, 48
Lean and Energy Toolkit, 69
The Lean and Environment Toolkit, 117
Lean manufacturing, 24–25, 33
Lean Manufacturing and the Environment, 117
Life-cycle assessment, 33, 34, 45–46
    areas of concern, 46
    and EPA, 34
    and green building, 191, 201
    and green design, 210, 219, 225
    software and manual, 67–68
    and supply chains and purchasing, 176–178
Life-Cycle Assessment Tool, 177–178
Light Up the World, 225
Lighting
    compact fluorescent, 60, 77, 82
    cost analysis tools, 82
    cost payback analysis, 95
    and diffusers, 80
    and dimmers, 81
    and effect on workers, 78
    fluorescent, 79
    and fluorescent ballasts, 79–80
    fluorescent vs. incandescent, 18–19, 77, 78
    and green building design, 194–195
    high-intensity discharge (HID), 78, 79
    LED, 60, 77
    as major energy use, 58, 59, 77
    measures to take, 78–79
    and motion sensors, 81
    and pollution reduction, 77
    and reflectors, 80
    return on investment analysis, 96
    and time-based controls, 80–81
    and ultrasonic snesors, 81
    and waste heat, 77–78
Limited Life-Cycle Assessment Worksheet, 226
Lodging businesses, 61–62
Lovins, Amory, 31, 36, 213
    estimate of potential electricity savings, 57
Lovins, L. Hunter, 31, 36, 213
Lowe's, 57, 246
Lumina Decision Systems, 177

Marine Stewardship Council, 243, 246
McDonough, William, 37, 214–215
Merrill Lynch, 149
Micro-credit, 224–225

National Envelope, 246
National Environmental Performance Track, 48, 239, 240
    criteria, 239–240
    and Environmental Management Systems, 239
    Mentoring Program, 239
National Environmental Protection Act (NEPA) of 1969, 257
National Institute of Standards and Technology, 67, 199

Native Energy, 74
Natural capitalism
 and biomimicry, 36–37
 and green design, 213–214
 and investing in natural capital, 37
 and radical resource productivity, 36
 and service and flow economy, 37
Natural Capitalism: Creating the Next Industrial
 Revolution, 20, 31, 36
The Natural Step, 31, 35–36, 69
 and green design, 212–213
Natural systems, 212
Neenah Paper, 246
New England Friends Funds, 57
New Hampshire, University of, and Life-Cycle
 Assessment Tool, 177
New Jersey
 Clean Energy Program, 189
 SmartStart Building Program, 189
New York State Energy Research and Development
 Authority, 189
Nexus Energy Software, 68
Nike, 174

Office equipment and computers, 59, 162
 computer energy savings online tool, 166
 DC Pro (data center energy efficiency assessment
  tool), 164
 efficiency plan, 165–166, 170
 Energy Star specifications, 163
 energy use, 162
 energy use in computer manufacture, 162
 and EPEAT (Electronic Product Environmental
  Assessment Tool), 163
 power management, 171–172
 process map, 166
 purchasing, 168–169
 recycling, 164–165, 168–169
 upgrading rather than replacing, 163
 See also Electronics Survey Worksheet;
  Equipment and Computer Action Worksheet;
  Equipment and Computer Survey
Office-based businesses, 60–61
OpenLCA project, 65, 178
Oregon Business Energy Tax Credit, 190

Packaging, and extended product responsibility, 35
PE International, 46
Pennsylvania Governor's Green Government Council,
 190
Pepsico, 149
Pesticides, 19
Pollution prevention, 31–32
Portfolio Manager software, 100
Practical Guide to Environmental Management for
 Small Businesses, 252
Prahalad, C. K., 224
Process mapping, 41–42
Proctor & Gamble, 149
Product design. See Green design

Promoting Green Purchasing: Tools and Resources to
 Quantify the Benefits of Environmentally
 Preferable Purchasing, 176
Purchasing. See Supply chains and purchasing
Putting Energy Into Profits: Energy Star Small Business
 Guide, 69

Quick Plant Energy Profiler (Quick PEP), 66

Rain Forest Action Network, 246
RCRA. See Resource Conservation and Recovery Act
 (RCRA) of 1976
Recycled Content (ReCon) Tool, 178
Recycling, 114, 132
 contracting with buyers and collectors, 133–135
 electronic equipment, 164, 168–169
 and leased buildings, 198
 purchasing recycled products, 118–119
 See also Waste; Waste and Recycling Action
  Worksheet
Reduce-recycle-reuse concept, 34
 and extended product responsibility, 35
Rees, William, 63
Refrigeration equipment, 62
Reimagining, 29
Renewable energy, 69, 72
 and carbon offsets, 74
 Distributed Wind Energy Technology Program, 71
 geothermal, 71–72
 and green energy certificates, 72–73
 green power, 72–73
 and green pricing, 72
 and Green-e renewable energy certification
  program, 73
 solar, 69–70
 tax credits, 75, 76, 77
 wind, 70–71
Resource Conservation and Recovery Act (RCRA) of
 1976, 266, 276
Resources, 52
Retail businesses, 59–60
Return on investment analysis, 44–45
 green buildings, 208
 lighting, 96
 travel and transportation, 152, 159–150
 waste, 119–120, 147
 water use, 101, 111
Robèrt, Karl-Henrik, 31, 35–36, 212
Rocky Mountain Institute, 36
Roddick, Anita, 257

SA 8000 Social Accountability Standard, 48, 262
Schlaepfer, Andreas, 57
Schmidheiny, Stephan, 33
Scientific Certification Systems, 243
 certifications available and products certified, 243
Scott, Lee, 57, 173–174
Service design. See Green design
Seventh Generation, 30
Sierra Club Mutual Funds, 57

Small and medium-sized businesses, 10
    as percentage of all businesses, 10
SmartWay Transport Partnership, 151
    Technology Package Savings Calculator, 151
Social Accountability International, 48, 258. See also SA
        8000 Social Accountability Standard
Social responsibility reporting, 257
Solar America Cities, 70
Solar energy
    photovoltaic, 69
    thermal, 69–70
Stakeholders, 32, 257
Supply Chain and Purchasing Action Worksheet, 179,
        183–184
Supply Chain and Purchasing Questionnaire, 179, 180,
        185
Supply Chain Process Map, 179, 181
Supply Chain Worksheet, 179, 182
Supply chains and purchasing, 173–175
    and company purchasing policy, 175
    and consumer expectations, 174
    and government purchasing programs, 175–176
    green business purchasing plan, 179–180
    greening advantages, 173–174, 175
    and life-cycle assessment, 176–178
    and process maps, 41
Sustainability
    chemical, 34
    cutting energy inputs, 15
    cutting raw material inputs, 15
    defined, 13–14
    and elimination of toxic materials, 15
    four requirements for (The Natural Step), 35–36
    full, defined, 39
    as largest movement in world, 13
    and resilience to change and risk, 15
    three critical components, 14
SustainAbility, 258
Sustainability reporting, 257–258
    Ceres Principles, 259–260
    Climate Counts, 262
    economic indicators, 261
    EMAS (European Union Environmental
        Management and Audit Scheme and logo),
        262
    environmental indicators, 261
    Greenhouse Gas Protocol Initiative, 262
    guidelines, 261
    ISO 14031 Environmental Performance
        Evaluation, 262
    performance indicators, 261
    SA 8000, 262
    social indicators, 261
Sustainable development, 14
Sustainable progress, 14
Swan logo ecolabel (Scandinavia), 245
    products and services certified, 245
Swiss Re, 57
Sylvatica, 177

Texas, state of, and Life-Cycle Assessment Tool, 177
Toxic Substances Control Act (TSCA), 275
Toyota, 32
Travel and transportation, 59, 149
    audio or video conferencing as alternative, 150
    cost payback analysis, 152, 158–159
    cost savings from vehicle mileage upgrade, 149
    efficiency plan, 151–152
    employee commuting, 154–155
    facilitating alternative modes, 150
    plan implementation, 152
    pollutants from, 149
    return on investment analysis, 152, 159–160
    and shipping, 151, 155–157
    telecommuting as alternative, 150
    and truck idling, 150
    See also Business Transportation Carbon
        Footprint Worksheet
Travel and Transportation Action Worksheet, 152,
        154–157
Travel and Transportation Economic Analysis, 161
Triple bottom line, 47, 258
TSCA. See Toxic Substances Control Act

Unilever, 246
United Nations
    Environmental Program, 258, 259
    Global Compact, 48
    Intergovernmental Panel on Climate Change, 16
    and sustainability reporting, 258, 259
U.S. Department of Agriculture, 77
U.S. Department of Energy
    Best Practices software, 65–66
    Building Energy Software Tools Directory, 65
    Building Technologies Program, 65
    cost payback analysis software, 43–44
    DC Pro, 164
    Energy Efficiency and Renewable Energy
        Program, 65, 71
    on energy-efficient computers, 163
    EnergyPlus software, 66
    Federal Energy Management Program, 43, 67, 82
    Industrial Technologies Program, 66
    Quick Plant Energy Profiler (Quick PEP), 66
    Save Energy Now initiative, 66–67
    solar program, 70
    water efficiency software, 99–100
    See also Energy Star program
U.S. Environmental Protection Agency (EPA)
    Database of Environmental Information for
        Products and Services, 176
    energy efficiency guides, 68–69
    ENERGYPLUS software, 43
    environmental management systems guides, 252,
        256
    EPEAT (Electronic Product Environmental
        Assessment Tool), 163
    green purchasing guidelines, 176

Integrating Green Purchasing Into Your Environmental Management System (EMS), 176 t

Introduction to Environmental Accounting as a Business Management Tool, 47

The Lean and Environment Toolkit, 117

Lean Manufacturing and the Environment, 117

and Life-Cycle Assessment Tool, 177

National Environmental Performance Track program, 48

Office of Pollution Prevention and Toxics, 34

and penalty mitigation, 264

Portfolio Manager software, 100

Promoting Green Purchasing, 176

Recycled Content (ReCon) Tool, 178

SmartWay Transport Partnership, 151

Superfund, 265

Waste Reduction Model (WARM), 117

WaterSense program, 99

See also Energy Star program; Environmental regulations

U.S. Green Building Council. See Leadership in Energy and Environmental Design (LEED) Program

Universal Waste Rule, 140–141

Utility bills, information from, 83

Valdez Principles, 259

Von Weizsacker, Ernst, 31, 36

Wackernagel, Mathis, 63

Wal-Mart
emissions reduction plan, 57
supply chain greening effort, 173–174, 175
and trucking efficiencies, 150

Waste, 113–114
assessment, 118, 121–122
business waste reduction plan, 118–121
cost payback analysis, 119–120, 145–146
disposal, 18, 19, 114
and excess transportation, 116
management, 114
management, and process maps, 41
monitoring reduction program, 120–121
office and equipment, 128–129
organic reduction, 131
and overprocessing, 116
and overproduction, 115
packaging reduction, 130
plan implementation, 120
and production defects, 116
as raw material for other production, 34

reduction, 24–25, 113–115, 126–127

return on investment analysis, 119–120, 147

reuse, 131

treatment, 114

and unnecessary inventory, 115

and waiting (downtime), 116

See also Hazardous waste; Recycling

Waste and Recycling Action Worksheet, 118, 128–132

Waste Expense Worksheet, 118, 121, 123

Waste Process Map, 122, 125

Waste Reduction Economic Analysis, 148

Waste Reduction Model (WARM), 117

Waste Survey Worksheet, 118, 121–122, 124

Water Conservation Action Worksheet, 101, 106–109

Water Conservation Economic Analysis, 112

Water Consumption Worksheet, 101, 102, 103

Water heating, 61
solar, 69

Water Survey Worksheet, 101, 102, 104

Water use, 98
assessment, 100, 102
business water efficiency plan, 100–101
in commercial buildings, 98–99, 106–108, 198, 204
conservation resources, 99–100
cost payback analysis, 101, 110
federal plumbing fixture standards, 109
landscaping, 108–109
plan implementation, 101
and process maps, 41
return on investment analysis, 101, 111

Water Use Process Map, 100–101, 102, 105

WATERGY spreadsheet program, 44

WaterSense program, 99

WaterWiser, 99

Web addresses, 52

White House Apparel Industry Partnership Task Force, 175

Wind energy, 70–71

World Business Council for Sustainable Development, 33, 64, 262

World Resources Institute, 64, 262

World Wildlife Fund, 246

Wuppertal Institute for Climate, Environment, and Energy, 36

Xerox, 221

Yunus, Muhammad, 224